Reading and Writing in Babylon

Reading and Writing in Babylon

Dominique Charpin

Translated by
Jane Marie Todd

Harvard University Press

CAMBRIDGE, MASSACHUSETTS
LONDON, ENGLAND
2010

Printed in the United States of America

This book was published with the support of the French Ministry of
Culture - National Book Center / Cet ouvrage a été publié avec l'assistance
du Ministère de la culture - Centre National du Livre.

First edition published as *Lire et Écrire à Babylone,* © Presses Universitaires
de France, 2008.

Frontispiece: detail, Neo-Assyrian bas-relief representing two standing
scribes. See Figure 6, page 29 (Werner Forman / Art Resource, New York).

Library of Congress Cataloging-in-Publication Data

Charpin, Dominique.
    [Lire et écrire à Babylone. English]
    Reading and writing in Babylon / Dominique Charpin ; translated by
Jane Marie Todd.
        p.   cm.
    Includes bibliographical references and index.
    ISBN 978-0-674-04968-0 (alk. paper)
        1. Iraq—Civilization—To 634.   2. Cuneiform writing—History.
    3. Reading—Iraq—History.   I. Title.
    DS69.5.C4813   2010
    935—dc22   2010010148

To my parents

Contents

Preface

Since the publication of Samuel N. Kramer's famous book *History Begins at Sumer,* its title has become known worldwide. It aptly indicates that Western civilization is rooted in the Near East of the late fourth millennium. Some people are fascinated by the search for origins, but I must confess that is not so in my case. I am more interested in how a civilization that has reached its maturity functions. That is undoubtedly a matter of taste, but it also reflects a preoccupation with being able to find fairly speedy confirmation—or invalidation—for the hypotheses formulated, which the many unknowns associated with the most ancient periods scarcely allow. The reader is hereby given fair warning: it is primarily the "classical" period of Mesopotamian civilization that I shall study in this book, that is, the long millennium extending roughly from Hammurabi (1792–1750 B.C.) to Nebuchadnezzar (604–562 B.C.). Since these two rulers reigned in Babylon, their capital provides the title for this book. The content, however, is not limited to that city alone: since antiquity, "Babylon" has connoted Mesopotamian civilization as a whole.

This book came into being as a result of issues that have been of concern to me ever since I published *Le clergé d'Ur (The Clergy of Ur)* more than twenty years ago. In that book I showed, notably, that what was believed to be a "school" did not have the institutional character generally attached to that term. In reality, it was the residence of members of the clergy who, in the city of Ur during the eighteenth century B.C., transmitted their knowledge at home, training their apprentices—in the first place, their children—to read and write cuneiform. Since then, many other authors have dealt with other sites or other eras. One of the questions that has arisen with increasing urgency is the extent of literacy in Mesopotamia: did the restricted group of professional scribes hold a quasi-monopoly? My work on the Mari archives convinced me that the opposite was true. I have already presented some results of that inquiry in various studies, which provided me with the starting point for several chapters of this book. I shall not conceal the fact that I have deliberately placed the emphasis on the aspects I find inadequately accounted for elsewhere. That position emerges from my research, which is devoted primarily to the documents of the third, and especially, the early second millennium. I am aware that a different view could be expounded by someone who begins with the scholarly texts of the first millennium, but that perspective is precisely the one prevailing in the other studies, whose dominance I wish to call into question.

I have sought to present that view in an accessible manner, as I did previously in *Hammu-rabi de Babylone (Hammurabi of Babylon)*. I owe my thanks to all who encouraged me in this undertaking. It reached fruition through my teaching at the Sorbonne, both at the Université de Paris 1 and at the École Pratique des Hautes Études (EPHE); my research occurred within the framework of the UMR (*unité mixte de recherche*, or joint research unit) 7192, which brings together the Centre National de la Recherche Scientifique (CNRS; National Center for Scientific Research), the Collège de France, the EPHE, and the Institut National des Langues et Civilisations Orientales (INALCO; National Institute for Eastern Languages and Civilizations), directed by Jean-Marie Durand. My wife, Nele Ziegler, who is also an Assyriologist, has earned my gratitude by actively encouraging me to pursue this project. My sister, Claire de Chaisemartin, aided me by reading over the manuscript. Michel Prigent and his entire staff at PUF have also earned my thanks for their continued support. I wish to dedicate this book to my parents: on two occasions during my secondary and higher education, they expressed their confidence when I was making crucial choices. I am profoundly grateful for that—and for the rest.

Paris/Heidelberg, December 2007

Note to the English-Language Edition

The text that follows is a translation of a largely revised version of the book published in French. I have reworked certain chapters to avoid repeating sections of my *Writing, Law, and Kingship: Essays on Old Babylonian Mesopotamia* (University of Chicago Press, 2010), which has no French counterpart. I have also made numerous additions, responding to studies that were published recently or of which I became aware only after completing the first manuscript, or further developing aspects I found interesting. This is therefore a second, revised edition, which has not appeared in French as such. In it I use the author-date reference system, which has allowed me to reduce considerably the number of notes without impoverishing the content. My thanks go to all members of the staff at Harvard University Press for their openness and patience and to Jane Marie Todd, who has now translated a book of mine for the second time.

Paris, April 2009

N.B. The scientific transcription in use among Assyriologists has been simplified, though certain usages have been retained: the *š* corresponds to the English *sh;* the *ṣ* and the *ṭ* transcribe emphatics without any real equivalent in English (*ts* and *tt,* respectively); the *g* is always pronounced hard, as in "glue." Sumerian words are transliterated using a period to separate the signs *(um.mi.a),* whereas Akkadian words are transcribed with no divisions *(ummānum).*

In the quotations, passages [in brackets] are restorations, whereas those (in parentheses) are explanations.

All dates are B.C., except those referring to modern scholarship.

Chronology

Evolution of Writing and Language

Dates (B.C.)		Period
ca. 3200–3000		Uruk IV
ca. 3000–2900		Uruk III (or Jemdet Nasr)
ca. 2900–ca. 2500		Early Dynastic I and II
ca. 2500–2334		Early Dynastic III a and b
ca. 2334–2193		Old Akkadian
ca. 2200–2000		Neo-Sumerian
	South	*North*
ca. 2000–1600	Old Babylonian	Old Assyrian
ca. 1600–ca. 1000	Middle Babylonian	Middle Assyrian
beginning ca. 1000	Neo-Babylonian (until 539) Late Babylonian (last text dates from A.D. 75)	Neo-Assyrian (until 610)

Principal Kings and Dynasties

Dates (B.C.)		
ca. 2334–2193		**Dynasty of Akkad** Sargon (2334–2279) Naram-Sin (2254–2218) **Third Dynasty of Ur** Shulgi (2094–2047)
	South (Babylonia)	*North (Assyria)*
ca. 2000–1600	Lipit-Eshtar of Isin (1934–1924)	
	Rim-Sin of Larsa (1822–1763)	Samsi-Addu (1808–1775)
	Hammurabi of Babylon (1792–1750)	

ca. 1600–ca. 1000	**Kassite Dynasty** (1595–1155) **Second Dynasty of Isin** Nebuchadnezzar I (1124–1103) Adad-apla-iddina (1067–1046)	Tukulti-Ninurta I (1243–1207) Tiglath-pileser I (1114–1076)
ca. 1000–612		**Neo-Assyrian Empire** Sargon (721–705) Sennacherib (704–681) Esarhaddon (680–669) Ashurbanipal (668–627) *Fall of Niniveh* (612)
	Neo-Babylonian Empire Nebuchadnezzar II (604–562) Nabonidus (555–539) **Achaemenid Dynasty** (538–330) **Seleucid domination** (330–141) **Parthian domination** (141–A.D. 76)	

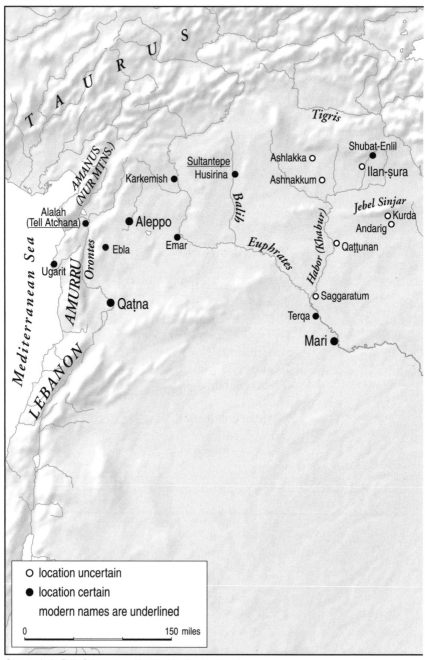

TAURUS

Tigris

Shubat-Enlil

Ashlakka ○

Ilan-ṣura ○

Sultantepe
Husirina ●

Ashnakkum ○

AMANUS
(NUR MTNS.)

Karkemish ●

Jebel Sinjar

Kurda ○

Andarig ○

Habor (Khabur)

Balih

Alalah
(Tell Atchana) ●

Aleppo ●

Qaṭṭunan ○

Euphrates

Mediterranean Sea

Orontes

Ebla ●

Emar ●

AMURRU

Ugarit ●

Saggaratum ○

LEBANON

Qaṭna ●

Terqa ●

Mari ●

○ location uncertain
● location certain
modern names are underlined

0   150 miles

Cartography by Philip Schwartzberg, Meridian Mapping, Minneapolis

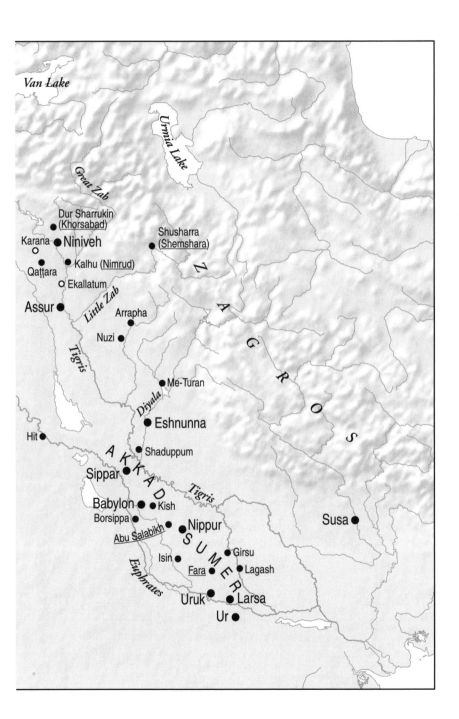

Reading and Writing in Babylon

Introduction

How did the inhabitants of Mesopotamia imagine the origin of writing? Berossos, priest of the god Marduk in Babylon in the early third century B.C., dedicated a book to King Antiochos I; written in Greek and titled *Babyloniaca,* it summarized the traditions of his country. In that book, writing appears as one of the essential elements that Oannes, a hybrid creature with a fish's body and a human head, gave to humanity at the dawn of time. While men were still living "without discipline and order, just like animals," at the start of the reign of Alorus—supposedly the first of the Mesopotamian kings—Oannes emerged from the Persian Gulf: "Berossos says that this monster spent its days, never eating anything, but teaching men the skills necessary for writing and doing mathematics and for all sorts of knowledge: how to build cities, found temples, and make laws" (Verbrugghe and Wickersham 1996, 44).[1] Given the close connection between Adapa, the indigenous name for Oannes, and the god Enki, patron of technology, it is clear that this gift of writing was, like kingship, "descended from heaven."

The epic *Enmerkar and the Lord of Aratta* presents a different view: the invention of writing was supposedly the act of a man, Enmerkar. To carry out his public works projects, that king of Uruk sought to procure the necessary raw materials from across the mountains, in the rich region of Aratta, but the ruler of that city issued a series of challenges in the form of riddles. Enmerkar managed to solve them all, until the messenger traveling back and forth between the two kings capitulated before the complexity of the message to be transmitted:

Because the messenger's mouth was too heavy, and he could
not repeat it,
   The lord of Kulab (Enmerkar) patted some clay and put the
words on it as on a tablet.
   Before that day, there had been no putting words on clay;
   But now, when the sun rose on that day—so it was!:
   The lord of Kulab had put words as on a tablet—so it was!
                 (Vanstiphout 2003a, 84–85, lines 501–505)

Imagine the perplexity of the lord of Aratta when he saw that
written message. The way writing was conceived is noteworthy:
the "spoken word" (*inim* in Sumerian) "held" in the clay. Writing
was only an oral discourse fixed on a support.[2] Ought we therefore
to place two different traditions in opposition, one that considers
the invention of writing a gift of the gods (through Adapa/Oannes),
the other, a human invention (attributable to Enmerkar)? Nothing
of the sort: for a bit earlier in the epic, we find that Enmerkar owed
his wisdom to the goddess Nisaba, who inspired him to solve the
riddles sent to him by the lord of Aratta.[3] And as a matter of fact,
Nisaba was the goddess of writing in the Mesopotamian pantheon.
Both accounts, despite their differences, place the emphasis on
something that coincides with the results of the most recent research: the birth of writing cannot be apprehended correctly in
purely evolutionist terms. Writing appeared in a sudden and
radical leap, constituting a complete system from the start (Michalowski 1994a, 54) (Figure 1).

Deciphering Cuneiform Writing

Cuneiform writing, which emerged in the late fourth millennium, met its demise in the early part of the Christian era: unlike
Aramaic writing, for example, it completely vanished from human knowledge. Hence, when travelers brought copies of cuneiform inscriptions—or the first originals—back to the West in the

FIGURE 1. An archaic tablet from Uruk, ca. 3200 (distribution of rations of different sorts of beer). The signs were not yet cut into segments at the time; this writing is therefore customarily called "protocuneiform." (Bolaffi Collection.)

seventeenth and eighteenth centuries, the "readings" proposed were utterly fanciful when compared with our current understanding. It has proved interesting to analyze them, however, to glean the conception of the sign and of the relation between language and writing that existed in Europe in the modern period

(Cancik-Kirschbaum and Chambon 2006). It was not until the early nineteenth century that the work of interpretation became truly rigorous.

The history of the decipherment of cuneiform writing has often been written, and I shall confine myself here to recalling the chief stages in that process (Bottéro 1987; Daniels 1995a). It was the result of a collective, lengthy, and exacting effort, which therefore appears to the uninitiated less extraordinary than Jean-François Champollion's achievement. No doubt Assyriology would be more popular if cuneiform writing were as appealing as Egyptian hieroglyphs and if a genius had early on provided the key to it. But such is not the case.

The starting point for that history is located in present-day Iran, in the region of Persepolis. Inscriptions on rock were discovered there, and Carsten Niebhur was the first to recognize that, behind their common appearance—signs composed of "spikes" or "wedges" (*cunei* in Latin)—lay three different systems. The simplest of these had about forty signs: it was rightly concluded that this was an alphabetical writing system. George Frederick Grotefend had the auspicious intuition that these were inscriptions of Persian kings from the dynasty of the Achaemenids, in other words, the successors of Cyrus the Great. Thanks to Herodotus, it was known that Darius and Xerxes had moved their capital to Persepolis. As it happened, a later state of the Persian language was beginning to be studied at the same time: "Zend," or in other words, the language of the Avesta. Considering the shortest cuneiform inscriptions, Grotefend wagered that they were composed of the name of a king, his genealogy, and his titulature. By combining several of them, he managed to read: "Darius, powerful king, son of Hystaspes," and "Xerxes, powerful king, king of kings, son of Darius." From October 3, 1802, to May 20, 1803, Grotefend sent reports to the Königliche Gesellschaft der Wissenschaften (Royal Society for Sciences) at the University of Göttingen in which he detailed his discoveries. These discoveries therefore preceded by twenty years Champollion's famous *Précis du système hiéroglyphique (Abstract on the System of Hieroglyphics)*, but they did not immediately create much of a stir.

Several scholars, including Henry Rawlinson, took on the Persepolitan writing used to notate Old Persian. Between 1836 and 1847, Rawlinson successfully copied out the long Behistun inscription and, thanks to it, was able to completely decipher that writing. But Persepolitan writing, invented for the Achaemenid kings, was used for little other than the notation of their commemorative inscriptions.

Two other "cuneiform" writing systems remained to be deciphered. Between 1838 and 1851, Edmund Norris was the principal scholar to work on the second of these. Thanks to the proper names, he managed to read the text of the second column of the Behistun inscription, which was in a completely unknown language. It is now called Elamite, but the truth is, for lack of a sizable corpus and especially of sufficient variety, that language, spoken on the Iranian plateau from the third millennium B.C. on, remains poorly understood.

During the first half of the nineteenth century, several scholars concurrently tackled the task of deciphering the third writing system. It was the most difficult one, since it made use of several hundred signs. Ultimately, they came to understand that it combined phonetic signs notating syllables with others that notated words (called "logograms"). The language so written was called "Assyrian," since it belonged to the emperors whose capitals in the northern part of present-day Iraq, in Nineveh, Nimrud (the ancient Kalhu), and Khorsabad (Dur Sharrukin), had just been discovered. It constitutes the eastern branch of the Semitic languages, and that affiliation allowed for very rapid progress in deciphering Assyrian, thanks to its kinship to Hebrew and Arabic. In 1857, barely more than 150 years ago, it was decided that the time had come to take stock. A long inscription had just been exhumed in Nimrud,[4] and a copy of it was given to four scholars: Rawlinson,

Edward Hincks, William Henry Fox Talbot, and Jules Oppert. Without consulting one another, they were to send their translation of the text to the Royal Asiatic Society in London. The results were sufficiently concordant for the decipherment to be considered successful.

Nevertheless, the mixed character of that writing system, partly syllabic and partly logographic, raised a problem. After bitter debates, scholars reached the conclusion that it had originally been invented to notate Sumerian. The discovery in Tello of numerous inscriptions in that language beginning in 1880 confirmed that view. It was only with the 1905 publication of François Thureau-Dangin's *Inscriptions royales de Sumer et d'Akkad (Royal Inscriptions of Sumer and Akkad)* that Sumerian could be considered altogether deciphered. Even in our own time, the lexicon and grammar of that language and its parentage are far from being known with any certainty.

"Classical" cuneiform writing was not only used to notate Sumerian and Akkadian. Over time, many peoples borrowed it, adapting it to their own languages. In second-millennium Anatolia especially, it served to notate Hittite and Hurrian; in Armenia of the early first millennium, Urartian.

How to Read a Cuneiform Tablet

Whereas the history of this decipherment has often been written, explanations of how specialists in the writing system, traditionally called Assyriologists, proceed are much less common. Generally, when a photograph of a cuneiform inscription and the translation of its text are placed side by side, the uninitiated remain perplexed, wondering how one got from one to the other. This is often a long and difficult labor, about which specialists do not expatiate; in that respect, they are like old-time chefs who disliked divulging their recipes. I should now like to invite the reader to a visit to the Assyriologist's workshop.

Three-Dimensional Writing

We must first recognize the radically different character of cuneiform writing when compared with our own: it consists of incisions made in the surface of an unbaked clay tablet with the aid of a triangular-shaped calamus made of reed or bone (see Figure 14). The impression of that stylus produces a "spike" or "wedge" (*cuneus* in Latin, whence the name given to that writing in the eighteenth century). Combinations of several wedges form a sign: the simplest is constituted by a single horizontal or vertical wedge, while the most complex may consist of a dozen. It is the play of shadow and light that makes the written signs visible, and lighting from the left is necessary if the signs are to be read accurately.

Page Layout and Paleography

The "page layout" of the tablets changed over time. At first tablets were round, and their surface (front and back) was divided into columns, themselves subdivided into cells. In about 2300 B.C., a linear orientation prevailed. Henceforth the tablets were rectangular: the written lines were usually parallel to the shorter side, but the reverse sometimes occurred. Whatever the language, the signs were written from left to right.

The form of the signs themselves evolved between their appearance in about 3200 and the last datable text, written in A.D. 75. They were originally pictograms, that is, signs depicting visually what they signified. But very quickly, unlike Egyptian hieroglyphs, cuneiform signs lost that connection and became a more cursive writing. The different stages of that evolution as well as the regional variants have been painstakingly inventoried.

Hence, at a single glance, as a function of the shape of the tablet, the layout, and the paleography, an experienced epigraphist will be able to say, even before he starts to read the text, whether the tablet before him is, for example, a bookkeeping document from the pre-Sargonic period, a letter from the Old Babylonian period, or a Neo-Assyrian scholarly text.

A Repertoire of Several Hundred Signs

Next comes the reading of the document. The first task consists of identifying the signs. This is not always easy, for several reasons. Cuneiform is not an alphabetical writing system with twenty-six characters: the "standard" repertoire contains nearly 600 different signs. Moreover, the legibility of the written signs varies by era. The most outstanding period in this respect was the age of Akkad (ca. 2340–ca. 2200 B.C.). At that time, signs were incised with an elegance and uniformity that were never again equaled. By contrast, the end of the Old Babylonian period (seventeenth century B.C.) is characterized by sloping writing that is often difficult to decipher. Distinctions must also be made based on the kind of written material at issue: a copy of a literary text intended for a royal library such as that of Ashurbanipal will naturally be much neater than a memorandum that a merchant drew up in haste.

One Writing System, Several Languages.   But identifying the signs is only the first stage. Assyriologists must then select the value of each one and arrange them into signifying units, since there are no word separators or punctuation. That, no doubt, is the most complex mental process.

It must first be determined in what language the document was written, since cuneiform was used for very diverse languages (Woodard 2004). The Akkadians adopted it to notate their language in about the mid-third millennium B.C. In about 2000, their language, Akkadian, split into two branches: Assyrian and Babylonian. But cuneiform was also used to notate an Indo-European language, Hittite, not to mention languages that are still poorly understood, such as Hurrian and Elamite. Of course, Assyriologists in the broad sense of the term are obliged to specialize, but they must still have a good general background. Hence it is not possible to study Sumerian without knowing Akkadian: in fact, it is in good part thanks to the dictionaries constituted by the Akkadian scribes that we are able to understand the meaning of Sumerian words, for which there are no available resources to serve as the basis for comparison. Those who specialize in Akkadian are not required to know Hittite, but the reverse is not true. And so on.

Logograms or Syllables. Once the language in which the document is written has been identified, the Assyriologist's second instinct comes into play, producing reactions that vary depending on the language. Take the example of a text composed in Akkadian. The notation of that language may be done with phonetic signs. Each sign in that case represents a syllable: a vowel by itself, a consonant plus a vowel, or a consonant plus a vowel plus a consonant.

The problem is that a single sign may have several phonetic values. Hence the sign NI, when preceded by BE, will be read /LI/: in Akkadian, *bēlī* means "my lord." But in the sequence PA NI, NI will be read /NI/, *panī* meaning "my face."

Things become even more complicated in that a sign, in addition to its syllabic value(s), may have one or more logographic value. When the Akkadian scribes borrowed cuneiform writing, they kept the ideogrammatic value that certain of the signs had had in Sumerian. Recall that an ideogram (or logogram) is a sign that conveys both a sound and a meaning: the sign 𒅗 is pronounced KA and designates "mouth" in Sumerian. An Akkadian scribe could therefore use that sign to notate the word *pūm,* which designates "mouth" in his language. In a passage containing the word KA, if a syllabic reading of the sign does not make sense, the possibility of an ideogrammatic reading must be considered.

Ideograms have a disadvantage: they multiply the number of signs in the repertoire, thereby taxing the memory. But they also have a considerable advantage, which explains why ancient scribes valued them so: they take up less space on the tablet surface and required less time to write, since a single ideogrammatic sign suffices where three or four syllabic signs would be necessary. Let me demonstrate this point with a passage from a divinatory treatise. The first line is a copy and transcription of the text from the Old Babylonian period (2000–1600 B.C.), in syllabic notation. Below it is the same text notated in ideograms, in the Neo-Assyrian version (eighth–seventh centuries B.C.): BE is the ideogram for *šumma*, SAL for *sinništum*, and so on. The third line is the Akkadian text with the signs written in cursive:[5]

šum-ma	*sí-in-ni-iš-tum*	*ú-li-id-ma* (eleven signs)
BE	SAL	Ù.TU-*ma* (five signs)
šumma	*sinništum*	*ûlid-ma*
if	a woman	has given birth

The use of ideograms thus appears to have been a kind of shorthand, but with principles very different from those usually conveyed by that term at present.

Seen from outside, the system appears very complicated. Traditionally, Assyriologists have believed that its use was reserved for a very limited group, that of scribes, the only ones who could master that writing system and then only after a long training period. In this book, I shall call into question that view of Mesopotamian civilization.

Establishing the Text. The first decipherment of the text may be done quickly, if it is a well-preserved tablet and if the text belongs to a well-known literary genre. Hence a sales contract for a piece of land can be read at sight if the specialist has mastered the models used by the notaries of the period and is well acquainted with the proper names of the region. For a letter, the task will take longer, inasmuch as that genre is by definition much less stereotyped.

If the tablet is damaged, an Assyriologist must begin by determining whether "joins" (to use the professional jargon) with other fragments are not possible. There are two complementary ways of proceeding. He can base himself on the shape of the fragments and connect those that seem to complete each other as a function of the shape of the break (oblique, for example). Or he can make joins as a function of the content: for example, if a very rare proper name appears on two different fragments, it is possible that they belong to the same tablet.

Sometimes the search for joins is not fruitful, or the surface of the tablet itself is damaged beyond repair. Then the problem of restoring the lacunae arises. When the text corresponds to a well-established model, the task is relatively easy. It is much less so in the case of a letter, despite the existence of a certain rhetoric. Restitution is an area where scientific proficiency reaches its limit: despite the greatest ingenuity, no one is ever assured of the complete reliability of the result.

When the text belongs to the category of "literary" works, the labor will be rather painstaking because of the plurality of manuscripts. The lacunae in one are often filled in by another, which constitutes an appreciable advantage. But the existence of duplicates raises another problem: how to publish the variants? At present, Sumerologists provide a reconstituted text, with what is called a "score" underneath it—that is, the text of all the manuscripts that attest the line in question, in the state found on the tablet.

That type of work presupposes, then, that all the originals can be collated, that is, that all the tablets can be reviewed. Since some were published a great while ago, improvements in the interpretation are likely to be possible, particularly if duplicates have been discovered in the meantime. An Assyriologist is thus obliged to travel to the world's great museums. To edit a Sumerian text, for example, he must in the first place plan a visit to the United States, to consult the Babylonian section of the University of Pennsylvania Museum of Archaeology and Anthropology in Philadelphia; another to the Museum of the Ancient Orient in Istanbul; and a third to the University of Jena in Germany. The tablets discovered in Nippur, one of the most important sources of Sumerian manuscripts, are in fact dispersed among these three institutions. But in not unusual cases, he will also have to go to the British Museum in London or to the Vorderasiatisches Museum in Berlin, not to mention the Iraq Museum in Baghdad or the Louvre in Paris.

Translation. Once the transcription of the document has been established, the Assyriologist will go on to translate it. In reality, the two processes are intimately linked, as can be deduced from my previous comments. Of course, the translation problems will vary depending on the language of the text in question. In Akkadian, the vocabulary is fairly well known for the most part; only certain technical terms continue to raise problems. Akkadian's kinship to the family of Semitic languages allows for many comparisons that may contribute to delimiting the meaning of new words, which, indeed, we continue to discover on a regular basis. In addition, the task is simplified by the existence of two large dictionaries, one in German (W. von Soden's *Akkadisches Handwörterbuch),* the other in English *(Chicago Assyrian Dictionary).*

For texts composed in Sumerian, matters are less simple. Specialists in Sumerian do not have the opportunity to make comparisons but rather depend greatly on the "lexical lists" established by the ancient scribes, from which apprentices learned the Sumerian vocabulary. Although there is now an electronic dictionary (ePSD), it has not been possible as yet to overcome all the remaining problems related to vocabulary.

The Problem of Reproduction. Tablets are reproduced for two different purposes. For a long time, reproductions were intended to give access to the sources, and cuneiform tablets were simply

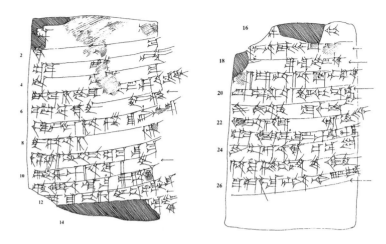

FIGURE 2. A copy and a photo of the same text (letter from Mari A.2692). (Courtesy of D. Charpin.)

published in the form of copies, with each reader deciphering them independently. Copying amounted to transposing, in ink, signs of a three-dimensional writing system onto a two-dimensional support (Figure 2). But by definition, however faithful the copy, it is still an interpretation. For tablets that have been broken, it is often very difficult to discern the marks; it is in such cases that an improvement in the reading will often become possible subsequently. Currently, a transcription and a translation of the text are often published together. The copy thus no longer serves as anything but verification. It is therefore possible to replace it with a photograph, which is by definition more reliable than a copy. All the same, one of the key problems of reproduction remains: the transformation from three dimensions to two. In general, at least six shots of each of the inscribed parts of the tablet are required to make it legible. Recent attempts at three-dimensional digitalization with a scanner have produced interesting results. The problem of the quality of the photo also arises: the lighting must be undertaken with special care. The use of vaporized ammonium chloride may improve the quality of the photo: when a fine white coating of it is deposited on the surface of the tablet, it does not penetrate into the wedges. That process markedly accentuates the contrast. The type of film, chemical products, and paper can all be experimented with as well. And since the advent of digital cameras, the electronic photo file can be manipulated through the use of a computer program.

Even more than the quality of the photo, that of the reproduction is crucial. At this point, financial considerations arise. The use of microfiche has been indispensable for some time; that of CD-ROMS is currently very common.

Plasticity and Durability of the Support. The work performed by the Assyriologist, then, includes not only the transcription and translation of ancient texts, but also their transfer onto new supports: the sheet of paper on which he writes his first transcription, the hard disk on his computer, the film on which he photographs the tablet. These supports have many advantages over the clay of the tablet: it is very easy to rework a text on a computer or to annotate it on a sheet of paper, which clay allows only with difficulty or not at all. Conversely, clay possesses one considerable advantage: it is resistant to fire, water, and magnetic disturbances. In short, in a few thousand years, our photographs, books, and hard disks will no doubt have disappeared, but our collections of cuneiform tablets will still be there.

For historians, the term "Mesopotamians" is problematic, since the former inhabitants of that region did not designate themselves as such and did not think of themselves that way. From the geographical point of view, the contrast is striking between the northern and southern parts of present-day Iraq, which correspond, respectively, to Babylonia and Assyria. But what we call "Babylonia" in no wise formed a unity in the third millennium or even at the start of the second: Akkad in the north (the region of present-day Baghdad) was distinct from Sumer in the south. Moreover, the borders of that "Mesopotamian" world were far from fixed. Mari, on the Middle Euphrates, about 15 kilometers west of the present-day border between Syria and Iraq, is a textbook case: depending on the period and the point of view, it was closer to Mesopotamia or, on the contrary, more oriented toward the Western Mediterranean. Such is the lot of all hubs. I shall make only brief excursions beyond Mesopotamia, to the west (Syria, Anatolia) or east (Iran).

Many have spoken of the long duration of Mesopotamian civilization, but they are far from agreeing on the ideal temporal divisions that would need to be respected in following its evolution (Van De Mieroop 1997). A combination of political and linguistic considerations have given rise to the designations currently in use, which I shall also employ in this book (see Chronology), despite their unsatisfactory nature. The expression "Old Babylonian period" will therefore designate the four centuries at the start of the second millennium dominated by the figure of Hammurabi, king of Babylon (1792–1750). Reference will also be made to the "Neo-Assyrian empire," and so on.

I shall begin by presenting the contexts and methods associated with an apprenticeship in the cuneiform writing system, in an attempt to evaluate the scope of literacy (Chapter 1). I shall then examine what writings were produced: first, archival documents (Chapter 2), and then correspondence, which I treat separately (Chapter 3). The complex relationship between the oral and the written was not limited to letters; hence I shall consider that situation in the realm of law and politics (Chapter 4). In the modern view, libraries constitute the site par excellence for reading, but that situation looked different in Mesopotamia (Chapter 5). Rarely were texts written "for eternity": nevertheless, a portion of those that have come down to us were intended for the deities and for posterity (Chapter 6). When a specialist reads a letter, we surmise that he is committing an indiscretion. By contrast, when he deciphers the commemorative inscription of a Mesopotamian ruler, he is fulfilling the wishes of the person who commissioned it in antiquity. He is acting in such a way that the ruler's name will not fall into oblivion.

chapter one

Apprenticeships in the Art of the Scribe: *Frameworks, Methods, Demographics*

In a traditional society like that of Mesopotamia, most professions were hereditary and instruction was given through apprenticeships. Research by social historians has in great part demonstrated this phenomenon, and the ancients spoke of it explicitly: "The fate that the god Enlil fixed for humanity is that the son should inherit his father's position" (Sjöberg 1973, 115–116). The education of scribes can be situated largely within that context, but by its very nature it entails an essential difference: it left written traces. For every period, the exercises done by apprentices have provided a large proportion of the Mesopotamian texts belonging to what A. Leo Oppenheim has called "the stream of tradition," in contrast to business documents (such as letters, contracts, administrative texts, and so on). To these pedagogical materials can be added a certain number of descriptions of activities taking place in schools, known through manuscripts dating from the eighteenth century B.C.

Evidence on Apprenticeship

The Third Millennium

Our knowledge of schooling and education in Mesopotamia, from the origin of cuneiform writing in southern Iraq in about 3200 B.C. to the end of the third millennium, is very fragmentary. But in reality, that is the case for data about the Mesopotamian world generally.[1]

The Origins in Uruk. The most ancient written tablets were discovered in Uruk. The writing on them has been termed "protocuneiform" because it differs rather appreciably from the cuneiform that emerged subsequently (Figure 3). For the following phase,

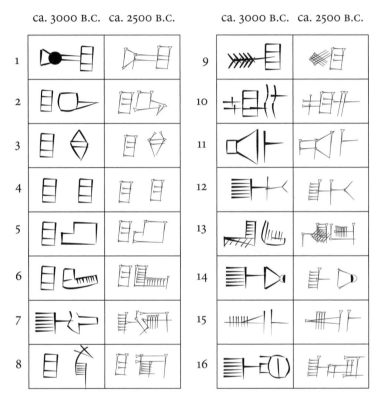

FIGURE 3. Table of the list of titles and trades (known as *Lu A*), illustrating the shift from protocuneiform to cuneiform: at left, signs from the Uruk period (about 3000 B.C.); at right, signs corresponding to the Fara period (about 2500 B.C.). (Courtesy of Robert K. Englund, after Nissen, Damerow, and Englund 1993, 111, fig. 88.)

between about 3000 and 2900, the number of places where tablets have been discovered is growing: in addition to Uruk and perhaps Larsa in the south, two cities in northern Babylonia have yielded texts, Tell Uqair and Jemdet Nasr. But the uniformity in the appearance of the tablets and in the writing conventions is so striking that it has been suggested there was a centralized education system for scribes.

The pedagogical methods for that most ancient period cannot be known exhaustively, of course, but material attesting to different stages of apprenticeship has been found (Veldhuis 2006). For the beginning level, there are tablets on which apprentices practiced inscribing "wedges." Some administrative texts that contain neither proper names of persons nor account totals may also have been school exercises. In addition, we possess lexical lists in which the entries are arranged thematically and which provide a complete semantic inventory of each rubric: metals, animals, fish, woods, toponyms, birds, and so on. Thirteen lists of this type have come down to us, in several copies. That lexical corpus contains a great many signs not found in the administrative documents of the time: the masters believed it necessary for their apprentices to learn "superfluous" signs to have sufficient mastery of the system. All the same, we must avoid falling into any sort of mysticism about the lists. They have sometimes been presented as the means for apprehending the universe as a whole. But it is very doubtful that theological or cosmological preoccupations lay behind them: none is devoted to the names of the deities, stars, rivers, mountains, or wild animals. By contrast, protocuneiform writing was from the start created as a system for administrative purposes. That meant being as complete as possible, so as to deal with every imaginable situation. It is surprising that the archaic lexical corpus does not devote more space to writing numbers, given their importance in the administrative texts and the complexity of the system of weights and measures used. There were actually no fewer than five different systems, depending on the nature of what was to be counted: the volume of cereal grains was not notated in the same way as that of dairy products. But in fact, metrology was a departure from the scribes' area of specialization, and apprenticeships in that subject matter must have taken place in the business world. A few computation exercises have been uncovered, however.

One of the most important discoveries was surely the lexical list of titles and profession names. Known as *Lu A*, it is attested by more than 185 manuscripts (Figure 3). That discovery was possible because the list was transmitted practically without changes until the early second millennium. As a result, it points to an altogether remarkable phenomenon: beginning from the most ancient phase in the history of cuneiform writing, scribes were trained in a rigorous manner, and that training quickly became an immutable tradition. The diffusion of cuneiform writing in the Sumerian world—but also beyond it, as the texts of Ebla in western Syria have shown—occurred rapidly, but it did not lead to divergent local developments, which would have resulted in chaos (Waetzoldt 1986; Archi 1992; Civil 2008).

The Early Dynastic II Period. After 2900, there is a lacuna of several centuries in the cuneiform documentation, and it is only the third and last phase of the so-called Early Dynastic period (ca. 2500–2334) for which we again have texts. These were found primarily at the sites of Fara and Abu Salabikh. The texts of Fara, exhumed before World War I by German excavators, were published by A. Deimel, who devoted a volume to the eighty-two texts that he called "school texts." Subsequently, researchers came to understand that these included texts customarily designated "literary," a designation that actually makes little sense. Unexpectedly, these "literary texts" bear striking similarities to tablets discovered in 1963–1965 by an American team in Abu Salabikh. The repertoire is identical in both cases: hymns to the temples, incantations, and wisdom literature (collections of proverbs and so on). Not only are the texts the same at both sites; at times, so too are the divisions of the written signs into cells within the columns.

These so-called literary texts were found at the site in Fara in eight different places, in four instances alongside administrative texts. It is highly improbable that each of these eight places was an independent center for copying and diffusing that type of text. More likely, the texts were preserved in different locations but written at a single site; or at least, they represent the work of a single school (Pomponio 1983). It is certain that the same scribes, called *sanga* at the time, kept the administrative bookkeeping records *and* oversaw the training of apprentices (Visicato 2000, 233). Nearly half the names of scribes from Abu Salabikh given in the colophons of the lexical and literary texts are Semitic:[2] it seems these were students from Kish who had come for training in the south (Foster 2005b, 88). It is they who exported their knowledge to Ebla via Mari.

The site of Lagash (Tell al-Hiba) has yielded a particularly interesting school tablet from the Early Dynastic IIIb period. On it are indications of how the master accompanied his lessons with commentaries, which in principle were never set down in writing (Civil 1983).

The Akkad Period.   Most of the school texts dating from the Akkadian empire (twenty-fourth to twenty-third century) come from Girsu (Tello). It might be surmised that the building holding them was a school, but the excavation took place so long ago that nothing is known of the archaeological context of the discovery; thus the building may have been an office where apprenticeships took place. The simplest writing exercises are on round or lenticular tablets: lists of the names of persons, gods, objects, and so on. There are also maps or plans, which may attest to apprenticeships in surveying. A business document containing far-fetched figures (30 talents of silver, 10 talents of gold, 3,600 head of cattle, 3,600 equids, 3,600 slaves, and 3,600 [*gur*] of grain) could also be the sign of an apprenticeship. Other texts, discovered especially in the region of the Diyala River, show that it was the empire's future managers who were being trained there. They had to have at least a rudimentary knowledge of Sumerian, even in northern Babylonia, where administrative documents were written in Akkadian at the time.

Shulgi and the Creation of the Institutional Edubba.   It is only for the age of the Third Dynasty of Ur (twenty-first century) that we possess more detailed information about the scribe's profession and place within society. The title "scribe" *(dub.sar)* covered various occupations, from royal secretary to modest pen-pusher assigned the accounts of a small store. Fundamentally, however, the scribe was considered an artisan and was remunerated as such (Waetzoldt 1991, 638; Charpin, Hunger, and Waetzoldt 2009). We also know that certain high officials in the administration, who bore a title different from that of scribe, had received an education in reading and writing. Paradoxically, this was one of the periods in Mesopotamian history that left the smallest number of exercise tablets.[3] The reason is simple: very few private houses dating from that period have been excavated. And we know from the following period, the Old Babylonian, that school tablets are usually discovered in the masters' houses.[4]

King Shulgi (2094–2047 B.C.) seems to have played an essential role in the evolution of scribes' training.[5] He undertook major reforms toward the middle part of his reign, which resulted in a significant increase in the number of administrative tablets. That means the number of scribes grew, though estimating how many there were is a risky enterprise. It has been calculated that in Girsu at the end of the Early Dynastic period, thirty scribes at most were working at the same time; there may not have been a hundred in the entire Akkadian empire. That number jumped to a few hundred in the Ur III period: we know of 1,600 in all, spread out over about four generations (Visicato 2000). Shulgi believed that training these scribes was a task of the highest priority, to judge by the place this theme occupies in the writings about him. But the creation of the *edubba*, literally, "the house of tablets,"[6] must not be attributed to him, at least according to Hymn B, in which that king recalls the training he received in his childhood. In addition, the principal task Shulgi assigned to the *edubba* was not to train bureaucrats but to make copies of hymns addressed to the deities in behalf of the kings, or to the kings themselves. Hymns were one way to perpetuate the memory of the sovereign, as Shulgi claims he had done for his predecessors: "When I have discovered *tigi* and *zamzam* hymns from past days, old ones from ancient times, I have never declared them to be false, and have never contradicted their contents. I have conserved these antiquities, never abandoning them to oblivion" (Hymn B of Shulgi, 272–275).[7] As a result, he expressed the wish that others would do the same for him (Figure 4). That request appears in Hymn E, sometimes considered a sort of "testament" of the king, which contains an impressive enumeration of the different kinds of hymns composed for Shulgi: "In the cult-places, let no one neglect the songs about me, whether they are *adab*, whether they are *tigi* or *malgatus*, *šir.gida* or praise of kingship, whether they are *šumunša*, *kungar* or *balbale*, whether they are *gi.gid* or *zamzam*—so that they shall never pass out of memory and never lapse from people's mouths. Let them never cease to be sung in the shining Ekur! Let them be played for Enlil in his Shrine of the New Moon!" (Hymn E of Shulgi, 53–61). Nevertheless, the transmission of these hymns was problematic: the human chain could be broken. And the principal written support that had existed until that time consisted of statues. That was particularly true for King Gudea of Lagash. These statues, located in the temples, ran the risk of being pillaged or destroyed at some point. Aware that the performance of songs of praise for the king was in danger of ending rather quickly, Shulgi created a school of scribes under the patronage of

FIGURE 4. Copy of a hymn to Shulgi, king of Ur: all the manuscripts of these hymns date from the Old Babylonian period and are copies by apprentice scribes. (Courtesy of Nederlands Instituut voor het nabije oosten [NINO].)

the goddess Nisaba. His decision to have the text of these hymns recopied continuously onto tablets in the *edubba* figures especially at the end of Hymn E: "May my hymns be in everyone's mouth; let the songs about me not pass from memory. So that the fame of my praise, the words which Enki composed about me, and which Gelštin-ana joyously speaks from the heart and broadcasts far and wide, shall never be forgotten, I have had them written down line by line in the House of the Wisdom of Nisaba in holy heavenly writing, as great works of scholarship. No one shall ever let any of it pass from memory" (Hymn E of Shulgi, 240–257). This decision produced excellent results: in the school curriculum, the copying of hymns held a major place until the mideighteenth century. Pupils did not confine themselves to the written dimension of these works: they also had to be able to sing them. Hence, in a text mocking a pupil is this comment: "When he sits before the student of the master, he is unable to declaim a *tigi* or *adab* hymn." The ruins of schoolmasters' houses have yielded copies of these hymns by the hundreds.

The Old Babylonian Period

The question of schools and education can be treated in the most detailed manner for the Old Babylonian period (twentieth to seventeenth century): not only are scholastic materials abundant, but there are also descriptions of the lessons and their spatial and institutional context.

The Framework for Scribal Apprenticeship and the Problem of Schools. It was traditionally believed that during the Old Babylonian period there was a school institution, the *edubba,* that subsequently disappeared, replaced by a familial transmission of knowledge. Such an evolution would have been very odd, since it would have moved in the opposite direction of what is known elsewhere. It is therefore fitting to look more closely at the question (Charpin 1986a).

What is known about these *edubba* is based in large part on literary texts describing the activities that took place in the schools, sometimes called "academic" literature.[8] The most famous example is the one popularized by Kramer under the title *Schooldays*. A pupil who was constantly being reprimanded at school had his father invite his master over; the teacher, well treated and showered with gifts, then praised his pupil. There is also the dialogue between Enki-mansum and Girni-isag. Girni-isag, who held the position of monitor ("big brother"), accused his student of incompetence; Enki-mansum defended himself, and the resulting text provides a very interesting catalog of the subjects taught. The text titled "A Father and His Delinquent Son"[9] depicts a scribe who wishes his child would pursue the same training he had rather than wandering the streets. Other texts of that kind exist, such as a conversation between a supervisor *(ugula)* and an apprentice scribe, or the instructions of a master *(um.mi.a)*. Then there are the texts that Benno Landsberger calls "Exams": they are known only through bilingual copies from the first millennium, but they certainly date back to a more ancient time.

It was believed that these texts proved that schools existed as independent institutions at particular sites reserved for teaching. The advice that students not dawdle in the streets on their way to class, for example, has been interpreted in that sense. In addition, the schools supposedly had a "playground," since among the auxiliary staff is the *lú.kisal.lá,* or "recess attendant" (literally, "yard man"). At the head of the *edubba* was the *um.mi.a* (expert), also called the "father of the school" *(ad.da é.dub.ba).* He was assisted by a "big brother" *(šeš.gal).* The students themselves were sometimes called the "children of the school" *(dumu.é.dub.ba).* That vocabulary may betray the familial origins of the institution. Such is the case for commercial firms, where the "employer" was called the "father": many commercial firms were in fact based on familial relations among their members. Most authors agree that teachers were directly remunerated by the students' parents, though there is little evidence of this.

How studies were organized is still poorly understood. There are a few allusions to the school schedule: "My days of vacation are three per month; the various holidays are three days per month; with that, there are twenty-four days per month that I spend at school, that is not a long time" (Civil 1985, 72 [Edubba D: 22–25]). It was not only the schools that provided three days off a month; similar indications are found in employment contracts. Pupils were sometimes directed to do exercises at home; these were called *im.šu*, literally, "hand tablets": "They assigned me my homework, in the evening they assigned me my 'hand tablet'; (when I returned home,) I read my 'hand tablet' to my father, I recited my tablet to him, he was delighted" (Civil 1985, 75 [Edubba A: 6–10]). Requests for assistance from Nisaba, patron goddess of scribes, were sometimes made: "May Nisaba make your writing reed beautiful, may she lead you to correct the mistake in your 'hand tablets'!" (Civil 1985, 75–76 [Edubba A: 75–76]).

When we read these texts, many questions remain unanswered, such as the age at which pupils started school and how long a scribe's training lasted.

The discovery of a school or library is often considered "sensational": it is therefore not surprising that some excavators believed in good faith that they had discovered schools when in fact they had not. The most spectacular example is the one in the Mari palace: André Parrot identified room 64 as a school, primarily because of the parallel benches filling the space, where he thought the students had sat (Figure 5). That interpretation can be refuted in several ways. In the first place, such a view of school is a glaring anachronism: classrooms equipped with rows of benches are a very recent phenomenon. In addition, the unfortunate students would have had to contort themselves horribly to fit their feet and legs into that very restricted space. And even though Mesopotamia,

FIGURE 5. The pseudo-school of the Mari palace: in reality, it was likely a storeroom where jars of wine were wedged between the benches. (From A. Parrot, *Le Palais, architecture: Mission Archeologique de Mari II/1* [Paris, 1958], plate 42.)

unlike Egypt, did not leave behind any representations of "squatting scribes," that must have been their usual posture (Charpin 2007a) (Figure 6). Let me add to these criticisms that the tablets discovered in that room were by no means school texts but rather administrative documents, including a good number relating to wine.[10] In reality, the room was used to store large jars, whose pointed end rested between two benches. Another example is the building in Ur located at 1 Broad Street. Often presented as the quintessential school, that house actually contained school tablets only in the foundations, in the form of documents discarded along with others of an administrative nature. The schoolmaster Igmil-Sīn, who emerged fully formed from the imagination of the excavator, Sir L. Woolley, vanishes as a result (Charpin 1986a, 434–485).

FIGURE 6. Neo-Assyrian bas-relief representing two standing scribes (southwest palace of Niniveh). The scribe depicted in the foreground (second figure from the right) is drawing on a sheet of papyrus or leather; the scribe behind him is writing on a wax tablet (probably a diptych in wood, whose hinge is visible). (Werner Forman / Art Resource, New York.)

Nevertheless, excavations have not failed to exhume real schools, though we must understand what that term means. In the first place, what conditions allowed the school tablets to survive? One of their essential characteristics was to be perpetually recycled: just as (even today) people employ reusable slates, pupils of the past, to save on clay, constantly remodeled the exercise tablets (Scheil 1937, 55). School tablets are therefore found at ground level only if the building was a place of learning immediately before its destruction (Tinney 1998). A few indisputable examples can be cited, such as the house of Ur-Utu in Sippar-Amnānum, the present-day Tell ed-Dēr (Tanret 2002). Among the some 2,000 tablets discovered in that residence of the chief lamenter *(gala.*

mah) of the goddess Annunitum, a building destroyed in year 18 of Ammi-ṣaduqa (1629), was a batch of seventy-one tablets, extracted from a stone container in the middle of the yard or nearby. Most had been twisted and misshapen, obviously when they were recycled. Inscribed on them were the most elementary exercises for learning cuneiform. Another clear case is in Ur, at house no. 7 on Quiet Street (Charpin 1986a, 420–434). A family of priests lived there for nearly a century, from the beginning of the reign of Rim-Sin to year 11 of Samsu-iluna (1739). Their archives have been unearthed, but so too have texts bearing witness to the scribal training that took place in that house. This time, they are not elementary texts but those belonging to the intermediate or even advanced stage of instruction. Let me also cite the case of the "TA quarter" in Nippur. School tablets were found in three adjacent houses, designated F, G, and H. The excavator believed that these could not possibly have been schools, since he could not imagine three of them located next to one another. He therefore thought that these tablets represented the "homework" done by apprentice scribes after school. But given that one of these houses yielded more than 1,400 school tablets, that explanation hardly seems credible. Much more likely, these were the houses of masters *(um. mi.a)* who taught from their homes (Robson 2001). The thousands of exercise tablets from Nippur have been classified into four categories, based on their shape (Civil 1979, 27–28). Type 1 are either large tablets with several columns or cylinders or prisms. Type 2 are tablets divided into two parts (Figure 7): the master's model appears in the left-hand column, while the student's practice exercises are in the right-hand column. As a result of being erased and reinscribed, the right part of the tablet sometimes became too thin and would finally be cut off. On the front is a short excerpt of a lexical list or of proverbs or model contracts. On the back of tablets of that kind are copies of lexical lists different from those on the front, or mathematical tables. Type 3 are single-column tablets containing a short excerpt from a series that continues on

FIGURE 7. An example of a so-called type 2 exercise: on the left-hand column, the master has written the model (here, a list of kinds of wood). The right-hand columns were used for different exercises, which were effaced one by one; prints from the fingers that smoothed out the surface are visible. (Courtesy of Michel Tanret.)

the back; type 4 are lenticular tablets containing only a few lines. Generally, only the flat side is inscribed, the curved side remaining anepigraphic.

For the moment at least, no school attached to a palace has been discovered—we now know what to make of the case in Mari. Nonetheless, scholastic materials have been exhumed from the palace of Sin-kashid in Uruk (Cavigneaux 1982). A few scholastic, lexical, and literary texts have also been uncovered in the palace of Enlil-bani in Isin (Sallaberger 1996, 179n16).

The term "school" appears to be misleading, then, in that it confers an institutional character on the training of young scribes. It also suggests a certain continuity of that activity at a single site. The archaeological evidence yields a different image: that of houses of literati who trained apprentices at home. All in all, scribal apprenticeships may hardly have been different in their sociological reality from the other ways of transmitting knowledge. That is, they occurred primarily within the context of the family. The opposition that Landsberger felt necessary to establish between "lay scribes" and "illiterate priests" cannot be maintained (1960, 98). Although not all literati belonged to the temple staff, part of that staff was trained in reading and writing.

The status of "academic" texts arises as a result. The term obviously does not apply to the reality of the eighteenth and seventeenth centuries as the excavations have revealed it: does that mean that these texts are idealized fictions? A. George has recently formulated an interesting hypothesis (2005): the school (edubba) described in these texts may correspond to the situation that existed in the twenty-first century, under the Third Dynasty of Ur, and that continued into the twentieth and nineteenth centuries under the kings of Isin. Later on, scribes were more often trained by masters at their homes: education would therefore have followed the same movement toward "privatization" as the rest of the economy. In addition, when Shulgi speaks of the schools of Ur and

Nippur, he designates them by terms that resemble temple names: "House of Wisdom of the heavenly Nisaba" or "Place of Knowledge." It may well be that the schools of his time were located in the temples of Nisaba, patron goddess of writing, just as the temples of Gula, goddess of medicine, served as "hospitals," those of Kittum, goddess of justice, as "bureaux of weights and measures," and so on (Charpin forthcoming a).

Techniques for Transmitting Written Knowledge. It is possible to reconstitute the masters' pedagogy by combining information about the *edubba* provided in the texts with an analysis of the exercises discovered at excavations.

The order in which beginning studies occurred is reflected in the tablets used to train apprentices. A pupil was first taught to hold the calamus properly in his hand: witness the exercises sometimes described by the medieval term *probatio calami* (Figure 8). Pupils learned the basic signs of cuneiform writing: vertical wedge (DIŠ), horizontal wedge (AŠ), and oblique wedge (U), then simple signs such as A or BAD. The apprentices went on to copy the syllabaries, beginning with the lists of signs. The ABC's of cuneiform were the series called *a-a-me-me* (the "Silbenalphabet B" in modern Assyriological jargon). Apprentices began with the signs that had the simplest shapes (A, KU, ME), repeated in various combinations; then new signs were introduced. That series is attested only in Nippur; elsewhere, another, similar series ("Silbenalphabet A") was used. The pupils continued with the *tu-ta-ti* series, based this time on a principle no longer visual but phonetic: each consonant was combined in turn with one of the three basic vowels of the writing system, in the order *u-a-i* (Figure 9). The first lines of the exercise were thus *tu/ta/ti, nu/na/ni, bu/ba/bi,* and so on, covering in all about eighty syllables. Apprentices then moved on to writing proper names. Lessons in anthroponyms were one of the first assignments given to young scribes (the so-called

FIGURE 8. Example of the *probatio calami*. The beginner learned to hold his calamus in his hand, always tracing the same sign, the simplest one (a vertical wedge). (Courtesy of the Penn Museum.)

Inanna-téš series, named after the first entry on "list A," the names of persons). The advantage of this course of study was that it was based on the scribes' concrete knowledge and on the fact that in Sumerian (as in Akkadian) names of persons always have a meaning.

The pupils then tackled the lexical lists. The master first made use of what was once viewed as a sort of "encyclopedia," the *Urra* series, a thematic enumeration of all sorts of animals, plants, objects, and so on. Such lists attest to the "science of the concrete," sometimes considered the mark of traditional societies. The master likely indicated orally the pronunciation of each Sumerian ideogram and its meaning in Akkadian, and the students had to learn them by heart. Clearly, such lists in no way constituted "dictionaries," in that they were not designed to supply the meaning

FIGURE 9. Example of a so-called *Tu-ta-ti* exercise. The scribe first inscribed each sign on a line, then three in a row: *[tu]/ta/ti*, then *tu ta ti; nu/na/ni,* then *nu na ni; bu/ba/bi,* then *bu ba bi;* and so on. (Courtesy of the Penn Museum.)

of a sign or word. The aim was primarily to increase the apprentices' vocabulary. In the Old Babylonian period, the series was divided into six sections and contained about 3,300 lines. The later tradition divided the content into twenty-four tablets (Veldhuis 1997, 47), as follows:

Section	Content	Tablets
1	trees and wooden objects	3–7
2	reeds and reed objects; vases and clay; skins and leather objects; metals and metal objects	8–12
3	domestic animals; wild animals; cuts of meat	13–15
4	stones and plants; fish and birds; clothing	16–19
5	geographical names and terms	20–22
6	foodstuffs	23–24

Once the pupil was familiar with the signs, he had to learn to associate them with the various possible pronunciations. That was the purpose of the so-called *Proto-Ea* series. The signs were arranged by shape and repeated as many times as there were different readings. The series began with the sign A, no doubt considered one of the simplest. It was repeated five times, with a gloss indicating its pronunciation; the translation into Akkadian was not written down. The notation "a A" means "a (is the pronunciation of the sign) A (when it means 'water')"; "du-ru A" is to be understood as "duru (is the pronunciation of the sign) A (when it means 'wet')"; and so on.

Apprentices then proceeded to the so-called *Proto-Lú* list, devoted to titles and the names of professions, terms of kinship, and descriptions of human beings. That series dates back to the origins of cuneiform writing. Precisely because it was so ancient, it lagged somewhat behind the social reality of the Old Babylonian period, since certain of the titles found on it had by that time disappeared from usage. The *Proto-Lú* was followed by other lists to be copied. It was undoubtedly at this stage in the apprenticeship that the study of mathematics was introduced, particularly in the form of multiplication tables or inverse tables (Robson 1999, 2008). Future scribes also had to learn the legal phraseology necessary for drawing up contracts. That was the aim of the series known as *ki.ulutin.bi.šè,* or *ana ittišu,* which was composed in Nippur in the Old Babylonian period, though most of the manuscripts are of more recent date. Some copies of the Code of Lipit-Eshtar do seem to be the work of a student. There are also many model contracts on which the list of witnesses and the date have been omitted. Hence a young student boasts to a comrade that he is able to write "marriage contracts, company contracts . . . sales contracts for houses, fields, slaves, securities in silver, lease contracts for fields, contracts for cultivating palm groves, and even adoption contract tablets" (Civil 1985, 70 and 72, lines 43–48).

The young scribe could then begin to copy "literary" texts. These were primarily texts in the Sumerian language, which thus played roughly the same role as Latin not long ago in Western civilization. The constitution of a corpus of Sumerian literature during the Old Babylonian period therefore did not come about so much from the desire to rescue it from oblivion as, more prosaically, from the masters' need to have available "anthologies of selected passages," so to speak. In any event, the situation is not very different from that of Greek literature, where what has survived corresponds primarily to the choices made by Byzantine schoolmasters. The first exercises consisted of copying proverbs, which had the dual advantage of being brief and easy to memorize (Veldhuis 2000a; Alster 2007). Like many exercises in imitation, these were done on lenticular tablets. First the master wrote the two or three lines of the proverb, and then the student recopied them underneath (Figure 10). After that, the exercise became more complicated: once the master had inscribed a proverb on the obverse, the student had to recopy it from memory on the reverse of the tablet. Hundreds of lenticular tablets of this kind have been

FIGURE 10. Lenticular tablet: the first two lines were written by the master. The student recopied them underneath with a less sure hand. (Courtesy of the Penn Museum.)

discovered: it is not difficult to distinguish on them the sure hand of the master from that of the student, hesitant and often error-prone.

That phase was followed by the copying of short excerpts, then of entire compositions. That level of the curriculum has been reconstituted on the basis of unearthed school tablets but also of "catalogs" of a particular genre. Some are inventories of manuscript collections held in the house of one educated person or another. They thus usefully complement the discoveries of archaeology for reconstituting the corpus of Sumerian literature. But other "catalogs" are near duplicates, and some have argued that they should be considered education "programs" of a sort (Civil 1975, 145n36; Vanstiphout 1995, 9n20; Shaffer 2000).

A set of four texts played a very important pedagogical role in the transition between the two phases: these were hymns with an extremely simple grammar. Hymn B of Lipit-Eshtar, a sixty-line composition, was the first that the apprentices had to copy (Vanstiphout 1979). It was followed by Hymn B of Iddin-Dagan, Hymn

A of Enlil-bani, and Hymn A of the goddess Nisaba, the four constituting what one Sumerologist has proposed to call "the tetrade." That first set was followed by a group of ten more texts, called the "decade" (Tinney 1999). Sometimes the master dictated: the student first had to repeat the lesson orally, then write it down. Hence the possibility of this reproach: "Your hand cannot follow the rhythm of (your) mouth" (Enki-mansum/Girni-isa dialogue: 12; Vanstiphout 1997). In house no. 7 on Quiet Street in Ur, two copies of a work have been found, identical but for variations in the signs (*mu.ši.na* on one tablet and *mu.še.na* on the other, for example). This suggests that a dictation was given simultaneously to two students, which is particularly likely in that two of the sons of Ku-Ningal, the master of the house, were his successors. In another example, the mistakes made by the apprentice give the impression that he was taking dictation but was afflicted with dyslexia (Foster 2003, 86). In other cases, a manuscript was provided the student, who had to recopy it, then carefully collate his tablet. Most of the exercises are on single-column tablets: these are often short excerpts of ten to fifteen lines but are sometimes texts as long as 120 lines. The longest texts were copied on tablets with two or three columns on the obverse; several tablets were sometimes required to hold a large work in its totality.

The works thus recopied belonged to diverse genres (Vanstiphout 2003b), first and foremost to the realm of literature: myths; epic narratives of the great deeds of legendary kings such as Gilgamesh; lamentations for destroyed cities; hymns to the gods and temples; and debates on antithetical realities, such as "the palm tree and the tamarisk" or "summer and winter." It is possible that a pair of students "acted out" these debates. The status of Sumerian "literature" is far from clearly established, but it seems evident that, for a good portion of these works, their only use was pedagogical. That explains the difficulties Sumerologists encounter in attempting to establish the text of these compositions: they are working from apprentices' copies of variable quality, some obviously produced by dullards.

Copying letters composed in Sumerian, particularly "historical letters," was also part of the curriculum. The correspondence of certain rulers has come down to us in that way—particularly that of the monarchs of the Third Dynasty of Ur, but also that of certain Amorite kings of Larsa (Michalowski 1981, forthcoming). The training of apprentices also entailed copying royal commemorative inscriptions.[11] That practice is particularly well documented for Nippur, where many copies from the Old Babylonian period of more ancient inscriptions (dating back to the Akkad and Ur III periods) have been discovered on statues or stelas that were on display in the courtyard of the city's major sanctuary, the Ekur. Students usually respected the forms of the signs in the original, but the exercise sometimes consisted of modernizing them. Apprentice scribes sometimes indicated on their copy on what support (now lost) the inscription appeared, or even its precise location: on the shoulder of the statue, for example (Buccellati 1993).

Training was not limited to "belles lettres": apprentices also received practical training to qualify them for their future tasks. To write an inheritance contract, they not only had to have learned by heart the corresponding model, they also had to be able to divide up the land area to be distributed among the heirs. Arithmetic, knowledge of the systems of weights and measures, and surveying were thus part of the curriculum. The same was true for other subjects, by definition less indispensable, such as music and song: students had to know the different musical genres *(šìr)* and be able to sing different compositions (Vanstiphout 1995, 8n16).

It is therefore clear that this training was what would now be called "multidisciplinary." But the pedagogical methods rested on principles we would consider "traditional," constantly depending on memorization, emulation, and even corporal punishment (Volk 1996).

Silent Reading? In the cuneiform world, was reading aloud the only practice, or is silent reading also attested? That question has never been the object of systematic research in Assyriology (but see Grayson 2000, whose conclusions I do not always agree with), though specialists in classical antiquity have addressed it many times.[12] The response to that question will be found not in the documents relating to apprenticeship but in various business texts, especially letters. When someone read a tablet to another, he "had [him] listen" *(šušmūm)* to it. The one who learned of its content "listened" *(šemūm)* to it. In all cases, then, the text was read aloud, as the following letter found in the Mari palace shows: "Tell Shu-nuhra-Halu: thus speaks Habdu-Malik. I did not send you a duplicate of the tablet intended for the king, since there is never anyone but you to read aloud the news contained in a tablet addressed to the king, and no one else has ever had occasion to do it. So I had one tablet taken twice: once for the king and (once) for you. I am sending a very urgent message. Listen to this tablet. If it is appropriate, have the king listen to it" *(ARM 26/2 396)*. Habdu-Malik does not distinguish here between the reading that Shu-nuhra-Halu does for himself and that which he must do for the king. The same verb is used, either in the active voice *(šemūm, to hear)* or in the factitive *(šušmūm, to make heard)*. In fact, the verb "read" *(šitassūm)* is a form of a verb whose primary meaning is "cry out, call" (Maul 1994a, 50, no. 18, note h); what is at issue, then, is reading aloud. Note as well this significant omen: "If the diviner sprays saliva while reading the oracle query . . ." *(CAD Š/II, 166b [RA 61, 36: 14])*. And on the colophon of a chronicle from Mari: "Hand of Habdu-Malik. Reader *(muštassūm):* Limi-Dagan." (Birot 1985, 232 [M.7481: r. 8']). An opposition clearly exists between the one who reads the text aloud and the one who takes it down in writing as it is being dictated.

One text may suggest, however, that some scribes practiced silent reading. Hulalum, private secretary to Samsi-Addu, wrote as follows to Samsi-Addu's son, Yasmah-Addu, king of Mari: "Tell my lord: thus speaks your servant Hulalum. With the tablets that they brought for the king (Samsi-Addu) from Qaṭna, the Qatnean messengers brought the king by mistake a tablet intended for my lord (Yasmah-Addu). Having opened it, I saw that it was written to my lord and I thus did not have the king listen to it. At present, I have just sent that tablet to my lord" (Charpin 1995a, 48–50 [A.2701]).

In this case, then, Samsi-Addu's secretary prepared to read the mail by breaking open the envelopes of the letters and familiarizing himself with their content before reading them to his master. It is interesting to observe the distinction Hulalum makes between the reading he himself practices (line 15: *āmur,* "I saw") and that which he may do for the king (line 16: *ul ušešme,* "I did not have him listen"). We might of course surmise that in this case Hulalum chose his words in haste. Nevertheless, he could have written, "having opened the letter, I listened *(ešmēšu)* to it and I observed *(āmur)* etc.," and he did not do so.[13] This might be taken as evidence that the Mesopotamian scribes were already practicing silent reading. There are in fact two words for "reading" in Akkadian: *šitassūm* and *tāmartum* (from *āmārum,* "see"):[14] the first term designates reading aloud, the second silent reading. That explains why the two words are combined on certain colophons, for example, that of Ashurbanipal: "I deposited (this tablet) in my palace to read it *(tāmartum)* and to have it read aloud to me *(ši tassūm).*"[15]

The Problem of "Bilingualism." The Old Babylonian period was noted for its bilingualism, Sumerian and Akkadian both being used at that time (Vanstiphout 1999). Even today, the date at which the living language of Sumerian became extinct is the object of bitter debates (Sallaberger 2004; Woods 2006; Michalowski 2006). According to some, it occurred at the end of the Early Dynastic period. For others, Sumerian was still alive in the Old Babylonian period. The question is complex, but let me simply point out that the use scholars make of certain texts in the attempt to prove that Sumerian was still spoken in the Old Babylonian period is inadmissible: Latin, for example, was still spoken in rhetoric classes less than a century ago (Charpin 1994a). The case of Shulgi, king of Ur, is particularly interesting (Rubio 2006). In Hymn C of Shulgi, the king responds to the Amorite messengers in Amorite and to the Elamite messengers in Elamite, languages he claims to know as well as Sumerian. Hymn B of Shulgi claims that it is impossible to deceive the king with a translation, since he knows five languages: Sumerian, Elamite, Amorite, Subarean (no doubt Hurrian), and Meluhhan. The absence of Akkadian from that list cannot fail to astonish. But it has been noted that no one never boasts of knowing one's native language: these two passages can therefore be considered evidence that Shulgi's mother tongue was Akkadian and that Sumerian was already a dead language at the time.

In the Old Babylonian period, then, Sumerian was a language of prestige, used for worship, commemoration, and so forth. Its use in legal texts varied by region: though almost always used in the south, it was employed only in set formulas in the north, where scribes used Akkadian whenever a special clause had to be inserted. In Upper Mesopotamia, the presence in Shubat-Enlil of a copy of the Sumerian king list (Vincente 1995) must not deceive us; knowledge of Sumerian was not very widespread. Samsi-Addu replied to his son Yasmah-Addu, who had demanded from his father a scribe able to read Sumerian, that there were none available at the moment (Ziegler and Charpin 2007). To enter into the good graces of King Zimri-Lim of Mari, a scribe undertook to send him a bilingual letter (Charpin 1992a; Durand 1997, no. 22)—but our judgment of what was supposed to be considered an achievement can only be harsh.

At first sight, the place of Akkadian in the training of scribes seems to have been limited. Recall that, for a long time in the West, students learned to read only in Latin, hence in a dead language. Lessons in reading French were a veritable revolution introduced by the Brothers of the Christian Schools,[16] which earned them the nickname "Ignorantine Brothers." It is therefore quite possible that a cultural phenomenon of the same order existed in Mesopotamia. Hence the famous proverb: "A scribe who does not know Sumerian, what kind of scribe is he?" (Alster 1997, 54, no. 47). Speaking Akkadian in the schools may have been forbidden, if we are to believe the text Samuel N. Kramer baptized *Schooldays:* "The Sumerian monitor, 'You spoke in Akkadian!' He beat me" (George 2005, 1228 and n2). In addition, the unrepresentativeness of the sources must no doubt be taken into account: most are from Nippur and Ur and thus reflect the southern, very Sumerianized traditions. It would be helpful to have a complete inventory of what was discovered in Shaduppum (Tell Harmal) in the lower Diyala Valley, that is, in the region of Akkad. It appears that the copying of literary texts in Akkadian was fairly advanced there.

Unlike the case for Sumerian literature, there are usually no duplicates of Akkadian literary texts: some have therefore argued that these were "masterpieces" of a sort, composed by students at the end of their training. More prosaically, apprentice scribes also practiced writing letters in Akkadian. Nearly identical copies of letters have been discovered at different sites (Sallaberger 1999, 149–154); only the proper names vary. These were clearly exercises, given their content, which often mention rather ordinary situations, as in this example: "To PN speak: thus PN_2. May Šamaš keep you in good health! Concerning the field of PN_3 which you had taken away and given to PN_4—PN_3 went (and) petitioned the king and the king became very angry. Hurry! Before the officer of the king reaches you, return the field to its owner. It is urgent!" (Michalowski 1983, 222–226).

A recently published text seems to show that lessons were sometimes given in the form of dialogues: the master would ask questions in Akkadian, and the student would have to respond in Sumerian, or vice versa (Civil 1998). A student, boasting of his success at school, proudly announces: "I can manage in the Sumerian language, writing, archiving, bookkeeping, computations; I can even hold a conversation in Sumerian!" (Civil 1985, 70 [*Edubba D*: 36–38]).

Diversified Training Programs? The problem arises whether all scribes had the same training: it is clear that there must have been a difference between an employee in a warehouse, who needed only a minimum number of signs for writing down his expenses and receipts, and the educated person able to compose a hymn in Sumerian glorifying the king. Did they both receive the same initial training, with the educated person simply pursuing his studies further, or are we to assume that different training programs existed? For the moment, it is impossible to reply to that question. And although we are beginning to have a good sense of the education of members of the clergy, we still do not know where and how the countless bureaucrats necessary for the daily functioning of the palace were trained. Our current view of the education of scribes, in which an apprenticeship in Sumerian literature seems to occupy a preponderant place at the expense of more practical training, may therefore have been distorted by an unrepresentative sample. And there may have been local differences: it has been noted that the school texts of Uruk contained more glosses in Akkadian than those of Nippur (Veldhuis 1997–1998, 362b). In addition, the importance placed on the copying of epics, legends, royal hymns, commemorative inscriptions, and so on, is surely not attributable to chance. Fidelity to a certain notion of kingship had to be inculcated in the scribes from the earliest years. And training was not only technical: it was necessary to foster an *esprit de corps* in individuals who, one way or another, would spend their lives in the king's service, either directly in the administration or indirectly in the temples, appealing to the gods for their benevolence toward the sovereign.

Familial Transmission of Knowledge in the Later Periods

For a long time, the data on apprenticeships in writing from the mid-second millennium on were less fully exploited than those for the Old Babylonian period. They have been the object of recent studies, which document the enduring quality of many of the practices but also significant changes.

The Middle Babylonian Period. According to the middle chronology, the Old Babylonian era ended in about 1600. It was followed by a period that is totally obscure; even its duration is unknown (between 50 and 150 years, depending on the chronology). The second half of the second millennium seems to have been a key period for the transmission of Akkadian literature, but on that matter only indirect evidence is available. The rare school texts extant for that era show the permanence of the techniques of Old Babylonian apprenticeship, but with a significant innovation: the introduction of Akkadian literary texts into the curriculum (Veldhuis 2000b). The most remarkable phenomenon in that era, however, was the considerable expansion of cuneiform beyond its traditional geographical area. Henceforth, Babylonian was written in cuneiform as far away as Hittite Anatolia (Beckman 1983), Syria-Palestine (van der Toorn 2000; van Soldt 1995), and Tell al-'Amarna in Egypt. There is no dearth of evidence regarding apprenticeship in the different hubs. Archaeological discoveries have sometimes confirmed influences that had long been suspected. The excavations of Emar have verified the role played by northern Syria as a relay point in the acculturation of Anatolia. But how were the students in Emar itself trained? It has been possible to establish the role played by a certain Kidin-Gula from northern Babylonia

(Y. Cohen 2004): the colophons of several tablets mention that they were copied by this individual's students. The curriculum in effect at the time has also been reconstituted (Civil 1989).

The Evidence from the First Millennium. There are no extant descriptions of schools for the later periods. That is undoubtedly why the theme of apprenticeship in the scribal craft has been treated primarily for the Old Babylonian period. The only sources available for the first millennium are made up of exercise tablets, and the difficulty of deciphering them accounts for why few researchers have been drawn to them. For a long time, they were considered only a lode from which to extract a few particularly interesting lexical or literary passages. It is only recently that an effort has been made to study them for themselves (Gesche 2001; Veldhuis 2003; George 2003–2004).

Some batches were discovered during regular excavations and are all the more precious as a result. The excavations of Kish during the interwar period exhumed exercises whose interest lies in their excellent state of preservation.[17] These include, notably, the tablets discovered in 1979 in Babylon, west of the Processional Way, in a building that a foundation inscription of Esarhaddon identifies as a temple of Nabu. In the floors of certain rooms, or in the adjacent fill, more than 2,000 exercise tablets were uncovered (Cavigneaux 1981, 1999a). They clearly served as construction material to raise the ground level for the building when Nebuchadnezzar renovated it. Some were even incorporated into the steps of a staircase. Although these were discarded tablets, they are related to the temple in which they were discovered. Some contain a colophon with a prayer to Nabu, for example: "To Nabu, preeminent heir, supreme master, quintessence of wisdom, master of ingenuity, who resides in E-gidri-kalama-suma, the well-named residence that confers the scepter and the throne in view of kingship, Nabu-zer-iddina composed a tablet and offered it for his salvation and the development of his understanding. O Nabu, supreme master, develop his understanding!" (Cavigneaux 1981, 49; cf. Cavigneaux 1996a). These were therefore ex-votos. More precisely, indications sometimes show that the tablets were given to the gatekeeper of the temple to deposit in the *gunna,* a kind of receptacle. These votive deposits likely took place during a ceremony, at the time of a feast of the god Nabu. There is therefore no reason to believe that the temple of Nabu included a school, and nothing is known about the places where and conditions under which these apprentices received their training.

The excavations of Uruk in 1969–1971 unearthed, in a residential quarter, many "literary and scholastic" tablets from the Hellenistic period (Hunger 1976; von Weiher 1983–1998). The image they provide of the training of apprentices is scarcely different from what the excavations of Ur and Nippur have revealed for the second millennium. Many of the commentaries, however, show that apprentices were sometimes trained orally by a master (*ummānu*).

An Education in Two Stages.   In studying the exercise tablets from the first millennium, whatever their provenance,[18] researchers have discovered two different formats that correspond to two stages in the beginning level of apprenticeship. The type 1 tablets are square and large in size, their surface divided into many narrow columns. On them are found the first elements of training, with exercises on holding the calamus, syllabaries, and excerpts from the *Urra = hubullu* series. The apprentices who completed that course of study were qualified to become part of the administration. The type 2 tablets are narrow and divided into two columns at most. They often contain several excerpts separated by a horizontal line. The texts belong to a well-delimited corpus: bilingual incantations, hymns and prayers in Akkadian, the *Enūma eliš,* the *Tintir = Bābilim* series, and various lexical lists. One cannot fail to be struck by the significant place occupied by the city of Babylon and its god Marduk in that corpus: it truly seems that the primary aim of that second stage was religious.

From the start, the extraordinary continuity of traditions is remarkable, but a key change must be pointed out. There was now clearly an "advanced level" of training that allowed apprentices, once they had mastered reading and writing *(ṭupšarrūtu),* to specialize in one of three distinct branches: the art of the diviner *(bārūtu),* that of the exorcist *(āšipūtu),* or that of the lamenter *(kalūtu).*[19] Each of these three disciplines had its own curriculum and its own body of texts. The diviner was responsible for interpreting the signs sent by the gods (Veldhuis 1999a). Lunar or solar eclipses, meteorological phenomena, or abnormal births, for example, could be warnings that ought not to be overlooked. The diviner could also inquire of the gods at the request of an individual. When he sacrificed a sheep, Shamash and Adad inscribed their responses on the animal's liver: the diviner had to decipher its signs, that is, any sort of malformation or perforation, for example (Leiderer 1990) (Figure 11). When the diviner read an inauspicious sign, the evil predicted was not ineluctable: it could be diverted from its target. It was at that point that the exorcist intervened. Through rituals, particularly the *namburbū,* he transferred the evil onto an item such as a strand of wool or a clay figurine, which was then destroyed (Maul 1994b, 1999). Lastly, the individual harried by the wrath of his god had to be able to reconcile with him. That was the task of the *kalū,* to "appease the hearts of the great gods" by chanting lamentations.

A few individuals vaunted their competence in every area. Wishing to enter the king's service, a certain Marduk-shapik-zeri wrote to the ruler, claiming he was more than a simple lamenter-*kalū:* "I fully master my father's profession, the discipline of lamentation *(kalûtu);* I have studied and chanted the Series *(iškarû).* I am competent in . . . , 'mouth-washing,' and purification of the palace. . . . I have examined healthy and sick flesh (i.e. good and bad *omina).* I have read the (astrological omen series) *Enûma Anu Enlil* . . . and made astronomical observations. I have read the (anomaly series) *Šumma izbu,* the (physiognomical works)

FIGURE 11. Models of clay livers (Mari palace, early second millennium), which may have been used in the training of diviners. (Courtesy of D. Charpin.)

[*Kataduqqû, Alandi*]*mmû* and *Nigdindimmû* [. . . and the (terrestrial omen series) *Šum*]*ma âlu*. [All this I lear]ned (in my youth)" (*SAA* 10 160: 36–43).[20] The list is impressive: in addition to his own field, Marduk-shapik-zeri claims to have mastered exorcism and all the divinatory techniques: extispicy (examination of a sheep's liver and other organs), astrology, physiognomy, and so on. The very fact that this individual emphasized his multiple skills shows he was an exception; the other twenty people he lists in the rest of his letter as being available to work for the king all have more narrow specializations.

Dynasties of Specialists. That letter provides an example of a succession from father to son in the same area of specialization. This seems to have been a universal phenomenon and helps explain the gradual fossilization of the scholarly tradition in Mesopotamia. Such successions were not limited to scholars, however: a

Neo-Babylonian example shows that a businessman from the Egibi family, having adopted a baby, "raised him from his early childhood and taught him to read" (Baker 2003, 251n45).

Not just anyone could become a "scholar" *(ummānu),* as demonstrated by the following anecdote dating from the Neo-Assyrian period. A goldsmith from the House of the Queen had hired a Babylonian to teach his son the texts on exorcism and divination. He was denounced to a royal agent, who accused him of wanting to imitate the king and crown prince. The unfortunate man had unintentionally committed the crime of lèse-majesté.[21] In the first millennium, people habitually took the names of ancestors. Many scribes of Uruk cited as a common ancestor a certain Sin-leqi-unninni, famous for having "edited" the Epic of Gilgamesh in the second half of the second millennium. It is difficult to know whether this was a real lineage or a way for scribes to place themselves under the patronage of a famous educated man from the past (Beaulieu 2000).

A Fossilized Transmission? The process of organizing the texts of the tradition, which is sometimes called, not without ambiguity, the "canonization" of the texts, began in the second half of the second millennium, during the Kassite period (Rochberg-Halton 1984). The Old Babylonian period that preceded it did not yet have established series such as the large compendia of omens. The *Šumma ālu,* for example, includes a few Old Babylonian texts, such as one dealing with the flight of birds (Weisberg 1969) and another relating to insects (Joannès 1994); but the series as such is not attested before the first millennium (Freedman 1998, 2006a). How was such an organization into series undertaken? One of the best-known cases is that of the medical series *Sakikku* (Finkel 1988). The establishment of that major collection is attributed in texts from later epochs to a certain Esagil-kin-apli, who was supposedly a schoolmaster *(ummānu)* living in the age of King Adad-apla-iddina (r. 1068–1047). Given that ruler's particular devotion to the goddess of medicine, for whom he rebuilt the principal temple in Isin, declaring himself her son, it seems likely that Esagil-kin-apli performed that work as a royal commission. The texts that were organized already existed: hence this was a work of compilation, not of creation. It is striking that specialists in the history of mathematics believe that nothing important was discovered in their field after the Old Babylonian period—J. Friberg speaks of "stagnation" (1987–1990, 583). In addition, apprentices copied texts that no longer had any relation to the practices of their time: the Code of Hammurabi, which continued to be copied in the first millennium, was no longer the source of legal expertise but had become the subject of esoteric commentary (Lambert 1989). An analysis of duplicates of documents from the Achaemenid period shows, moreover, that scribal apprenticeships at the beginning of that period still included the copying of contracts, which was already attested in the Old Babylonian period (Jursa 1999, 13–19).

Secret Knowledge and the Development of Esotericism. The conservatism of the Mesopotamian scribes is striking. By the end of the second millennium, they were facing formidable competition from alphabetical writing, especially Aramaic, which had considerable advantages. Because these systems notated only consonants and not syllables, they had a much more limited repertoire: some thirty signs, which made learning them decidedly less tedious. But that is not all. They also allowed for greater speed in writing things down. At first, tradition required that scribes continue to write on clay. Hence, for thirteenth-century Ugarit, tablets inscribed in "alphabetical cuneiform" have been found alongside those inscribed in "classical" cuneiform (Watson and Wyatt 1999). But very quickly, it became clear that the advantages of speed and economy could be truly exploited only by changing the support. The Egyptian experience was put to good use by the Levantines: henceforth, alphabetical writing systems were notated in ink, on papyri, skins, or shards (ostraca). Given that situation, Mesopotamian scribes tended to make their writing more complex, as if, having understood that it was impossible to compete, they deliberately chose to highlight the esoteric character of their knowledge.

Thus the diviner who began to initiate his son in cuneiform had to make him swear not to divulge the learning he would acquire: "The learned savant *(ummānu),* who guards the secrets of the great gods, will bind his son whom he loves with an oath before Šamaš and Adad by tablet and stylus and will instruct him" (Lambert 1967, 132 [K.2486+ ii: 20–21]).[22] Many colophons from the first millennium impose strict limits on communicating the text: "The knowing (one) may show (the tablet) only to the knowing, not to the 'unknowing'!" (Borger 1957–1971, 188–191; Rochberg 2000, 362). Correlatively, the nature of wisdom changed: from a human quality at the start of the second millennium, it became divine revelation (van der Toorn 2007). Witness the transformation of the Epic of Gilgamesh. The editor of the later version added to the beginning of the prologue twenty-eight lines that insist on the hero's wisdom;[23] he complemented them with an account of the Flood, the sermon of Uta-napishtim (the Babylonian Noah), and an epilogue. In addition, he omitted the episode of the innkeeper who, in the ancient version of the text, had advised Gilgamesh—with a great deal of common sense—to give up his quest for immortality and to take pleasure in the present. The later version, by contrast, concerns only the hidden knowledge held by the survivor of the Flood and transmitted to Gilgamesh.

Who Could Read and Write?

The study of how cuneiform writing was taught leads naturally to the question of how many in Mesopotamia were able to master it (Charpin 2010, chap. 1). For a long time, the prevailing image was of a world where writing was the monopoly of a small number of specialists, the professional scribes. A few exceptions were conceded—a few sovereigns and a few merchants. That is still the view of some very good Assyriologists, such as P. A. Beaulieu (2007, 473): "Cuneiform writing was the preserve of a small caste of professionals. In a letter to his employer the Assyrian king Esarhaddon, the Babylonian scholar Ašarēdu the Younger alludes to the restricted diffusion of writing with a touch of wit when he warns that 'the scribal craft is not heard about in the market place'" (SAA 8:339). Several recent studies, however, have demonstrated that the mastery of writing, especially in the late third millennium and in the second, was more widespread than is usually believed.

The Exceptions Traditionally Recognized

In general, studies on Mesopotamia cite three rulers as having presented themselves as "literate": Shulgi, king of Ur, in the first half of the twenty-first century; Lipit-Eshtar, king of Isin, in the second half of the twentieth century; and, much later, Ashurbanipal, king of Assyria in the mid-seventh century.

In Hymn B, Shulgi mentions the training he received:

> When I was young, I learned at school
> the scribal art on the tablets of Sumer and Akkad.
> Among the highborn no one could write like me.
> Where people go for instruction in the scribal art
> there I mastered completely subtraction, addition, calculating,
>   and accounting.
> The fair (goddess) Nanibgal Nisaba
> provided me lavishly with knowledge and understanding.
> I am a meticulous scribe who does not miss a thing!
>   (Veldhuis 1997, 24–25; Volk 1996)

Elsewhere, that king of Ur also boasted of his skills in divination and in music.

The literacy of Lipit-Eshtar, king of Isin, is also celebrated in Hymn B, where the ruler is addressed as follows: "Nisaba, the woman radiant with joy, / the true woman scribe, the lady of all knowledge, / Guided your fingers on the clay, / Embellished the writing on the tablets, / Made the hand resplendent with a golden stylus" (Vanstiphout 1978, 36–37, lines 18–22).

The largest body of evidence has to do with Ashurbanipal (Fincke 2003–2004, 120–122; Livingstone 2007). In the first place, there are inscriptions in which the king enumerates all the qualities the deities bestowed on him:

> Marduk, the sage of the gods, gave me wide understanding and broad perceptions as a gift. Nabu, the scribe of the universe, bestowed on me the acquisition of all his wisdom as a present. Ninurta and Nergal gave me physical fitness, manhood and unparalleled strength. I learnt the lore of the wise sage Adapa, the hidden secret, the whole of the scribal craft. I can discern celestial and terrestrial portents and deliberate in the assembly of the experts. I am able to discuss the series "If the liver is a mirror image of the sky" with capable scholars. I can solve convoluted reciprocals and calculations that do not come out evenly. I have read cunningly written text in Sumerian, dark Akkadian, the interpretation of which is difficult. I have examined stone inscriptions from before the flood, which are sealed, stopped up, mixed up. (Streck 1916, 252 [Asb.⁴i 10–18]; Livingstone 2007, 100)

In this text, Ashurbanipal presents himself as an expert in divination, mathematics, languages, and even epigraphy (Figure 12).[24] But he was also a sage and an accomplished sportsman, each god having attributed to him all the qualities in the deity's field of choice. According to another text, the god Assur even gave him knowledge of all the languages of the world. In other words, what we have here is a heroic description of the ruler, which in itself

FIGURE 12. A "paleographical exercise" from the Neo-Assyrian period (syllabary A). Each column is subdivided into cells, with at left the archaic form of the sign and at right its equivalent in the writing of the time. (Courtesy of the British Institute for the Study of Iraq [BISI].)

might inspire skepticism about the king's real proficiency in reading and writing. As a matter of fact, it has been noted that this self-portrait of Ashurbanipal was no doubt influenced by the beginning words of the Epic of Gilgamesh (Pongratz-Leisten 1999, 312): "He (Gilgamesh) saw the secret and uncovered the hidden / He brought back a message from the antediluvian age" (George 2003, 538–539 [Gilgamesh I 7–8]).

But there are also more conclusive types of evidence concerning Ashurbanipal's literacy. Hence in the summer of 671, a year after Esarhaddon had decided the question of his succession and had designated Ashurbanipal as the future king of Assyria, the scholar Balasī wrote the sovereign: "To whom indeed has the king done such a favour as to me whom you have appointed to the service of the crown prince, to be his master and that I read with him his exercise?" *(SAA* 10 39: r. 4–9, trans. Livingstone 2007, 101–102). In fact, a letter from Ashurbanipal to King Esarhaddon, obviously written at a still elementary stage of his training, has been unearthed (Livingstone 2007, 107, fig. 2). Ashurbanipal seems to have bowed to the same custom as every other apprentice: he dedicated copies of texts he had written to the god Nabu, as the colophons of certain tablets indicate: "Ashurbanipal, great king, strong king, king of the universe, king of Assyria, son of Esarhaddon, king of Assyria, son of Sennacherib, king of Assyria. Following the content of the clay tablets and wooden polyptychs, versions of Assyria and of the region of Sumer and Akkad, I wrote, verified, and collated this tablet in the assembly of scholars and, for my royal reading, I placed it in my palace. Whoever shall efface my inscribed name and inscribe his name, may the god Nabu, scribe of the universe, efface his name!" (Hunger 1968, 97, no. 318).

In addition, the mail Ashurbanipal received from an astrologist named Nabu-ahhe-eriba contains many glosses. Pierre Villard revisited this case a few years ago and drew a moderate conclusion regarding Ashurbanipal's skills: "There is no reason to place in doubt his interest in the scribal disciplines; conversely, we must refrain from exaggerating the importance of the theme of the literate king in royal propaganda. The motif is, for example, totally absent from the bas-reliefs, though their programs were elaborated in accordance with the ruler's directives" (Villard 1997, 148–149; cf. Fincke 2003–2004, 119–122). This last observation was important, but it has been superseded in the meantime: on several bas-reliefs, an object tucked into Ashurbanipal's belt has recently been identified as a calamus (Figure 13).[25] Note that these are hunting scenes and that they aptly demonstrate the scope of the

FIGURE 13. Ashurbanipal on a hunt (north palace of Niniveh): a calamus is tucked into the king's belt. (©The Trustees of the British Museum / Art Resource, New York.)

sovereign's abilities, as both an accomplished scribe and an expert hunter. Once again, the complementarity between the text and the image is striking.

Were Shulgi, Lipit-Eshtar, and Ashurbanipal merely exceptions? Evidence has proliferated in recent decades. In addition to Lipit-Eshtar, other kings of Isin are portrayed as being literate: allusions to the mastery of writing can be found in hymns about Lipit-Eshtar's predecessor Ishme-Dagan and about Enlil-bani (Veldhuis 1997, 25). Were these kings of Isin truly literate, or did their hymns plagiarize other similar compositions? It is difficult to decide: since Ishme-Dagan characterized himself as a champion of footraces in terms that closely resemble those of Shulgi, he might also have imitated the theme of the scribe king. But it may also be that Sin-iddinam, king of Larsa, can be counted among the literate kings (Ludwig 1990, 187). In addition, in one of his inscriptions, Esarhaddon, father of Ashurbanipal, also claims to know how to write (Frame and George 2005, 279). He is actually the one who began to collect tablets in Niniveh: Ashurbanipal, in constituting his library, was only continuing his father's work.

Let me add, finally, the case of the Neo-Babylonian king Nabonidus (r. 555–539). In one of his inscriptions, it is asserted that "Nabu, administrator of the universe, gave him the art of writing" (Beaulieu 1989, 79). But in a satirical tract, probably composed by priests of Marduk from Babylon against the king, he is made to say the opposite: "Although I (Nabonidus) do not know the art of writing in cuneiform, I have seen secret [things]" (Beaulieu 1989, 79n10, 217). It is obvious that such a "confession" was aimed at discrediting the ruler and casting aspersions on his religious reforms,[26] and surely this polemical text must not be taken seriously. On one hand, then, is the topos of royal rhetoric that Ashurbanipal inherited; on the other, polemics. It is therefore impossible to know whether or not Nabonidus was really able to write cuneiform; another tradition, favorable to Nabonidus, in fact credits him with that knowledge (Machinist and Tadmor 1993, 149b). It may at least be suspected that he had mastered Aramaic writing.

Alongside kings, another category of individuals has long been recognized as having engaged in writing without the use of professional scribes: merchants. The best-known case is that of the traders from Assur who, in the first quarter of the second millennium, established trading posts in faraway Anatolia. Since the 1970s, a consensus has been reached that most of these businessmen were able to read and write.[27] The repertoire of Old Assyrian signs, it has been noted, was particularly limited, which suggests that the mastery of writing by the merchants themselves must not have raised tremendous difficulties. That point of view was elaborated by Mogens T. Larsen: "There are indications that a great many Assyrians knew how to read and write so the need for privately employed scribes may not have been so great. The system of writing was highly simplified with only a limited number of syllabic signs and quite a few logograms, and many of the outrageously hideous private documents constitute clear proof of the amateurishness of their writers. We know for certain that some of the sons of important merchants were taught the scribal art in As-sur" (Larsen 1976, 305; see also Larsen 1989, 133; Ulshöfer 1995, 35). G. Kryszat has recently argued that, because the writing of Old Assyrian merchants was reduced to the minimum, "a substantial part of their community was able to write a letter or any other document in such a way that everybody with at least the same level of knowledge of the script was able to read it" (2008, 232).

The Old Assyrian merchants were in no wise an exception, as Larsen himself has shown. In particular, we know of merchants from Larsa, in southern Iraq, who in about 1780 were visiting the kingdom of Eshnunna, east of present-day Baghdad. Leemans (1960, 73–74) has noted that the letters they wrote at the time all had the characteristics of the letters from Larsa, not those from Eshnunna. Hence these merchants did not have recourse to the services of local scribes. Leemans concluded that they had taken a scribe with them; Larsen argued, with much more likelihood, that this was evidence that they themselves wrote their corre-spondence (1987, 220n51).

The famous Assyriologist Benno Landsberger vigorously called into doubt the mastery of writing by members of the clergy: "One must castigate as false romanticism the conception of the so-called *Priesterweisheit,* still to be found in secondary handbooks. The scribes, although a great number of them were deeply religious, were completely a lay group. The priests as well as the kings (not counting some exceptions among the latter), and the governors, and the judges were illiterate" (Landsberger 1960, 98). Such a view has proved to be erroneous. The epigraphical discoveries in the houses of certain priests in charge of the great temple of Nanna-Sīn in Ur attest to the training in letters they provided in their homes (Charpin 1986a). Then there is the evidence provided by the house in Sippar-Amnānum where nearly 100 school tablets were discovered (Tanret 2002). In all probability, the teacher was the scribe who often worked for the owner of that residence, Inanna-mansum, who was the chief lamenter *(gala.mah)* of the goddess Annunitum; the pupil must have been his son and successor, Ur-Utu. That son, therefore, was given an education in literacy. But an analysis of the curriculum revealed by these tablets indicates that the level of proficiency he reached was not very high. It was enough that he know the basics: how to read and write. Let me add to Michel Tanret's comments that the trade of *gala.mah* must have been taught orally to Ur-Utu by his father. That no doubt explains one of the disappointments of the excavation: there were almost no texts of a religious nature among the exhumed tablets.

A Few Recent Approaches

Claus Wilcke has argued that literacy was much more widespread than is generally believed (Wilcke 2000). His book, which deals primarily with the period from the late third to the second millennium, is based on three inquiries. The first of these is archaeological: he hypothesizes that, if the residents of ancient Mesopotamia were able to read and write, traces must have been left in the settlement areas. Unfortunately, most of our documentation comes from illicit or old excavations, undertaken at a time when little care was taken to observe and record the archaeological context. Wilcke attempted to collect all the cases where tablets were found in houses. He shows that in every era, the proportion of residences where tablets were preserved was large, between one quarter and one third in Assur, more than half in Ur, and so on. It seems to me that this inventory must be qualified in two ways. On one hand, the districts excavated were those inhabited by members of the elite. On the other, preserving one's property deeds, debt records, and so on in one's archives does not necessarily mean one could read these texts, much less write them.

Wilcke's second approach consists of identifying, in the texts themselves, evidence that they were written by the interested parties. He cites a few documents that use the first person in a way he considers revealing. He also systematically studies two expressions frequently found in letters—"*upon seeing* my present tablet" alternates with "*in listening to* my present tablet"—and argues that the permutation is significant. In the first case, we may deduce that the letter's recipient was able to read it himself without resorting to the services of a scribe.

Wilcke's third approach is to study the deviations from the norm found in the texts, especially in phonetic notations of Sumerian from contracts of the Ur III period. He considers them a sign that they were written by a nonprofessional. His conclusion is twofold. First, he maintains that the mastery of writing was not confined to professionals alone, that is, to scribes: writing was also practiced by members of the social elite. Second, Wilcke qualifies his assertion by arguing that a passive knowledge of writing (knowing how to read) was certainly more developed than an active knowledge (knowing how to write).

Up to now, the data from the royal archives of Mari have rarely been put to use in support of this matter. Yet they provide a great deal of information on the subject. For a long time the view was that members of the elite were fundamentally illiterate. That is the belief of Jack Sasson, a good specialist in the Mari archives. He writes, concerning the reading of letters: "Written statements were read aloud by scribes to illiterate officials" (Sasson 1995, 607n21). It is not possible to give an exhaustive list of the officials who knew how to read. But the idea that, in this kingdom on the Middle Euphrates in the eighteenth century B.C., the possessors of power depended entirely on professional scribes to have their mail read to them is manifestly inaccurate. Many texts show that high officials in Mari—administrators, members of the military, diviners, and even kings—were able to read and write letters on their own (Charpin 2010; Charpin forthcoming c).

How had the situation developed a millennium later? Simo Parpola has republished a letter dating from the apogee of the

Neo-Assyrian empire. A few collations and an evaluation of the particular syllabary of that letter allowed him to provide a new translation: "To the king my lord: your servant Sin-na'di. Good health to the king, my lord! I have no scribe where my lord sent me to. Let the king order either the governor of Arrapha or Aššur-belu-taqqin to send me one" (*ABL* 151 [*SAA* 15 17]; Parpola 1997). That letter dates from the reign of Sargon II (721–705 B.C.), and Assur-belu-taqqin was governor of Me-Turan at the time. Its author was undoubtedly on a mission in the upper Diyala Valley without a scribe to accompany him. He therefore must have written the letter himself, which accounts for the peculiarities, even blunders, it contains. The analysis Parpola conducted (1997, 321n17) led him to conclude that the author of that letter had to have mastered 112 signs (79 syllabic signs and 33 logograms).[28] He concluded: "I submit that the alleged 'drastic' second-millennium change in Mesopotamian literacy actually never took place, and that the level of literacy in first millennium Mesopotamia was at least as high (if not higher) as in earlier times" (Parpola 1997, 321–322).

Women Scribes?

Within the Sumerian pantheon, the patronage of scribes fell to the goddess Nisaba. That does not mean, of course, that the scribal craft was not primarily a man's profession. Nevertheless, women scribes are occasionally attested, especially in the Old Babylonian period, though in two rather special contexts. First, in the world of the temples: some of the nuns-*nadītum* in the city of Sippar had obviously learned to write cuneiform,[29] and a woman belonging to that milieu defined herself as a "scribe" (Lion 2001a; Lion and Robson 2005). In addition, within palace harems, the scribes were women: two of them kept the accounts of the foodstuffs consumed by the king and his table companions (Ziegler 1999, 91–92). And in the dowries of princesses a woman scribe sometimes appears among the servants bestowed.[30] For the Neo-Assyrian period, a woman is attested as "scribe to the House of the Queen" in the archives of Kalhu.[31] That reality was transposed to the world of the gods: in the description of the Netherworld in the Epic of Gilgamesh, the goddess Ereshkigal has a tablet read to her by a woman scribe, the goddess Beletṣeri: "Before her was squatting Belet-ṣeri, the female-scribe of the Netherworld, holding a tablet and reading aloud in her presence" (George 2003, 644–645 [Gilgamesh VII: 204–205], commentary 851).

It has recently been argued that all the members of the royal Assyrian family during Esarhaddon's time were probably literate, including the women. Hence the daughter of that king wrote to her sister-in-law, Ashurbanipal's wife: "Word of the king's daughter to Libbi-âli-šarrat. Why do you not write your tablets and recite your exercise, or people will say: 'Is this the sister of Šeru'a-eṭirat, the eldest daughter of the house of Administration of Aššur-etel-ilani-mukinni, the great king, the strong king, king of the world, king of Assyria?' And you are a daughter, a wife of first rank *(kallatu),* the lady of the house of Ashurbanipal, the great crown prince of the house of Administration of Esarhaddon, king of Assyria'" (*SAA* 16 28; cf. Livingstone 2007, 104). The princess's criticism of her sister-in-law for not being sufficiently dedicated to writing and to her exercises rests on an argument related to her prestige, which applies only if her entire entourage had mastered cuneiform.

A Writing System Less Difficult to Master Than Believed

If it was long believed that knowledge of cuneiform in antiquity was very limited, that is no doubt because the art of the scribe was considered difficult—a manner, no doubt unconscious, for Assyriologists to assert their own value. Since it appears that the practice of cuneiform, at least at a rudimentary level, was actually rather widespread, how to explain the possibility of that phenomenon? Some authors have shown that the writing system was not as difficult as is currently believed. Of course, there are about 600 different signs, each possessing several values, syllabic or ideogrammatic. But not all these values are attested for a single period or in every kind of text: the present-day epigraphist's knowledge must not be confused with that of the person in antiquity, who needed to know only the repertoire in use in his or her time. It was thus possible for Old Babylonian scribes to write with a minimum syllabary of eighty-two signs, provided they did not use heavy syllables (that is, provided they wrote not *kum* but *ku-um*). But even without that restriction, the syllabary remained fairly limited: Goetze, in publishing divinatory texts, tallied 112 syllabic signs and 57 logograms in the corpus he was editing, figures that can be taken as representative (Goetze 1947).

All in all, knowledge of cuneiform, at least as of the late third millennium, was not exclusive to scribes, but was in part shared by members of the ruling class as well. Slaves could also occasionally receive training as scribes (Dietrich 2001). No doubt that was possible in part because cuneiform writing was less complex than is generally indicated. But let us also not forget that there is no direct link between the supposed difficulty of learning a writing system and the percentage of the population able to use it (Powell 1981, 435–436): contemporary Japan has a lower illiteracy rate than France or the United States.

Conclusion

In the Netherworld as Enkidu describes it to Gilgamesh, the well-being of the dead is directly correlated to the number of children they had. Someone who had five children is as happy as a scribe in service of the palace; he is surpassed only by someone who had six children, happy as a plowman, and someone with seven, who sat beside the Judge of the Netherworld. Despite what might be supposed, this was not a social classification: the number of children is linked to the occupation. The five children of the scribe corresponded to the five fingers on the hand with which he wrote, and the six children of the plowman to the six animals used to pull the plow (Radner 2005, 84). Of course, that does not mean that the scribe's status was not considerable, but there is no extant text from Mesopotamia that exalts the scribe at the expense of members of the other trades, as happened in Egypt.[32]

Among the proverbs about the scribe's profession are the following: "A scribe without a hand (is like) a singer without a voice" (Alster 1997, 53 § 2.43); and "A scribe whose hand cannot keep up with the mouth, he is indeed a scribe!" (Alster 1997, 58 § 2.40). It is significant that the emphasis is placed on the manual dexterity involved in that work and not on the intellectual qualities that such a craft entails. But note the irony in the proverb "An unsuccessful scribe, he will be an incantation priest" (Veldhuis 1999b, 36n4).

Significantly, no one ever said "learning to write" but rather "learning the art of the scribe" *(ṭupšarrūtam ahāzum* or *lamādum)*. Hence this notation in an Old Assyrian letter: "To be sure, we are learning the art of the scribe."[33] The author of the letter simply means, "we are learning to read and write." Similarly, the god Nabu is described as the "creator of writing, of the art of the scribe," as if the two expressions were synonymous.[34] That undoubtedly explains why it was so long believed that writing was exclusive to professional scribes, but the terminology simply reflects an archaic situation. The expression "art of the scribe" *(nam.dub.sar* in Sumerian) goes back to the mid-third millennium, at a time when writing was in fact in the hands of specialists. By the end of the third millennium, that knowledge had been diffused beyond the sphere of writing professionals. Knowledge was likely passive for the most part: once someone had learned to read, he no longer wrote very much. It is surely not by chance that there are more attestations of *reading* than of *writing* on the part of nonprofessionals. Nevertheless, we must abandon our prejudices, which are linked to an ethnocentric assessment of the supposed superiority of the alphabet. Despite what has been written, the "Greek miracle" was not directly connected to the advent of an alphabetical writing system, which had already existed for several centuries (Michalowski 1994a). And of course, the different kinds of writing must be taken into account. In the "dispute" between Enki-mansum and Girni-isag, the apprentice scribe is heard to say: "You wrote a letter, but that is the limit for you!" (Vanstiphout 1997, 589, line 20). Knowing how to write a letter was thus considered the minimum requirement. The interesting thing is that, in the second and first millennia, that minimum was obviously not exclusive to professional scribes. Finally, let me note an essential difference between Mesopotamian civilization and that of classical antiquity. In Mesopotamia, there was no "free" reading: no one is ever depicted reading for pleasure.

chapter two

The Archival Documents

Mesopotamian writings can be grouped into three broad categories: archival documents, library texts, and commemorative inscriptions. The first group depicts the daily lives of individuals
and of large institutions (temples and palaces) and comprises correspondence, legal documents, and bookkeeping texts. For nearly
thirty years I have pointed out the need to study these documents
in themselves by importing the methods of diplomatics into Assyriology. As G. Teissier has written, "the eminent philologists
and jurists who look at Mesopotamian tablets or Greek papyri
from the Nile Valley would undoubtedly find it nothing but ad-
vantageous to apply to them the methods elaborated in diplomatics for medieval documents" (Teissier 1961, 668). A good portion
of my research has come in response to that invitation from the
former director of the École des Chartes.[1]

The External Characteristics of the Documents

Although the most ancient inscribed tablets discovered thus far
date to the late fourth millennium B.C. (Nissen, Damerow, and
Englund 1993; Talon and Van Lerberghe 1998; Englund 1998) and
the most recent to the early years of the Christian era, the use of
cuneiform may have persisted until the third century A.D. (Geller
1997; and, with a different view, A. Westenholz 2007).[2] Over that
period of more than three millennia, the external appearance of
the documents—the support for cuneiform writing, the shapes of
the signs themselves, and the authenticating marks—changed
considerably (André-Leicknam and Ziegler 1982). No books have
been devoted to that question, just a few specialized articles (Post-

gate 1986a; Radner 1995). In that field, individual experiences and an intuitive approach usually prevail.

Writing Incised in Clay

In Mesopotamian civilization, it was the particularity of the clay support for writing[3] that produced the appearance of cuneiform writing itself, whose signs are incised in the soft surface of the tablet. The calamus could be carved from a reed (Driver 1976, 23–26; Saggs 1981; Powell 1981) or from bone (Tanret 2002, 25–26) (Figure 14), more rarely from metal. Gold or silver calami are mentioned in literary texts: were these "deluxe" exemplars or simply metaphors? In any event, bronze styli have been found in the Ugarit palace and at the site of Hammam et-Turkman (Bleibtreu 2003). Whenever cuneiform writing was borrowed, so too was the clay tablet, in Hittite Anatolia, for example. A few other cultures in the Eastern Mediterranean also made use of it: in the first place, the entire Creto-Mycenaean world (Godard 1990); and in the second, Egypt, where, however, clay was used only under special circumstances (Pantalacci 2008b). In both these cases, the peoples were obviously imitating the Mesopotamian practice, which had spread to the Mediterranean coast. By the eighteenth century B.C., contacts between Cretans and Mariots were occurring at the port of Ugarit (Guichard 1999), and the king of Haṣor maintained regular relations with the king of Mari (Bonechi 1992; Horowitz and Wasserman 2004; Ziegler and Charpin 2004).

Unlike papyrus or skin, clay was an inexpensive raw material, but special care had to be taken in its preparation so that it would not crack as it dried. The most explicit allusion to the preparation of a tablet appears in a scholastic text (Civil 1998). We should therefore probably take seriously the king of Ashnakkum's declaration that he wrote so many letters to the leader of the nomads that his stock of clay was depleted: "My servants tired themselves out going to the leader of the nomads, and I used up the clay of

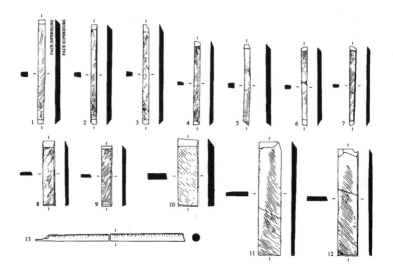

FIGURE 14. Bone calami found in the house of Ur-Utu in Sippar-Amnāmum (seventeenth century). (Courtesy of Michel Tanret.)

Ashnakkum for the tablets I am continually sending there" (*ARM* 28 105: 9–10). A workstation for preparing tablets was excavated in Hammam et-Turkman in the Balih Valley (Meijer 2004). It is a circular basin about 20 inches (50 cm) deep, supplied with water by a rivulet from a well; next to it was a rectangular space where purified clay was discovered, with kneading marks and finger-prints still visible in some spots. In Susa, what Roman Girshman took to be a school turned out to be a repository for school tablets that were to be recycled: they had to be mixed with fresh clay and fashioned into small rods from which new tablets were prepared (Gasche and De Meyer 2006).

The use of clay had both advantages and disadvantages (Charpin 1989). The first constraint was that of space: the scribe had to cal-culate in advance the surface area needed. We know of tablets that were fashioned but never inscribed (Al-Rawi and Dalley 2000, nos. 3, 49, and 50). Based on their format, it is possible in some

FIGURE 15. Example of anepigraphic tablets (Mari palace,
eighteenth century B.C.): given
their format, they were
probably fashioned for a short
bookkeeping text. (Courtesy of
D. Charpin.)

cases to discern the nature of the text they were intended to con-
vey (Figure 15). There is reason to wonder whether, in all cases, it
was the scribe himself who fabricated the tablet before inscribing
it: assistants may in fact have been used. If so, examinations of the
fingerprints made in the surface of the tablets for the purpose of
identifying the scribes would be misguided.[4] Another fundamental constraint resulted from the fact that clay, once inscribed,
dries rather quickly, making any later modification of the text
impossible. By definition, then, a text was written all at once. On
the large tablets, the appearance of the writing sometimes changes
near the end of the text. That transformation is a consequence of
the clay hardening. Sometimes additions were made once the tablet had begun to dry. It is fairly easy to identify them, since the
signs are incised more superficially.

Contrary to a prevalent idea, tablets were not normally baked;
that treatment was for the most part reserved for certain library

copies (Veenhof 1986b, 1n2; Fincke 2003–2004, 243). It was believed that a kiln had been found in a courtyard of the Ugarit palace (thirteenth century B.C.), in which various tablets, including letters *(received* by the king), were placed to be baked. This was an error in interpretation.[5] By contrast, many documents were baked to a greater or lesser extent when the building that sheltered them was destroyed by fire. That accidental baking generally led to a modification in the color of the tablet: an oxidizing atmosphere produced a red tablet, a reducing atmosphere, a black one. That is also the case for the baking sometimes conducted in museums to extract the salts and thereby slow the deterioration of the tablets.

Because the tablets were not baked, the clay from outdated ones could be remoistened and used again (Faivre 1995). That practice is primarily attested in schools, but also in administration archives. The scribes, having drawn up a summation, could reuse the clay of the small tablets written day to day (Figure 16). We sometimes find archives that have "self-destructed" up until the final phase of their existence. There are also cases in which an individual who was traveling, needing to reply to a letter, reused the clay from the tablet he had received (Larsen 1987, 220n51).

Clay was not the only support for cuneiform writing, however.[6] When there was a desire to confer a particularly solemn character on a document, it could be engraved in stone. Such was the case for royal deeds of donation or exemption dating from the second half of the second millennium, which were designated by the Babylonian term *kudurru.* These stones had a two-part inscription: the first part explicitly reproduced the text of the tablet sealed by the king; the second was composed of a series of curses against anyone who did not respect the content or who damaged the monument in some way (Slanski 2003; Charpin 2002b; Brinkman 2006). At least some of the deities invoked in the text were represented by their symbol sculpted in the stone (Slanski 2003–2004) (Figure 17). The Hittites engraved certain international documents

FIGURE 16. Example of an administrative tablet in the process of being re-cycled (Mari palace, eighteenth century B.C.). (Courtesy of D. Charpin.)

in metal. The famous treaty concluded between Hattusili III and Pharaoh Ramses II was inscribed in silver, though only a copy in clay survives (Edel 1997). A bronze tablet of large dimensions, weighing 5 kilograms and reproducing the text of the treaty of the Hittite king Tudhaliya IV with Kurunta of Tarhuntassa, was un-covered a few years ago in the Hittite capital of Hattusha (see Figure 35).[7]

For their economic and administrative documents, the Hittites seem to have used wooden tablets covered with wax.[8] This could be the reason why that type of text has been so little attested—though lucky finds may yet lie in store. The use of wax was not unknown in Mesopotamia (Stol 1998, 343–344); for a long time, it was be-lieved to have been used primarily as a support for manuscripts of "literary" works. In fact, certain catalogs list writing boards along-side "classical" tablets (Parpola 1983). Sometimes these wooden tablets had only a single element (these were called *daltu* in Akkadian), but some were polyptychs *(le'u)*. The excavation of

FIGURE 17. *Kudurru* of King Meli-shihu (Middle Babylonian period). The donation had been noted on a tablet sealed by the king. The beneficiary had a copy engraved in stone; the engraved divine symbols correspond to the deities invoked in the curses. (Erich Lessing / Art Resource, New York.)

Nimrud, the ancient Kalhu, has yielded, next to fragments of wooden writing boards, a polyptych in ivory with no fewer than sixteen panels (Wiseman 1955; Howard 1955) (Figure 38). It is now known that writing boards were also used to record administrative texts between the Middle Assyrian period (Postgate 2003, 133–136) and the Neo-Babylonian (MacGinnis 2002). The writing on these wax tablets was done with a calamus different from the one used to inscribe the clay tablets (Seidl 2007). That type of tablet undoubtedly had an advantage over traditional clay tablets in that it more easily allowed scribes to write long texts, and especially, made it easier to modify the text.

In the first millennium, skin scrolls *(magallatu)* were used as a support for cuneiform writing, which was set down in ink. That practice is mentioned for a legal text[9] but also as being used to copy divinatory texts.[10] Human skin was sometimes inscribed, always under unusual circumstances and only in the first millennium: slaves were tattooed with inscriptions in Akkadian but also in Aramaic and even Egyptian, so that they could be tracked down if they ran away (Stolper 1998; Reiner 2004).

Tablet Formats

Because a clay tablet is by definition three-dimensional, in order that it not become too fragile, its thickness had to increase proportionate with the size of the surface. Let me cite two extremes: a tablet measuring ⅝ × ⅝ inches (1.6 × 1.6 cm) and ½ inch (1.1 cm) thick, and others measuring 14¼ × 13 inches (36 × 33 cm), with a thickness varying between 1⅝ and 2 inches (4 and 5 cm). In spite of these physical constraints, there were major differences in the shape of the tablets: hence, the corners could be relatively rounded or instead sharp. Generally, the obverse was almost flat and the reverse more curved, but other configurations are attested. Round tablets were usually for school exercises, but administrative documents with a more or less oval shape have also been found. Square tablets were much rarer than rectangular ones: usually the writing runs parallel to the short side, but the opposite is also known. To move from the obverse to the reverse, one generally flips it bottom to top (and not right to left as one does with a piece of paper).[11] As a result, the scribe could use the top and bottom of the blocks but also the left edge. Practices varied a great deal depending on the kind of text and the era. It was during the most archaic period that the greatest amount of information was conveyed by the page layout (Green 1981). In the archives of Ebla as well, the nature of an administrative text (an annual report on the distribution of precious metals or a monthly report on the distribution of textiles) is evident simply by the large format of the tablet (Archi 2003).

A fundamental reform came about shortly after the middle of the third millennium. Whereas previously scribes had written in columns subdivided into cells (Figure 18), now they wrote in lines, with the signs inscribed left to right.[12] Large tablets were sometimes divided into columns, as before; these ran left to right on the obverse, but right to left on the reverse. There was normally no enjambment: not only did the scribe finish a word at the end of a line, he usually also strove to justify the margin. If the line was ever too long, the scribe would use indentation, a practice now reserved for writing verse.

Letters posed a particular problem, since by definition they are texts of variable length. In the Neo-Assyrian period, two very different formats coexisted, depending on the nature of the message (Villard 2008). Letters proper, called *egirtu,* were written parallel to the short side; the names of the recipient and the sender, as well as the customary salutations, appeared at the top. Conversely, reports-*u'iltu* were written parallel to the long side; they bore no salutation, the name of their author simply appearing at the end of the text.

The existence of envelopes is well attested. Once the tablet was dried, the scribe covered it with a thin layer of clay (about ⅛ in.,

FIGURE 18. Pre-Sargonic tablet discovered in a building of worksite B in Mari (about 2350). The signs are still divided into columns subdivided into cells. (Courtesy of D. Charpin.)

or .2 cm, thick).[13] Envelopes were used for two different types of texts: letters and contracts. In the case of letters, the purpose was obviously to keep their content confidential. The envelope, on which only the recipient's name appeared, was broken once the recipient had familiarized himself with its message. The envelope also made it possible to verify the sender, who impressed his seal on the envelope (Figure 30). For other eras, contracts have also been found in envelopes. Sometimes only a summary appears on the envelope, but usually the scribe recopied the entire text.[14] Subsequently, if the envelope was damaged or if someone suspected that the text had been tampered with, judges had only to break open the envelope to gain access to the text of the internal tablet (Charpin 2000a, 72) (Figure 19). Envelopes also provided a larger surface area than tablets: a margin was therefore set aside on the left for seal impressions. In the later part of the Old Babylonian period, scribes no longer placed contracts in envelopes but laid

FIGURE 19. An Old Babylonian legal document: the complete text of the internal tablet is recopied on the envelope, on which cylinder seals are also impressed. (Réunion des Musées Nationaux / Art Resource, New York.)

out the tablets as if they were envelopes (Van Lerberghe and Voet 1991). The use of envelopes continued until the Neo-Assyrian period, but in practical terms ended in the Neo-Babylonian period (Baker 2003, 244–245).

Cuneiform Signs

Cuneiform writing is made up of wedges precisely because of the support used: it is difficult to trace curves in clay. That explains why the original pictograms were quickly replaced by signs broken down into "spikes" of varying sizes and orientations. These signs underwent a considerable evolution over the three millennia constituting the history of cuneiform writing (Walker 1987a; Edzard 1976–1980).

Unfortunately, the paleography of cuneiform was underdeveloped for a long time and in large measure still remains so. Paleographical observations generally begin, at the earliest, only with the most ancient Semitic writing systems of the alphabetical type. As Alphonse Dain has aptly observed, "A scholar who studies Sumerian cylinders will not be said to be a paleographer. Therein lies an unfortunate restriction, sanctified by custom." And, he adds, "In fact, only three areas of paleography have been constituted into an autonomous science: the Greek, the Roman and Latin, and the medieval West and Renaissance" (Dain 1961, 530). That under-development can be explained in part by the reproduction techniques used. For a long time, the high cost of photographs meant that Assyriologists were restricted to publishing documents in the form of hand-made copies. In not unusual cases, the copy did not respect the layout of the original or the exact shape of the signs. In the worst cases, the normalization went so far that the copies be-came in reality disguised transcriptions.[15] The case of the Neo-Assyrian letters published in printed form in fourteen volumes (Harper 1982–1914) is no better. Even with very careful copies or excellent photographs, an essential characteristic of cuneiform writing cannot be reproduced: its three-dimensional quality.

In addition, paleography fell victim to the very success of cu-neiform writing, whose length of use surpassed three millennia. That explains why only overly general studies have been written (Daniels 1995b). In R. Labat's classic *Manuel d'épigraphie akkadi-enne* (*Manual of Akkadian Epigraphy,* 1988), the evolution of cunei-form writing is treated on the left-hand page in very large blocks of time:[16] the third millennium, the first and then second half of the second millennium (Old and Middle Assyrian, Old and Mid-dle Babylonian), and finally, the first millennium (Neo-Assyrian and Neo-Babylonian). Most of the studies deal more extensively with the geographical differences perceptible at a single moment (Biggs 1973; Sallaberger 2001) than with the evolution over time in a single region. And the remarks generally have more to do with the repertoire of signs in use (the syllabary) than with their form.[17] A general survey is currently being prepared under the director-ship of A. Livingstone and J. Taylor.[18]

Epigraphists who have worked intensely on certain archival lots such as those of Mari have become skilled at recognizing scribes' "hands." That experience is very difficult to transmit, however, since it is necessary to elaborate a descriptive code, though certain efforts have led to interesting results. By studying the correspondence of the chief musician Rīshiya, Nele Ziegler has been able to demonstrate the existence of two "hands": a portion of Rīshiya's letters was no doubt written by him personally (2007, 93–98). A study of the texts of "king's meals" has also made it possible to show that these bookkeeping documents were written by two different "hands." Lists of rations distributed to the palace staff have yielded the names of two women scribes, obviously in charge of those accounts: in that case, prosopography has confirmed the results of the paleographic analysis (Ziegler 1999, 106).

It is primarily for the areas "peripheral" to the cuneiform world—for example, among specialists on the Hittites (Rüster 1972; Rüster and Neu 1975; Klinger 2003)—that paleography is the most developed. In that case, there was no need to study the archival documents. The essential concern was to succeed in dating the copies of manuscripts from the royal library. It is undoubtedly because the contracts and administrative documents of Mesopotamia can be dated with relative ease by other means that paleography has remained underdeveloped. These texts often include a date; when they do not, their chronology can often be established by a prosopographical inquiry.

How is cuneiform writing to be analyzed (Daniels 1995b)? One must first try to reconstitute the shape of the stylus and observe the angle at which it was held in relation to the tablet and how deeply it was pressed into the clay. One must then examine the wedges, and especially, the order in which they were inscribed in combination to form a sign (Edzard 1997a, 39). The slant is significant: late Babylonian and Seleucid texts are characterized by signs that slope rather than being perpendicular to the line. One must also observe the relative size of the signs, their distribution along the horizontal line, the length of the vertical strokes, and so on. Experimentation can produce very interesting data (see especially the photos in Powell 1981).

As it does everywhere, paleography must take into account the nature of the support and the kind of text. Inscriptions on stone always have a more archaic-looking writing than the cursive of the same period. A famous example is the Code of Hammurabi: the characters on the stela in the Louvre, engraved a little before 1750 B.C., nearly correspond to the cursive in Sumerian tablets from the twenty-fourth century B.C., not at all to that of its own time (Figure 20).

In any event, it must not be imagined that paleographical changes were the result of a slow evolution: they occurred in sudden leaps. Writing reforms were generally decided on at the impetus of the political authorities. During the Dynasty of Akkad (twenty-fourth to twenty-third centuries B.C.), for example, the central administration under Naram-Sin imposed a uniform style across the empire. Local archives therefore display the coexistence of two types of bookkeeping tablets: those for internal usage, which followed the old writing habits, and those intended to be presented to the imperial inspectors, which conformed to the new criteria. The imposed nature of the exercise is observable on one large tablet. The scribe began it in the "imperial style," then changed his mind near the middle and ended in his usual mode of writing. It has been noted that, had the tablet been broken, the two fragments would have been dated with a chronological difference of at least a generation (Foster 1986, 49).

A second reform occurred in the kingdom of Mari in the late nineteenth century B.C. The tablets described as "Shakkanakku" suddenly disappeared in favor of a more "modern" style consistent with the habits of the scribes from the neighboring kingdom of Eshnunna (Charpin and Ziegler 2003, 40 and n99). We possess an administrative document—a rarity in the history of

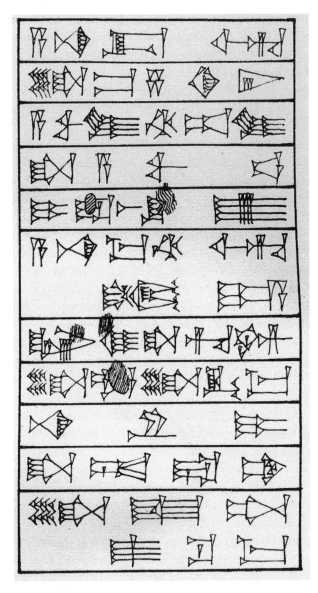

FIGURE 20. The archaic monumental writing of the Code of Hammurabi: excerpt from the epilogue ("May the wronged man who faces trial go before my representation as just king..."). (Courtesy of Gregorian & Biblical Press, Rome.)

writing—written in accordance with the old norms, then recopied in the modern way (Durand 1985a). A comparison between the two shows that the changes had to do with the form of the tablets, the configuration of the signs, and the syllabary all at once.

The Values of the Signs

A sign could be read in different ways depending on whether it had a logographic or a syllabic value. The value of a logogram (one sign representing an entire word) also changed depending on the era and the type of text. Syllabic values were also multiple, the context making it possible to recognize the proper reading without difficulty. The proportion of logograms to phonetic signs varied by kind of text and by era. In general, an inventory list would contain a greater proportion of logograms than a letter. But the use of logograms increased between the Old Babylonian period and the beginning of the first millennium.

Seals

In ancient Mesopotamia, seals were impressed on the clay tablet itself: the written text and the seal impressions were thus on a single support. Matrices took different forms, depending on the era. Cylinder seals predominated in the ancient periods, to be gradually replaced by rings and stamps.

As in all civilizations, the use of seals fulfilled three needs: "to close (and guarantee the integrity or confidentiality of a text), to assert ownership, and to authenticate an act (by manifesting that it truly expresses the will of an individual or of a moral person)" (Metman 1961, 393). Hence a chest, jar, or door would be closed with a piece of clay that was then sealed (Figure 21). Letters were sent in clay envelopes bearing the name of the recipient and the impression of the sender's seal. The importance of seals in legal matters is very clear. The person who was abandoning a right or

FIGURE 21. Label used in the Mari palace to close a chest where the census tablets of the district of Saggaratum were preserved. (Courtesy of D. Charpin.)

making a pledge had to seal the tablet: the seller, who renounced forever his rights to an alienated possession, or the debtor who entered into an obligation to repay his creditor, for example. Very often, there were also the seal impressions of a certain number of witnesses, whose names were inscribed on the contract and who were in some sense guarantors of the authenticity of the act.

A contract in due form, sealed by the seller, was considered unassailable in court, as the following case demonstrates. A certain Yahgunum, having sold a plot of land to Etel-pi-Marduk, sought to prevent the buyer from building a house on it. Even though the new owner had already incurred expenses, Yahgunum was able to pressure him to stop work. But Etel-pi-Marduk went to see the authorities in Babylon, who advised Yahgunum not to persist in his attitude, since any tribunal would decide the matter in the purchaser's favor.

Tell Yahgunum: thus (speaks) Ibbi-Sumuqan. May the god Shamash bring you life! As for Etel-pi-Marduk, son of Ikshud-appashu, to whom you sold a plot of land three years ago, and whom you made swear an oath by the king when he undertook to build a house on it, and whom you, in so doing, compelled to abandon his plan, he brought me his tablet (documenting) that he bought the house from you and I inspected it: it is unambiguous. The impression of your seal and (the names of) five witnesses are written on the tablet. If he shows the tablet to the judges, will they circumvent the law for you? That is why I am writing you this letter: return the plot to Etel-pi-Marduk, so that his investment will not be lost and he can build his house. If you wish, come here to Babylon and see what the situation is with your case. (*AbB* 3 82)

In ancient Babylonia, as in the Western Middle Ages, some seals were *bene cognitum et famosus* (well known and famous), as this example shows: "You have sealed (this contract) with the seal of the high priest–*šangūm* of Shamash, of the high priest–*šangūm* of Aya, and with your seals. . . . If the seal of the high priest–*šangūm* of Shamash, of the high priest–*šangūm* of Aya, and your seals are contested, whose seal will be accepted?" (*AbB* 11 90: 18–19, 27–29). It is clear that the loss of a seal by its owner was judged a grave matter, so much so that a certificate of loss was immediately issued: "On the first day of month xi, a seal in the name of Ṣilli-Urash was lost" (the names of four witnesses and the date follow) (Klengel 1968).[19] And a certain Sin-mushallim bought back his father's seal from a merchant for one shekel of silver; a certificate was then drawn up so that he would not be responsible for the contracts sealed with the seal between his father's death and the moment he bought it back (van Koppen 2002).

In an Old Assyrian lawsuit, one Sin-nada complained that two chests belonging to him had been stolen, and he detailed their content. After the description of a large number of tablets, one by one, come the following:

—1 seal belonging to Idi-Eštar, son of Aššur-nada—while he was still alive, 4 shareholders placed it under seal and entrusted it to me;

—the seal of Šamaš-tappa'i was entrusted to me under the seals of 3 shareholders' employees. (*CTMMA* 1 84a: 50–54)

Hence a seal could be entrusted to a colleague, but to avoid fraudulent use, it was placed in a sealed container. In the Old Babylonian period, cylinder seals usually bore both an image and a legend. The legend described the seal's owner in three ways: first, by his name; second, by his father's name; and third, as the servant of a king or god (Gelb 1977). The indication of the seal owner's name can be very valuable for the historian in certain cases, for example, when the tablet itself does not cite the individual's full name but only his hypocoristic (nickname). The second element appearing in the legend of a seal is the patronymic, following the usual manner of defining a person in ancient Babylonia, where "family names" were not in use. There again, this information may not appear in the text and is essential for prosopography. The third line of the legend indicates the king or deity of whom the seal's owner is said to be the servant. The individual who declared himself the servant of a deity was not a priest in the temple of the god but was referring to his family's patron god or goddess (Charpin 1990a). Those who belonged to the palace administration were described as "servants of the king." The legend of a seal sometimes included the owner's title, which is not always indicated in the text. The promotion of certain officials can be verified thanks to the appearance of a new title on their seals.[20]

By the late third and the early second millennium, the iconography on cylinder seals was deteriorating: "presentation" scenes and depictions of "human figure with mace" began to multiply (Figure 22). As a result, scribes did not roll the cylinder across the tablet (to the great displeasure of contemporary specialists in iconography), but simply impressed the part of it on which the legend appeared, taking great care to ensure that the legend would be visible.[21] In addition, when someone ordered a seal from a lapi-

FIGURE 22. Matrix of an Old Babylonian cylinder seal and modern impression in clay. The image represents the king ("figure with mace") before deities. The legend has been divided into three lines between the figures: "Ibni-Amurrum / son of Ilima-ahi / servant of the god Amurrum." (©The Trustees of the British Museum.)

cide, he was provided with a model of the inscription to be engraved; several tablets of this kind have been unearthed (Tanret 2008, 145). A letter from Mari indicates there were "readymade" seals: they already bore a decoration, and one had only to engrave the legend to match the purchaser's identity. In response to a request from the king's secretary, an official wrote him: "There are seals in Mari: a servant engraves them. Write: if there is a readymade one in Mari, have someone inscribe your name. If there is not a readymade one, write, in a message from you, to Ana'ish (a goldsmith), so that the matter of the engraving and the inscription will be finished."[22]

There is further—negative—evidence of the growing importance granted to the name of the seal's owner: cases in which the seal does not allow one to identify him. These may be, in the first place, seals with a religious legend, for example, a prayer in praise of a deity; or they may be anepigraphic seals. In such cases, the scribe often accompanied the impression with a notation in small characters indicating the name of the seal's owner (Figure 23),[23] but that was not always done.[24] Sometimes a seal may bear an ordinary legend that does not correspond to any of the parties to the contract or to the witnesses. This may have been a seal used by someone other than its owner, often a member of his family. In some instances, the scribes felt the need to explain that fact, as in YOS 8, no. 71, where a note indicates that Idin-Ea used the seal of his father, Balmunamhe, because his own seal was unavailable. But in others, the scribe explained nothing. Hence, in BIN 7, no. 214, the seller is Damiq-ilishu, son of Ana-Damu-taklaku, whereas the only seal impression appearing on the tablet is that of Amer-ilishu, son of Ana-Damu-taklaku. Despite the absence of any comment, it is clear that the seller had sealed with his brother's seal.[25]

These were ad hoc practices, which may have resulted from the momentary unavailability of the seal, as in the following text, in which the debtor uses a witness's seal. The envelope indicates: "Not having a seal, he sealed with that of Apilsha." It might be surmised that this was a case of someone too poor to own a seal, but the tablet offers a variant that leads us to set aside that interpretation: "Not having his seal on him, he sealed with Apilsha's seal."[26] Another possibility is that a seal had recently been lost, as indicated by the sender of this letter: "My cylinder seal was lost in Mashkan, that is why I sealed (the envelope of this letter) with someone else's seal" (*AbB* 11 77: 24). Sometimes individuals consistently used seals that were not their own: these were inherited seals. Although a seal was often buried with its owner, it could also sometimes be transmitted to the eldest son, less no doubt out of niggardly concerns for economy than to demonstrate familial continuity. There are cases in which the transmission of a seal by inheritance within a family continued over several generations. Hence, on a contract from year 13 of Ammi-ṣaduqa (1634) is the impression of the seal of Sin-iddinam, which he had had engraved about a century and a half earlier, under the reign of Hammurabi.

FIGURE 23. Tablet in the form of an envelope (Sippar, seventeenth century): seals were rolled over the left edge. Above, only the legend of the first seal is impressed. Below, since the seal bore no legend, someone impressed the image and inscribed over it: "seal of Sin-iddinam" (a judge, the sixth witness to this sales contract). (From H. Klengel, in H. Gasche et al. 1994, 171.)

A genealogical study has made it possible to establish that the seal belonged at the time to a certain Ibni-Sin, great-grandson of Sin-iddinam (Van Lerberghe and Voet 1989).

What are generally—though somewhat inaccurately—called "*bur.gul* seals" are a special case. These are cylinder seals engraved by a lapicide (*bur.gul* in Sumerian) in clay or soft stone and containing only the name and patronymic of the party to the contract. This type of seal never mentions of which king or deity the owner was the servant. When several people made a pledge, as in the case of adoptions or divisions of inheritance, their names appeared on a single seal of this sort; such tablets had no seal impresssions of witnesses, however. In addition, the so-called *bur.gul* seals were completely lacking in iconography (Figure 24). They were used for only a single transaction. In one case, two transactions were conducted by the same person within a short interval of time, yet the *bur.gul* seal used the second time was not the same as that impressed on the first contract.[27]

Why were these seals used? It is difficult to say. Sometimes it seems that they were for individuals who had to seal but did not own a cylinder seal.[28] Such is the case for the tablets from Uruk authorizing slaves to leave the house. A member of the slave's family served as guarantor: when the guarantor was a man, the impression was an ordinary seal, but when the guarantor was a woman, it was a *bur.gul* seal impression (Charpin and Durand 1993). There is at least one example, however, of a *bur.gul* seal impression in the name of an individual for whom the impression of a personal seal also exists. Note, moreover, that the use of these *bur.gul* seals was confined to certain regions and to a certain period of time (Leemans 1982). In any case, the great interest of these types of seal is that they show what was most important about seals in the Old Babylonian period: above all, they were used to impress in clay the name of the person making the pledge.

It is clear, then, that in the Old Babylonian period emphasis was deliberately placed on the name of the seal's owner. Iconography

FIGURE 24. Example of a *bur.gul* seal impression on the back of a contract, between the list of witnesses and the date (the seal has been impressed twice). The matrix contains only two lines: "Amurrum-malik, son of Erissum-mātum." He is the seller; no witnesses sealed it (Nippur, year 13 of Samsu-iluna [1737]). (Courtesy of the Penn Museum.)

was no longer considered an effective instrument for identification. This was not an isolated phenomenon: Babylonian civilization granted a privileged place to writing generally during that period. This example also shows that we must be cautious about adopting a linear view of evolution: seals from the first millennium usually had no legend, and, when one did exist, it was a prayer. In all cases at that time, the seal's owner was identified through a legend inscribed by the scribe.

When a tablet contains the impression of one or several seals, the epigraphist who publishes the text often has a tendency to overlook them, at times not even indicating their presence. At best, he or she will be interested only in the legend, leaving it to specialists in sigillography to copy and comment on the figures. No one will deny that a division of labor is inevitable because of the skills required, but an overall approach to the document is necessary. Indeed, sigillographers for their part long had a tendency to privilege the study of matrices over that of impressions, which are infinitely more difficult to study. All the same, impressions offer the advantage of appearing on documents that usually include a date or can be situated with some accuracy in time. Hence a stylistic study of seals can locate precise reference points, which sigillographers have often lacked. From that standpoint, a whole series of recent studies has made up for lost time.[29] How seals were impressed on the tablet (before or after the text was inscribed, in what place, in what order, and so on) has also begun to be studied with increasing precision (Hattori 2001).

One also sometimes finds on the tablets the imprint of the fringe *(sissiktum)* of a piece of clothing or even the imprint of a fingernail *(ṣuprum)*, which, like the seal, were used as a substitute for the person (Finet 1969).

The Internal Characteristics of the Documents

Studies of the internal characteristics of Mesopotamian documents focus in the first place on the language used by the scribes, which did not necessarily correspond to the language spoken at the time, and on the particular models for the different kinds of texts.

Languages of Culture and Vernacular Languages

In the history of writing, it is not uncommon for the language used to compose documents to be different from that used in daily life. In Mesopotamia, such differences are attested for several periods.[30]

During the Old Babylonian period, Sumerian was used in written texts, but that language was no longer spoken except in artificial situations, such as among priests or at school. Scribes also used it, especially for drawing up contracts. But gradually, beginning in northern Babylonia, Akkadian was increasingly employed,[31] a situation resembling that of deeds in the Western Middle Ages, where terms borrowed from the vulgate gradually infiltrated the Latin.

In addition to Akkadian, another language was spoken in the Near East at the start of the second millennium: Amorite, which belonged to the northwestern Semitic group. That language is known almost exclusively through many names of persons and a few technical terms (M. P. Streck 2000; Charpin 2005–2006a); as yet, no text written in Amorite has been found. The weight of the Sumero-Akkadian tradition undoubtedly compelled scribes not to set Amorite down in writing. Cultural prejudices may also have played a role: Amorite was primarily the language spoken by the Bedouins from the west, who were held in disdain by the settled populations of Mesopotamia (Charpin 2004a, 58–59).

A similar gap between the language of written culture and the spoken language occurred in the second half of the second millennium, as documented in the archives of Nuzi, a small city that belonged to the kingdom of Arrapha (Kirkuk region in the northeastern part of present-day Iraq). The written language was an Akkadian strongly contaminated by the locally spoken language, Hurrian.[32] Akkadian was also used by scribes at the other end of the Mittanian empire, in the Syrian city of Alalakh. That was true closer to the capital as well, in Tell Brak, though a letter composed in Hurrian has been found there.[33] In Qaṭna in central Syria, texts have recently been uncovered that display a curious mix: sentences begin in Akkadian and end in Hurrian (Richter 2005).

In the first millennium, new, alphabetical writing systems appeared and were used to notate languages such as Aramaic. The temptation to write in Aramaic and in ink is understandable, given the cumbersomeness of traditional cuneiform writing. This is demonstrated by an ostracon found in Assur. On that shard, an Assyrian official posted in Babylonia wrote a long letter to a colleague from Assur, in ink and in Aramaic (Fales 2007, 103n39). Neo-Assyrian bas-reliefs, in fact, sometimes represent side by side a scribe writing on a tablet and another whose calamus is inscribing a text on papyrus or leather, the first obviously notating Akkadian, the second, Aramaic.[34] The Assyrian empire was clearly bilingual from the standpoint of the written text: hence we possess an order from the king to bring together all available scribes, both "Assyrians" (that is, those writing in cuneiform) and "Aramaeans" (those writing in Aramaic), who were to escort the troops charged with levying the tax-*iškaru*.[35] The nature of the support explains the preponderance of Akkadian in the archives unearthed, since Aramaic was not often set in clay.[36] Nevertheless, in a missive written to an official posted in Ur (southern Babylonia), the Neo-Assyrian king Sargon II refused to receive mail written "on skin *(sipru)* in Aramaic"; letters to him had to be written "in Akkadian," that is, in cuneiform on a clay tablet.[37]

It is evident from this example that a link existed between the support, the writing system, and the language on one hand, and the symbolic value that could be attached to the use of cuneiform on the other. The letter from Sargon represents a very firm assertion of political and cultural identity and is in this respect remarkable for its awareness of the underlying issues.[38] Such determination is undoubtedly an essential factor for explaining the longevity of cuneiform in the first millennium. Hence the grandson of Sargon, Esarhaddon, gave scribal training in Akkadian to the sons of Babylonian dignitaries whom he kept as hostages in Niniveh (Fincke 2003–2004, 118). Nevertheless, beginning with his reign, most official correspondence was in Aramaic (Luukko and Van Buylaere 2002, xvii): found in Niniveh were many pieces of clay that were used to seal the skin scrolls serving as support for these letters, which have totally disappeared (Parpola 1986, 226n19).

Composing Texts

When scribes had to draw up a contract, they followed models that varied by region and by era. Hence the description of the cadastral location of a parcel in a sales contract for a plot of land in the Old Babylonian period would be different depending on whether the contract was drafted in Sippar or in Larsa. From the mid-second millennium on, scribes also indicated the orientation of each boundary line of the plot. Some clauses were typical of certain regions and were absent from contracts written elsewhere. In northern Babylonia in the late Old Babylonian period, for example, sales contracts included, following the price, an indication that an additional sum *(SI.BI)* had been paid to the seller (Tanret and De Graef 2003–2004).

Unfortunately, only a few manuals systematically present the formularies used by scribes for each category of acts in a given era: the one J. N. Postgate devoted to the Neo-Assyrian period is a fine example (Postgate 1976). For the Old Babylonian period, a few studies confine themselves to specific kinds of texts, whether sales contracts (San Nicolò 1922) or loans (Skaist 1994). The only systematic study of diplomatic discourse undertaken thus far deals with treaties and other "international" acts from the second half of the second millennium (Kestemont 1974).

Letters were less rigid in form than contracts, but a certain number of practices still had to be respected (Sallaberger 1999). Correspondents sometimes alluded to these practices, as in this example: "What is this behavior? Even when I write you by the rules, you don't send me any reply to my letter!" (*AbB* 9 264: 7). The school exercises that have been uncovered confirm the existence of models for letters used to describe various situations.

The Succession of Operations

It seems that scribes proceeded directly to the writing of the definitive deed. In the Old Babylonian period, only a single copy of the document was made, to be given to the person who might need a written text to prove his or her rights. Under special legal circumstances, several true copies were made (Van Lerberghe and Voet 1994). Such was the case for exchanges, when each of the two parties was supposed to keep a written record of the agreement concluded. In cases where both copies are found in the same archive, we may assume that one of the two parties subsequently bought back the plot he had first offered for exchange (Charpin 1980, 104). Divisions of inheritances gave rise to various practices based on local custom. In certain regions, each heir received a tablet describing everyone's share. These tablets, several copies of which were drawn up, may therefore be called partition documents. In other places, however, the tablet given to each heir described only what he inherited.

The Status of Scribes

The status of scribes remains poorly known (Charpin, Hunger, and Waetzoldt 2009). For the most part, a scribe was considered a kind of artisan: in an administrative text from Mari, among the thirty-one "specialists" (dumu.meš *ummēni)* listed are carpenters, singers, and gardeners, but also a scribe (*ARM* 9 27). There was certainly a variety of social statuses: a certain Yasitna-abum complained to Queen Iltani that he had taken her advice and learned the art of the scribe but that, for lack of support from her, he was unable to achieve the standard of living she had led him to expect (Foster 1993).

Many contracts include, at the end of the list of witnesses, the name of the scribe who recorded the text. Curiously, prosopographical studies based on this type of indication have developed only recently,[39] and much remains to be done. Nevertheless, a few figures are emerging from the shadows, such as the secretaries of certain kings, who read the mail addressed to the ruler and composed the missives the king sent out. It was obviously a privilege to be in the king's service, and it is clear that scribes who fell into disgrace made efforts to win back the sovereign's favor. One of the finest examples is that of a scribe from Mari who had served Yasmah-Addu; after that ruler's fall, he sent Zimri-Lim a letter written in both Sumerian and Akkadian, hoping that that feat would get him hired by the new king.[40]

The vast majority of references to scribes are in contracts: the last witness is very often the scribe who composed the text. A few rare figures are fairly well known, such as Shumum-liṣi, attested between year 33 of Ammi-ditana and year 13 of Ammi-ṣaduqa in 174 texts, including 151 from the archives of Ur-Utu discovered in Sippar-Amnānum (Tanret 2004). Even so, we do not know how these scribes were compensated. We can only conclude that they were paid by the person who needed to keep the tablet to prove his or her rights. Only "peripheral" texts, notably in Terqa, indicate the payment of small sums of money to the scribe (Tanret 2005). It seems that in certain cases, scribes attached to a palace or a temple could also occasionally work for individuals.

Local Traditions

Many examples of model contracts have been found in the schools of Nippur for the Old Babylonian period. Characteristically, they bear no names of witnesses or date. In place of these indications are "its witnesses," "its month," "its year."[41]

The weight of tradition was ultimately even stronger among schoolmasters than among "notaries." In the first millennium, that resulted in a paradoxical situation: the models that were recopied by apprentice scribes at the time no longer corresponded to those that appeared in contracts during the same period, but were still those that had been used in the city of Nippur in the first half of the second millennium (Landsberger 1937).

The Formation and Consultation of Archives

A definition is called for: "archives" are the accumulation of written traces left behind by the activities of a person, a collectivity, or an organization. The definition provided in French law no. 79-18 of January 3, 1979, applies perfectly to Mesopotamia: "Set of documents, whatever their date, form, and material support, produced or received by any physical or moral person, or by any public or private agency or organization in the performance of its activities." From that standpoint, I find María Brosius's approach unsatisfactory: she writes that "a collection of records reflects a deliberate choice or selection of documents" (2003b, 10). I prefer to adopt the definition of a medievalist: "The notion of an 'archive' stands in complete opposition to that of a 'collection' . . . On the contrary, documents are deposited in archives in exactly the same way that the sedimentation of geological strata occurs, which is to say, gradually, constantly" (Bautier 1961, 1120). That accumulation may be disrupted from time to time, when outdated documents are sorted and discarded, a process secondary to the fundamental one of accumulation, however. A label on a tablet basket from the early second millennium B.C. attests to the existence of that operation: "Basket of outdated tablets to be destroyed" (YOS 5 58; Veenhof 1986b, 18n76).

Assyriologists have taken an interest in studying archives only in the last few decades.[42] It is true that, at its inception, archaeology resembled more a hunt for objects—tablets included—than a scientific enterprise as it is now understood, and the archives of major sites such as Niniveh, Sippar, and Nippur have paid the price. In addition, museum storerooms were constituted in great part through the purchase of documents from "fortuitous discoveries," a term that often means illicit excavations. In this respect, the situation remains extremely worrisome.[43] Even texts from regular excavations were for a long time published typologically, without respect for the sets of objects among which the tablets had been discovered. The case of Ur is altogether representative in this regard. The Old Babylonian texts were divided into several volumes, devoted to "Royal Inscriptions," "Letters and Documents," and "Literary and Religious Texts," even though in the houses of certain members of the clergy the different types of texts were found together. Analyses of that documentation as a function of the different locales have produced very interesting results (Charpin 1986a).

It must not be forgotten that, even when the excavation is conducted very carefully, archaeologists discover ruins, so that they cannot expect to find archives as they existed during the life of the building before its destruction. Thus the discoverers of the Middle Assyrian archives of Tell Sheikh Hamad, after a very meticulous three-dimensional recording of the finds, ultimately concluded that the 600 tablets or so unearthed had fallen from the upper floor during the final fire (Pfälzner in Cancik-Kirschbaum

1996, 7). We must absolutely recognize that a catastrophe leading to the destruction of a building (usually a fire) has an impact on the survival of the archives, even in the most privileged cases such as Ebla (Archi 2003; Matthiae 2008) or the house of Ur-Utu in Tell ed-Dēr (Janssen 1996; Tanret 2008). Hence information from the excavations must be complemented by the data in the texts themselves. In not unusual cases, these texts indicate how the archives were classified or consulted. We thus possess an inventory of the possessions of an important person "deposited in the lower storeroom of the building-*šahuru*" in thirteenth-century Assur. After the mention of a chariot and different objects relating to it, and before the inventory of furnishings and metal or wooden objects, is an enumeration of twenty-four tablet chests, whose content is given in precise detail:

> 1 chest *(quppu)* of (obligations) on Šamaš-eriš;
> 1 chest of clearance(s) of people and fields, of the town of Šarika;
> 1 chest of (obligations) on Aššur-tahatti; . . .
> 1 *ditto* of (obligations) on Riš-Adad; 1 chest of herald's proclamations for houses in the inner city; etc. (*KAJ* 310; Postgate 2003, 129)

It is likely that these indications were taken from the labels on the chests.[44] The "classic" procedure for finding archived tablets is described in a letter from Queen Shibtu to Zimri-Lim, king of Mari:

> Tell my lord: thus (speaks) Shibtu, your servant. The palace is faring well. Here is what my lord wrote to me: "I am hereby sending you Yaṣṣur-Addu. Send inspectors *(ebbum)* with him; let them take the tablets he indicates to them and let these tablets be stored near you until my arrival." Now, since my lord wrote me, I sent Mukannishum, Shub-Nalu, and Usharesh-hetil with that man. In the workshop-*nepārum* under Etel-pi-sharrim's authority, Yaṣṣur-Addu showed a room to the in-

spectors I had sent with him. And they opened the door of the room—sealed with the seal of Igmilum, who is attached to the administration—which he had shown. They took two baskets of tablets, these two baskets of tablets having been sealed with the seal of Etel-pi-sharrim. With their seals, these baskets of tablets were placed near me in anticipation of my lord's arrival. And the door of the room they had opened I sealed with my seal. (*ARM* 10 12 [*LAPO* 18 1152]; Charpin 2001, 13–14)

Note the abundance of precautions surrounding that operation: not only was the room in which the baskets were archived closed with seals (Potts 1990) but the baskets themselves were sealed; and the queen insisted on the fact that the seals had remained intact, that is, that no one had opened these baskets before the king's return.

Family Archives and the Archives of Large Institutions

The usual opposition between "private" and "public" archives is meaningless when applied to ancient Mesopotamia. "Private archives" were in reality *family* archives. And there was nothing public about so-called public archives: they belonged to large institutions, that is, to palaces or temples.

Family archives often cover a period of one or two centuries, up to six generations. Among the finest examples, let me cite those of Ur-Utu in Sippar (eighteenth to seventeenth centuries B.C.) and those of the Egibis (seventh to fifth centuries B.C.) (Wunsch 2000 and Abraham 2004). For the most part, they contain property deeds, which were transmitted across the generations along with the property to which they refer, particularly land (Charpin 2010, chap. 4). Texts concerning the last generation are often more abundant and varied: when the final destruction of the houses sheltering these archives occurred, the outdated documents had not yet been sorted out from those that still had value (Joannès

1995). Depending on the case, these documents could be preserved in reed baskets, wooden chests, or earthenware jars.

Unlike family archives, palace archives generally cover only a very limited period of time. Hence, in the Mari palace, the living archives deal only with the decade when Yasmah-Addu was king of Mari and the thirteen years of Zimri-Lim's reign, less than a quarter century. The archives from the time of Yahdun-Lim and Sumu-Yamam actually constitute dead archives, covering only about twenty years; even if we take them into account, we arrive at a figure of under fifty years. The administrative archives of the "House of the Queen" in Girsu in the Early Dynastic IIIb period, which is to say, about 1,600 tablets, cover twenty-five years (Visicato 2000, 237), ending with the defeat of Urukagina. The most recent studies of the archives of Ebla (twenty-fourth century B.C.) have tended to reduce the duration of these archives to about forty years at most (Biga 2003). Those of the Urgarit palace, in the thirteenth century B.C., cover a slightly longer interval of time, but it would seem that a portion of those archives had been discarded on the upper floor.

Temples appear to have been less vulnerable to the vicissitudes of political-military life, since in some cases they preserved administrative archives for a longer period of time. The archives of the temple of Ninurta in Nippur, for example, extended over more than seventy-five years, from year 1 of Lipit-Enlil of Isin (1873) to year 28 of Rim-Sin (1795).[45] Those in the storeroom of the temple of Ningal in Ur (Ganunmah) cover 120 years, from year 9 of Gungunnum (1924) to year 19 of Rim-Sin (1804) (Figulla 1953; Spada 2007; Black and Spada 2008). In the first millennium, the archives of the temple of Shamash in Sippar, known as the Ebabbar, cover a period from the last third of the seventh century to year 2 of Xerxes (485 B.C.), that is, about a century and a half (Jursa 2005, 118).

There were never any truly "public" or "state" archives in Mesopotamia. From that standpoint, the title *State Archives of Assyria*, chosen for the corpus of Neo-Assyrian documents—remarkable in other respects—that have been published by the University of Helsinki since 1987 appears unfortunate. In the Ebla palace during the third millennium (Matthiae 2008), as in that of Mari during the second (Charpin 2008a) or Niniveh during the first (Parpola 1995), these were royal archives in the sense of "king's archives." In particular, the sovereign kept the correspondence he received, both from his peers and from his officials posted in the provinces or on missions abroad. Conversely, kings, like private individuals, ordinarily did not keep duplicates of the letters they sent out. For our knowledge of the letters *written* by the Neo-Assyrian kings we are primarily beholden to the quotations found in the replies to them (Watanabe 1985, 140). Archives thus provide only the passive correspondence of individuals, whatever their status.[46] Letters did not normally bear a date or the place of origin. The messenger who brought them could provide orally the desired details about the sender's place of residence and about when the letter was composed. When, in rare cases, a date does appear, only the day and month are indicated, almost never the year. It seems clear, therefore, that the ancients gave little thought to the archiving of letters. Nevertheless, the Babylonians who sorted out the archives of the chancellery in the Mari palace were able to distinguish the letters from the age of Yasmah-Addu from those belonging to that of Zimri-Lim (Charpin 1995b), which they could not have done unless the letters had first been organized by a filing system. That interest in preservation is particularly astonishing given that quotations from earlier letters, which in fact never date very far back in time, are almost always done from memory and not word for word.

The palace archives also preserved internal bookkeeping accounts: lists of rations of oil or clothing distributed to the women in the harem or to visitors, expenses incurred for the king's table and for his guests, and so on. The archives found in Ebla and Mari have preserved thousands of administrative documents of this kind. Texts concerning the kingdom as a whole are rare. One exception is the large census tablets, which were inscribed in the provinces and then brought together in the capital (Durand 1998a, 332–353). Every governor kept his own documentation. In the Ur III period, archives from the province of Umma seem to have been kept in a single building; but since they were exhumed by illicit excavators, we can only hypothesize about the organization of that administrative documentation. The 10,000 tablets currently published cover a period of thirty-eight years (from Shulgi 32 to Ibbi-Sin 3); they allow us to distinguish among different offices, charged, respectively, with agriculture, grain, labor organization, animals, wool, leather, metals, boats, and forests (Steinkeller 2003, 41–42). But we have no concrete knowledge of the conditions under which all these texts were elaborated, and especially, of the manner in which they were preserved.

Beginning with the mid-second millennium, the ruler also kept in his palace the text of the treaties he had concluded with foreign sovereigns.[47] The sites of Hattusha (Beckman 1996) and Ugarit (Lackenbacher 2002) have yielded many examples. In Assyria, it seems that the matrix of the god Assur, which was used in the first millennium to seal treaties, was preserved in the "city hall" *(bīt ālim),* while the texts of treaties were written, sealed, and preserved in an annex to the neighboring temple of Nabu (George 1986, 141). The title "bearer of the tablet of the fates of the gods" of Nabu can be explained by the fact that the god Nabu oversaw the writing of the most important state documents.

Living and Dead Archives

Unless I am mistaken, I was the first to introduce into Assyriology the distinction between "living" and "dead" archives.[48] The distinction is essential for properly evaluating the nature of the texts unearthed during excavations.[49] "Living archives" refers to an accumulation of texts that continued until the moment just before the building in which they are discovered was destroyed. For example, the archives of King Zimri-Lim were held in his Mari palace until Babylonian troops entered it in 1760 B.C. But often the documents uncovered during excavations are dead archives, that is, texts that were discarded by the ancients themselves.[50] Take the case of the archives of the temple of Ninurta in Nippur: hundreds of tablets written between 1873 and 1795 B.C. were found during excavations of a building constructed in the Parthian era on the ruins of the temple of Inanna (Sigrist 1984). The builders, in digging through the tell in search of clay for bricks, had obviously come across an archival lot more than a millennium and a half old. They decided that the clay tablets would make an excellent material for reinforcing the platform on which they wanted to build a fortress. Examples of this kind abound.

It is not unusual for a single building to contain both living and dead archives. In the Mari palace, several dozen bookkeeping documents from the time of Yasmah-Addu, predating the destruction of the site by some fifteen or twenty years, have been discovered sunk into the clay inside a bench used to hold large earthenware jars. And in effect, they are memos recording oil expenditures (Charpin 1984, 1987). Tablets that document the reigns of Yahdun-Lim and Sumu-Yamam, predecessors of Yasmah-Addu, have for their part been found under the floor in certain rooms. They were thrown down there when a new clay floor was made, at the time Yasmah-Adda moved into the palace. The texts that the ancients got rid of in that way had only a temporary value—memoranda, minor bookkeeping texts, and so on—and were regularly winnowed out.

Consulting the Archives

The problem raised by archives in every era is that of access to information: how to find what one is looking for? The Mesopotamians had techniques that, admittedly, were still rather rudimentary. In Ebla, the walls of the archive rooms were fitted with wooden shelves (Matthiae 1986) (Figure 25). Practically none of the texts bear a date, so that their chronology could only have been indicated by the place the tablets occupied on the shelves. But since these were destroyed by fire, modern historians have no external reference point at all: it is only through a patient analysis of the documents' content that we are gradually managing to reconstitute the sequence.

Most often, tablets were kept in baskets or chests. Evidence of a chest was discovered in the house of the chief lamenter Ur-Utu in Tell ed-Dēr (Tanret 2008). It had contained 207 tablets arranged in four layers. The receptacle itself, no doubt made of reeds, had disappeared, but the tablets were found stacked up in a space measuring $14\frac{1}{4} \times 9\frac{1}{2}$ inches (36 × 24 cm); the chest must have been some 8 inches (20 cm) deep. It was solid enough to bear the weight of 23 kilograms, which is what the 207 tablets weighed. Baskets and chests were often sealed and equipped with a label that gave some idea of their content. One of the most interesting cases is that of judicial trials (*di.til.la* in Sumerian) in Girsu from the twenty-first century B.C. Some of the labels for tablet baskets found there suggest that the trials were classified by year and by judge (B. Lafont 2000, 38n2). These texts obviously served as a record of legal decisions and had to be available for reading when required.

The most precise indications regarding the consultation of archived tablets come from the letters of Old Assyrian merchants. Since these merchants were often far from home, they sometimes wrote to their wives or to another correspondent, asking that a tablet be sought in their archives: "Open the two chests containing my tablets. Take from them the acknowledgment of debt belonging to Assur-rabi, son of Assur-malik, and have him pay you the $23\frac{1}{2}$ shekels of silver, then return his tablet to him" (Michel 2001, no. 390; see also, for example, nos. 390 and 398). An example

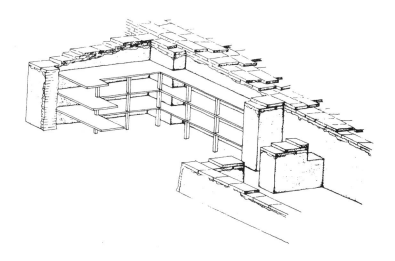

FIGURE 25. The archive room of the Ebla palace: photo of the room at the time of its discovery, and drawing reconstituting the wooden shelves where the tablets were stored. (Courtesy of Nederlands Instituut voor het nabije oosten [NINO].)

from the Mari palace shows that unpaid debts could be inventoried before being handed over to a person charged with compelling the tardy debtors to pay up (Charpin 2008b). In addition, in the early second millennium, the "judges of the cloister" of Sippar, assigned to look after the interests of the nuns dedicated to the god Shamash, kept in their houses law texts, such as a rescript of King Samsu-iluna (Janssen 1991). Finally, three of the ten jars containing the archives of offerings in the temple of Assur for the second half of the second millennium (650 tablets in all) include an inscription indicating their content, such as the following: "Sealed-tablet container of the accounts of the brewers of the Aššur temple under the supervision of Ezbu-lešir, the offerings-overseer of the Aššur temple, servant of Tiglat-pileser (I)" (Postgate 1986b, 170 and n8).

Old Babylonian texts were dated using a system of "year names." Every year was designated by a name that commemorated an outstanding event—military, religious, or other—from the previous year. Of course, such a system presupposes the existence of lists establishing the order of succession for the names. It has recently been observed that the year names for the late Old Babylonian period systematically mention the sovereign's name at the start of the formula, which is not the case for the more ancient texts. The reason for such a change is obvious: as time passed, the archives grew, and it became increasingly difficult for scribes to find their way around them. In addition, there is now evidence that some private archives were sorted chronologically. In the house of Ur-Utu in Sippar-Amnānum (Tell ed-Dēr), no fewer than four lists of year names have been found; they were obviously used to organize the property deeds of Ur-Utu's father at a time when the division of his possessions gave rise to a serious quarrel among his heirs (Tanret 2001).

The question arises whether administrative texts, once archived, were ever actually consulted. A study of texts of "king's meals" in Mari seems to show that the writers of the summations did not always take the trouble to consult the tickets composed day to day and that they often made estimates (Sasson 1982). There are contrary examples, however. Hence King Zimri-Lim gave instructions by letter that the census tablet chests be taken from where they were archived and the summations sent to him. His steward replied:

> My lord wrote me on the subject of the regular army rolls, composed of isolated individuals and domestics-*gerseqqum* from the district, which are sealed with the seal of Sammetar. Following my lord's letter, Lady Inibshunu opened the sealed room and the tablets *found there*[51] . . . Igmilum. . . . He pointed out to us the two chests containing the tablets from the district that were sealed with the seal of Sammetar. I, along with Ṭabat-sharussu, took them out with my own hands. In accordance with what my lord had written me, I did not open any chest. Having taken out the two chests, I sent them to my lord.
>
> (*ARM* 13 14 [*LAPO* 17 652]; Charpin 2001, 15)

The king's aim was clear: to learn what forces he could count on for his next military campaign. Some enumerations in fact give the breakdown, locality by locality, of the number of men who could be enlisted (information drawn from the census tablets), the number of men who actually responded to the royal summons, and finally, the deficit (*ARM* 23 428, 429). Similarly, Hammurabi wrote to Shamash-hazir, manager of the Crown lands of Larsa, to come join him in Sippar with all the tablets relating to the fields attributed in tenure for the preceding three years (*AbB* 4 22). Registries of names were in fact consulted when needed: "The palace registry was examined: Ahushina, son of Etelliya, is not listed on it for a work unit; he is listed as a replacement for Shumman-lā-Shamash."[52]

A recently published letter from Hammurabi would seem to show that, during negotiations with a foreign king, the diplomatic archives were consulted. The king of Mari sent him a draft treaty ("tablet of the oath by the god"):

> Hammurabi acquainted himself with the curses on the tablet of the oath by the god [and *he told me this*]: "The curse of that tablet is very harsh! [This is not (something) to be] meditated on [*within oneself*] or to have heard orally! Of course, there have been tablets of oaths by the god since (the time) of Sumulēl (and) Sīn-muballiṭ, my father; and since I [myself] ascended the throne of the paternal house, I have sworn an oath by the god to Samsi-Addu and to many kings! These tablets exist, but they are not as harsh as this tablet of the oath by the god!"
>
> (Guichard 2004, 22 [A.2968+: 73–78])

Perhaps we ought not to take too seriously that assertion by the king of Babylon: it is not certain that he had these ancient tablets read to him. In another case, the Mittanian king Tushratta invited the pharaoh to compare the inventory tablet of his sister's dowry, which he had just sent out, to that of his aunt, sent out during their fathers' time (*EA* 24 § 22). I doubt, however, that this is anything other than a rhetorical device (*pace* Abrahami and Coulon 2008, 19).

In the first millennium, summaries in Aramaic are sometimes found along the edge of a tablet, inscribed with a stylus in the clay, or in ink on the surface (Figure 26). This demonstrates that there was an assumption that the tablets would be available later for consultation and also that, for the scribes' convenience, the use of Aramaic was becoming obligatory (Fales 1986).

What Was Written and What Was Preserved

It is clear that the writings that have been preserved represent only a small fraction of what existed. The value of a large portion of the texts, especially the bookkeeping documents, was limited

FIGURE 26. Cuneiform tablet from the Achaemenid period with two lines inscribed in Aramaic writing. Here, the Aramaic summary was incised in the clay. (Courtesy of the Penn Museum.)

in time. They were regularly summarized and the originals discarded or recycled. The Mari palace has yielded complete text sequences composed by certain agencies, such as the meat department, for a very limited period of time (Charpin forthcoming e). For example, a batch of 153 tablets dates from the first three months of the reign of Zimri-Lim. If we extrapolate from it for the entire thirteen years of Zimri-Lim's reign, we find we ought to possess a set of 8,000 tablets just for that one type of transaction. The same number of texts should also exist for expenditures of oil, grain, and so on. Hence the some 15,000 tablets that have been uncovered represent only a tiny part of what was put in writing.

For the legal texts as well, certain types of documents had only a temporary value. Such is the case for debt contracts: on principle, at the time of repayment, the debt tablet was returned to the debtor, who was supposed to destroy it. An Old Assyrian letter indicates, for example: "As for the tablet concerning (a debt of) *x* silver, let him pay to you (fem.) the silver and the interest on it, then relinquish the tablet to him" (*TCL* 20 116: 3, 8; *CAD* 131a). How are we to explain the fact that so many debt tablets have come down to us? A first explanation lies in the duration of the loans.[53] Some creditors kept debt tablets for long periods of time; in Mari, an inventory of the lands of Inibshina, priestess-*ugbabtum* of the god Addu, has yielded thirty-two contracts for unpaid debts, some of which were already more than three years old (Charpin 2008b). Moreover, it has been possible to show that, when sovereigns canceled the debts following the proclamation of a *mīšarum* edict, some creditors kept their debt tablets regardless, even though the contracts had lost all value (Charpin 2000b; Van Lerberghe 2003; Suurmeijer 2006–2007).

In reality, texts were only rarely preserved, as a function of what Civil has called "the 'catastrophe' factor" (1987, 46). It was the sudden destruction of the Mari palace by the Babylonians that, paradoxically, preserved a good portion of the archives, and the same conclusion is valid in most other cases.

Conclusion: Memory and Archives

Periods of political upheaval created the need for conquerors to take stock of the wealth they had acquired. Inventories were therefore taken, such as those for the treasuries of the Mari palace after Samsi-Addu, father of Yasmah-Addu, seized it (Charpin 1983). But individuals' memories could sometimes fill in the gaps in the written record. Hence, when Samsi-Addu had a sudden need for large quantities of bronze to equip his armies, he considered taking the objects in that metal that were in the tomb of the former king of Mari, Yahdun-Lim. Officials from the time who could provide the weight of these objects were therefore questioned—and their reply proved a disappointment to the sovereign (Ziegler 2000, 18). Another example appears in a letter from one of Hammurabi's ministers to Shamash-hazir, reporting the claim of a certain Gimillum:

"My family's field is located in the district of the locality of Mehrum. Among the old tablets from the temple of Nisaba, I saw:

'—field of one *bur* four *ikū* belonging to the soldier Adallalum;
—field of one *bur* four *ikū* belonging to the soldier Wardum, Albana territory, district of Mehrum and Muhattat.'
That is what was written on an old service-*ilkum* tablet."
That is what he told me. At present, I am sending him to you. Have him bring you elderly men who know their family and their family's field and have the elders of the city and the elderly men stand up and establish (it) by the "arms" of the god of the city. Please establish for me, with the help of the "arms" of the god of the city, whether it is Adallalum or Wardum who is his father and which of the fields is his family's field. Send me a complete report regarding it, so that I can send a reply to his message. (*AbB* 4 118)

This letter shows, once again, that the ability to read was more widespread in Mesopotamia than is generally believed. Gimillum tells what he *saw* on the tablets and is able to quote the passage concerning his family's field. No scribe intervened in this case. In addition, there is a complementarity between the written text and memory. Despite the existence of a text, an appeal was made for personal recollections. I note in passing the distinction made between the "elders of the city" *(šīb ālim)*, who had an official role, and the "elderly men" *(awīlē labīrūtim)*, the repository of collective memory.

The letter from the Hittite king Hattusili III to Kadashman-Enlil II, king of Babylon, shows that, as of the second half of the second millennium, the idea that the archiving of data could supplement the memories of mortal men had made inroads. The Hittite king recalls that he had sent out letters just after the death of the father of the current king of Babylon: "At that time, my brother was a child, and they did not read the tablets to you. At present, the scribes from that time are no longer alive, and the tablets were not even archived in order that those tablets might be read to you now" (Hagenbuchner 1989, 281–289, no. 204, lines 17–20). The idea was explicitly emerging that the written text allows communication not only across space but also across time.

chapter three

Oral and Written, Part 1:
Correspondence

In the view of Mesopotamian scribes from the early second millennium, written communication was made necessary by the limitations of oral transmission, as we learned from the famous passage in *Enmerkar and the Lord of Aratta*. Because the message to be transmitted to the lord of Aratta was too complex and the messenger was unable to repeat it correctly, the king of Uruk invented cuneiform writing (Vanstiphout 1989). For Old Babylonian scribes, then, the raison d'être for writing was so that sovereigns could correspond with one another. The reality seems to have been different. Although the most ancient tablets go back to about 3200 B.C., the first letters to come down to us date from the period preceding the ascension to the throne of Sargon of Akkad in about 2400 B.C. They include those discovered in the royal archives of Ebla, particularly the famous letter from Enna-Dagan, king of Mari (Fronzaroli and Catagnoti 2003).

The Corpus

In general, the epistolary mode was widely used by historians writing during classical antiquity, and they produced many apocryphal documents. Very few "letters from Alexander" are considered originals. The question legitimately arises, therefore, as to whether the same was not true in Mesopotamia, where correspondence constituted one of the most important corpora.

Apocryphal Letters

There are clearly apocryphal missives in the Mesopotamian corpus, such as the famous letter of Gilgamesh (George 2003, 117–119). The ancients did not doubt the historicity of that king of Uruk, but our point of view differs from theirs. The status of other letters attributed to kings but known only through late copies must be studied on an individual basis. In a letter attributed to Samsu-iluna, the king of Babylon denounces the scandalous conduct of the clergy, whom he accuses of profanation and sacrilege. The letter may be rooted in an authentic incident, a theft that took place in the temple of Nippur, but many anachronistic elements reveal that it was a later text (Al-Rawi and George 1994). Long described as the "Weidner chronicle," it has proven to be an apocryphal royal letter, though the identity of the fictive correspondents is not certain (Al-Rawi 1990).[1] The extensive mutilations in both texts prevent us from assessing their exact import, but it is clear they were composed within a very precise theological-political context.

The correspondence between kings in the Third Dynasty of Ur (twenty-first century B.C.) is a special case: no original has come down to us, only modernized copies made by apprentice scribes in the early second millennium. Schoolmasters at that time selected about thirty letters and had their students recopy them as exercises. It seems clear that a political agenda governed that choice: the initial aim of the scribes in the service of the kings of Isin was to show their apprentices the legitimacy of the secession of Ishbi-Erra, who had founded a new dynasty in Isin. They did not hesitate to insert apocryphal letters into the corpus. As the leading expert on that corpus has cautiously written, "Although it is possible that all of these texts were fictitious, it is more probable that the core of this royal correspondence was based on actual archival texts, but revised, and that other texts of the same type were written long after the death of the kings of Ur" (Michalowski 1993, 4). More radically, a recent study has placed in doubt the authenticity of the *totality* of that correspondence. That analysis deals primarily with the language of the documents: the Sumerian in these letters appears too advanced to date from the end of the third millennium (Huber 2001; cf. also Charpin 2007b). The authenticity of other letters has sometimes wrongly been called into doubt.

Hence the letter from the Hittite king Hattusili I to Tuniya of Tikunanum (Salvini 1994; Durand 2006) has been characterized as a "later fictional text" (Van De Mieroop 2000). The other tablets found at the same time as that letter make the hypothesis totally improbable; on the contrary, the letter is "important, contemporary confirmation of the historicity of elements in Hittite legend and 'history' in general and the campaigns of Ḫattušili in particular" (Miller 2001, 421). That example demonstrates once again the dangers of hypercriticism. Let me also point out that the sincerity of "authentic" texts was not undermined by the possibility of their publication: there was not in Mesopotamia any case analogous to that of Pliny the Younger, who, while writing his letters, knew that they would later be published.

Authentic Corpora

The epistolary corpora that have been preserved are very diverse in nature and come from many different eras. For the third millennium, the first letters date only to the end of the Early Dynastic period, about 2350 B.C. (Kienast and Volk 1995; Michalowski 1993). In the Akkadian empire, correspondents wrote in Sumerian in the south, in Akkadian in the north. Under the Third Dynasty of Ur, in addition to royal correspondence, a great number of brief memos of an administrative nature were composed. Several hundred were discovered with the other documents belonging to the same archives (Sollberger 1966; B. Lafont 1990). The problem of authenticity therefore does not arise in their case.

The Old Babylonian period produced both "everyday letters" (Sallaberger 1999) and an abundant diplomatic correspondence.

The letters between private individuals clearly illustrate the extent of literacy among the elites of the time. The correspondence of the Assyrian merchants living in remote Anatolia is worthy of note: in the archives of their houses, letters received from their colleagues, but also from their wives remaining in Assur, have been unearthed (Veenhof 2008). There is thus a mix of business texts and letters of a private, even intimate nature (Michel 2001). The most important lot of diplomatic correspondence was uncovered in the Mari palace.[2] The archives left in that building by the Babylonians when they destroyed it in 1759 B.C. cover a period of about twenty-five years, during which the throne was occupied successively by Yasmah-Addu and Zimri-Lim. Alongside many administrative documents were several thousand letters, including 2,500 that have now been published in full. These have been complemented by the discoveries made at other sites in Syria and northern Iraq (Charpin and Ziegler 2003, 20–27).

The second half of the second millennium has primarily yielded royal letters. The most ancient lot comes from Tell al-'Amarna in Upper Egypt (Moran 1992 and 2003). In that capital founded by Akhenaton (Amenhotep IV), a batch of nearly 300 letters has been unearthed. It represents both letters written to the pharaoh by the great kings of his age (of Babylon, Mittani, Assur, and others) and the correspondence sent by his vassals from Syria-Palestine: Rib-Hadda, king of Byblos, was the most prolix of these. The Hittite capital of Hattusha has also yielded a vast royal correspondence, particularly with Egypt and Assyria (Edel 1994; Mora and Giorgieri 2004). Ugarit, between the Hittite and Egyptian worlds on the Syrian coast, deserves special mention: several hundred letters have been found in the royal palace but also in other buildings. A portion of the correspondence was written in Akkadian (Lackenbacher 2002; Bordreuil 1991; Yon and Arnaud 2001), but a not insignificant share was in the local language and writing system, Ugaritic (Caquot, Tarragon, and Cunchillos 1989).

For the first millennium, letters have been found primarily in palaces and temples. Correspondence between individuals is much rarer, no doubt because it was primarily written in Aramaic on skins and has consequently disappeared. It is in the palaces of Nimrud and Niniveh that the correspondence of the Neo-Assyrian emperors has come to light; it counts about 3,000 items. Depending on the region of origin, the letters they received were written in either Assyrian or Babylonian (Parpola 1987–2003). Particular mention should be made of the corpus of letters sent by the literati in the service of Emperors Esarhaddon and Ashurbanipal (Parpola 1993a). The great interest of this correspondence lies in the fact that it shows how these scholars put to concrete use the corpus of reference texts preserved in libraries. Letters from the Neo-Babylonian and Achaemenid periods (some 1,500) are for the most part closely linked to the administration of the temples.[3]

How Letters Were Put in Writing

In every period, the procedure for writing letters, when not carried out by the sender in person, seems to have taken two main forms: dictation or composition by a scribe. Once the tablet was inscribed, the scribe reread it to his master, made a few corrections if necessary, and then put it in an envelope, which he sealed with the sender's seal. The letter was then ready to be sent to its recipient.

Letters Written in Akkadian

Correspondence raises a specific linguistic problem: the sender and the recipient must understand each other, which is problematic if they do not speak the same language. That is why, from the early second millennium to the mid-first millennium, Akkadian became the language of choice for epistolary exchanges. The most unusual case is that of the letters exchanged between Pharaoh

Ramses II and the Hittite king Hattusili III, written in Babylonian, but the examples could be multiplied. Precisely because of that cultural domination of Akkadian, certain languages, such as Amorite, were never set down in writing. All the letters found in the archives of the Mari palace are written in the Akkadian language, with a single exception (a letter in Hurrian). The question therefore arises whether Akkadian was spoken in the kingdom of Mari and among its neighbors, or if we have here a case of bilingualism, where Akkadian was the language of written culture and Amorite the spoken language. Opinions on that subject vary. The elites could probably speak both Amorite and Akkadian (Durand 1992, 123–126), which would explain how they could have dictated their letters. A recently published text shows that Yasmah-Addu, king of Mari, spoke only Akkadian, but that most of the members of his entourage were bilingual (Ziegler and Charpin 2007). I therefore do not share the view of those such as J. Cooper, who believes that "we may read and understand letters from Mari, Tuttul, Emar, or Alakakh as the Akkadian texts they are, but we are very aware that they may have been dictated and read out in local languages that would have been very different from the Akkadian in which they were written down" (2006, 85).

Dictation or Composition?

Depending on the time and place, letters had either a standard form or were adapted to fit the content (Eidem 2002). As an extreme case, consider the practices of the chancellery of Rim-Sin, king of Larsa (1822–1763 B.C.). Letters there were all written on large tablets with a very elongated form. As a result, the reverse usually bore no writing, and sometimes the text occupied only part of the obverse (Stol 1981, 126n197a). It truly seems that these letters were dictated to a scribe who, not knowing the length of the message, used a "standard" format. The size of letter tablets was also fixed in the Neo-Assyrian period (Figure 27); very often,

FIGURE 27. Neo-Assyrian letter. This is the famous petition of Adad-shum-uṣur to Ashurbanipal at the time of Ashurbanipal's ascension to the throne (K.183 [*ABL* 2 and *SAA* 10 226]). (From Mattila 1995, 141.)

not all the available space was used (Radner 1995, 72). In the Mari archives, by contrast, letters varied in size: the scribe seems to have known the length of the message to be inscribed before he fashioned the tablet.[4] The archives of the Assyrian merchants in Cappadocia have revealed a few cases of letters with a kind of "second page," described as a "supplement" (ṣibtum in Akkadian) (Veenhof 2003a, 91). This was a piece of clay much thinner than a tablet, round or oval in shape, inscribed on a single side, and inserted into the same envelope as the letter.[5] The existence of "second pages" is also attested in the age of al-ʾAmarna (Abrahami and Coulon 2008, 12n45). In the Neo-Assyrian period, a letter from the exorcist Adad-shum-uṣur to Esarhaddon, SAA 10 197, continues in no. 198, which begins by indicating: "This is a continuation of the words of the previous letter."

In certain cases, the scribe seems to have written down the letter as it was being dictated. Several letters from King Samsi-Addu, in which he vituperates against his son Yasmah-Addu, were obviously dictated in the heat of anger. Some sentences are not even complete, others include long incidental clauses, and in still others the verb does not occupy the final position. An explicit example of dictation comes from the city of Andarig. In this letter, a prophet-āpilum of the god Shamash made this request to the representative of Mari: "Send me a discreet scribe, so that I may have (him) write the message that the god Shamash sent for the king through me" (ARM 26/2 414: 30–33). By a stroke of luck, that message has itself been preserved (ARM 26/1 194; Charpin 2002c, 15).

Nevertheless, the sovereign usually confined himself to indicating to his secretary the main points of the message to be written. A few tablets from Mari contain notes taken during such meetings (Joannès 1984, 87–104 and 1985); the same technique has been identified for the Neo-Assyrian period (Villard 2006, 25–26). These notes served as an outline for the scribe, who wrote the definitive text from it (Figure 28). He was therefore the actual writer: the style of the letters corresponds to a fairly rigid rhetoric, and

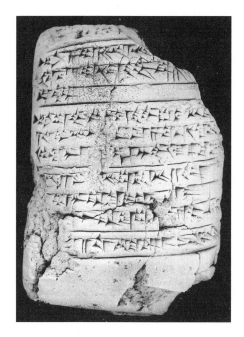

FIGURE 28. Example of a memorandum, notable for its sloppy appearance. The scribe divided the different subjects into separate paragraphs by a double line. For example, he noted in the penultimate paragraph: "Pertaining to the act of writing to Babylon about the two slaves who are in Babylon with Ahizu." (Courtesy of D. Charpin.)

that is what now makes it possible to restore the missing passages. When he did not take dictation but instead wrote from his master's instructions, the scribe was freed from various constraints, such as inscribing the text at high speed and anticipating the size of the tablet based on the length of the message. It may be that some letters that were never sent to their recipient were drafts.

The level of the scribe's skills as a stylist varied. At one extreme, some petitions are particularly ornate: such is the case for the bilingual letter (in Sumerian and Akkadian) sent by a scribe wishing to enter into the good graces of Zimri-Lim after that king had ascended to the throne (Charpin 1992a; Durand 1997, no. 22). Conversely, Ishme-Dagan complains to his brother Yasmah-Addu that he had received a letter that was not explicit enough,[6] a criticism Samsi-Addu also made to him.[7] Under such conditions, it is clear that the job of composing royal letters could not be performed by just any scribe; it was a position of trust that only someone close to the ruler could fill.[8] Sometimes a king might wish to keep a matter confidential, in which case he had to turn to a scribe other than his usual secretary. Hence, Hammurabi of Aleppo, wishing to write confidentially to Zimri-Lim, asked for the help of Shu-nuhra-Halu, who was on a mission to Aleppo at the time. As Shu-nuhra-Halu recounted to his master: "Here is what (Hammurabi of Aleppo) told me: 'There is a confidential matter that I want to discuss with you. (Tomorrow) at dawn, approach the palace gate so that I may tell you of it, so that you may write it down on a tablet and send it to your lord.' That is what he told me" (*FM* 7 45: 9–14).[9] Obviously, the young king of Aleppo had only limited trust in the discretion of his own scribe. As it happens, the queen mother had a major stake in the matter in question. Hammurabi likely feared that his secretary would immediately inform her of it. We have no knowledge of an "oath of scribes" similar to the "oath of diviners"—the text of which has been preserved in the Mari archives[10]—by which scribes might have pledged "professional confidentiality" like their diviner colleagues. Given the proliferation of oaths in the Old Babylonian period and in later periods, that gap must no doubt be imputed to the randomness governing finds.[11]

Some letters explicitly allude to the fact that the text could have been longer, but that it was pointless to expatiate on the subject. Minister Habdu-malik even justified the brevity of a report by citing the need not to surpass the physical limits of the tablet: "I went to Karana and transmitted to Asqur-Addu all the instructions that my lord had given me. Why should I tarry longer in writing to my lord? So that the information will not be so copious that it cannot be written on a single tablet, I have summarized the essential of the matter and have written it to my lord" (*ARM* 26/2 394: 3–8).

In some extreme cases, the information being given was clear only to the recipient, as in this letter from Samsi-Addu to the king of Shusharra: "Say to Kuwari: Thus (says) your Lord. I have heard the letters you sent me. All that you write to me I will do" (*ShA* 1 25). To our great frustration, the tablet contains nothing further.

Although it was traditionally believed that only professional scribes knew how to write, many indications, particularly in the Mari archives, show that was not the case. Not only administrators but also generals were able to read and possibly to write (Charpin 2010, chap. 1). Some letters of mediocre quality must be interpreted as having been written by their senders without the intermediary of a scribe.

In order to have a letter written, the king sometimes solicited the counsel of an adviser, or a close associate submitted suggestions to him. Hence Zimri-Lim asked his minister Sammetar to come see him, so as to write a reply to a letter from Hammurabi: "A tablet reached me from Babylon; come, let us listen to that tablet, let us have a discussion and reply to it!" (*ARM* 26/1: 6–10). Conversely, there is also a tablet on which Sammetar, at his own initiative, submitted a letter proposal for Zimri-Lim to send to the king of Aleppo.[12]

Royal Chancelleries?

The Mari palace, though of considerable architectural interest, no more yielded a "chancellery" in which the letters sent by the king were composed and the mail he received archived than it did a school. The famous "room 115," where more than 4,000 letters were discovered, housed only a few crates of tablets intended for Babylon (Charpin 1995b). Nevertheless, in the second half of the second millennium, Egypt had a place called the "site of the pharaoh's letters," both in Tell al-'Amarna and in Per-Ramesse (Abrahami and Coulon 2008, 10–11). It was there that the correspondence the sovereign received was stored, and there too that letters sent in his name were written: witness the discovery of anepigraphic tablets in building Q42.21, where the correspondence addressed to the pharaoh was discovered (Pantalacci 2008a, 43–45). There is no reason to think things were any different in Mesopotamian palaces.

Composing Letters

Among "business documents," a distinction is traditionally made between, on one hand, legal and bookkeeping texts, which are very formulaic, and, on the other, letters, which are much more vivid. Nevertheless, the epistolary genre also had its rules, though they appear to have been less constraining, and apprenticeship in the scribal craft included copying letters. Rather than speak of a single "model," it is more accurate to say that there were multiple models, dealing especially with the address formula and the closing, and with a certain number of recurring rhetorical figures. Some rules of composition had to do with decorum: an inferior always had to feign the belief that his superior was well informed about the matter being written about. When places were listed, those farthest from the person being addressed had to be given first, and the closest ones last (Charpin 1995c).

The formula that begins an Old Babylonian letter betrays the oral origins of the transmission of messages. The first lines are invariably formulated in two parts: "To X, say: thus (speaks) Y." (*Ana* X *qibi-ma umma* Y). To whom is the imperative "say" addressed? It is generally believed that the formula is addressed to the messenger (Kraus 1973, 40). Two examples reporting how diplomats orally transmitted a message from their master confirm this belief. Ishme-Dagan's envoys to Hammurabi of Babylon acquitted themselves of their mission as follows: "They were asked for the news. They therefore delivered their report: 'Thus (speaks) your servant Ishme-Dagan (and so forth)'" (*ARM* 26/2 384: 18′–19′). In the same way, when King Sharraya's messenger gave a neighboring king an oral message from his sovereign, he said: "Thus (speaks) Sharraya" (*ARM* 26/1 127: 18). The recipient was identified at the start by his name, his title, or both. In general, letters written by a subject to his king begin with the formula "to my lord"; when the name of the king follows ("to my lord Zimri-Lim"), it is because the sender is a foreigner.

The second part of the salutation identified the sender; he could be designated by a title rather than by his name, or his name could be followed by an epithet that situated him in relation to the recipient. Very often, a subject of the king addresses his ruler and defines himself as "your servant." Since the rest of the letter is written in the third person, the use of the second person shows that the second part of the salutation constitutes a speech placed in the mouth of the messenger who is speaking to the recipient. It is only after the address formula that the words the sender intends directly for his correspondent are given. The type of formulation that was used owed nothing to chance: strict rules of etiquette governed how a king addressed another king by letter. A few texts show that the ancients were very attentive to these rules. Depending on his hierarchical position, a king addressed another king as "father," "brother," "son," or "servant." He could turn political events to his own advantage in order to rise in the hierarchy of kings, as Samsi-Addu did in relation to the king of Eshnunna, as we learn in a later letter about his son Ishme-Dagan: "In all his messages to Hammurabi, Ishme-Dagan addressed him as his lord. That was his father's attitude: originally, all the letters from his father were addressed to the Eshnunnean as to his lord; then, once he had (re)taken the entire country following the Eshnunnean's troubles, he called him 'brother.' At the present time, it is likely that such is the calculation of Ishme-Dagan. It is only in word that he acquiesces to Hammurabi's wishes" (*ARM* 2 49: 6–11 [*LAPO* 16 309]). The salutation was never followed by blessings in letters addressed to kings or written by them; conversely, blessings were the rule in private correspondence (Dalley 1973). It was often the custom to reassure the recipient about what might be worrying him. Hence governors, but also other local leaders, generally indicate: "The district is faring well."

Generals on campaigns note: "The troops are faring well: may my lord not worry!" These formulas often appear after the salutation but are sometimes used to close the letter.

Frequently, the sender indicates in the closing that he is in need of a reply, often urgently so. In any case, the failure to reply demonstrated a grave lack of respect, as Samsi-Addu wrote to his son: "Why did you not send any reply to my tablet? Isn't not sending any reply to my tablet a form of contempt and a negation of the other? Is that your ethics?" (Unpublished A.4231: 13′–17′). In a letter Hammurabi wrote to one of his sisters, he states explicitly that considerations of decorum carried great weight in the code that governed the writing of correspondence: "I acquainted myself with the tablet from you that you sent me. In it you wrote me: 'Why did you not write me about your illness?' There are some for whom illness is a subject of correspondence with their brother(s). As for me, I write happy news: 'I was ill, now I am healthy'" (*ARM* 10 169 [*LAPO* 18 1267]).

Contrary to our customs, letters did not normally bear an indication of the time and place they were written. We may surmise that the bearer of the tablet orally delivered this information, of which we are now so cruelly deprived. In any event, subordinates had to make haste to keep their superiors informed. Otherwise, they might receive a bitterly ironic letter like the following, sent by the minister of finance to administrators in the Mari palace: "Tablets from you must be delivered to me on a regular basis, giving news of the palace and of the workshops. In fact, I listened to the tablet from you that you sent about people being dismissed; in fact, I was informed even before your tablet reached me!" (*ARM* 13 53 [*LAPO* 16 66]).

Rereading

Whether or not the letter was dictated, once the tablet was inscribed, the scribe had to reread it to his master before placing it

FIGURE 29. Passage of a letter in which a scribe's erasures are very visible: he effaced two lines and reinscribed three in the same space in smaller characters. (Courtesy of D. Charpin.)

in the envelope. This is confirmation that the Akkadian language was used, since such a procedure makes sense only if the sender was able to understand what the scribe was reading. During the rereading, the sender sometimes indicated changes to be made in the text. That is undoubtedly how we must interpret cases in which certain words, even entire lines, have been erased and rewritten (Figure 29). It was no doubt inevitable that a certain number of mistakes (forgotten signs and so on) would persist in the letters despite that rereading phase, given that scribes must have practiced "sight reading" just as we do. One episode shows that, having failed to reread, a scribe had confused one toponym with another, so that the king received false information about a city taken by the enemy (Charpin 1995a [A.427]; Sasson 2002).

Copies of Sent Letters?

Usually, no duplicates were kept of the letters sent out. What *was* kept of the letters written by the kings of Mari to people outside the capital[13] were either drafts[14] or letters that, for one reason or another, were never sent. That explains the dissymmetry in the content of royal correspondence from the Old Babylonian period (Charpin forthcoming f): the Mari palace preserved primarily the *passive* correspondence of Kings Yasmah-Addu and Zimri-Lim.[15] The corpus of letters from the governors of Zimri-Lim includes only the letters sent to the king of Mari: there are no replies from the king, in contrast to Book 10 of Pliny the Younger's letters, which almost always contains Emperor Trajan's replies. We possess only a portion of Hammurabi's *active* correspondence: these are the letters he wrote to officials such as Sin-iddinam and Shamash-hazir, which were exhumed in Larsa. Since the Babylon palace has not been found, none of the letters received by Hammurabi has been discovered.

There are a few exceptions to the general rule. A fair number of letters from Sargon have been found in the Niniveh palace. These are actually letters sent when the king was not living there: he sent a copy of the letters to the crown prince staying in Niniveh (Villard 1995, 106). In any case, the near nonexistence of duplicates accounts for a consistent rhetorical feature of the letters: the initial recapitulation of a previously sent missive by the person writing a reply.

Old Assyrian merchants would seem to have developed a different practice, usually keeping copies of the mail they sent out. A certain Imdilum even claims: "I am keeping copies of all the letters I send you" (*CCT* 2 6: 14–16; Ichisar 1981, 214). That claim must not be taken too seriously, however: the context is that of a quarrel with a colleague, whom the correspondent was thus attempting to intimidate. The archives found in the houses of the commercial sector *(kārum)* of Kanish show that the practice was not at all systematic.

Envelopes and Seals

Once the letter was composed and reread, it was placed in an envelope. One of the legendary texts about Sargon of Akkad presents the advent of the envelope as a radical invention by King Ur-

Zababa of Kish, a means to send the messenger bearing the letters, the cup-bearer Sargon, to his death without his knowledge: "In those days, writing on clay certainly existed, / but enveloping tablets did not exist. King Ur-Zababa, for Sargon, creature of the gods, / with writing on clay—a thing which would cause his own death—/ he dispatched it to Lugal-zagesi in Uruk" (Cooper and Heimpel 1983, 76–77, lines 53–56; Alster 1987). The theme had a long and notable posterity. Here it underscores the principal purpose of envelopes: to keep the text from the eyes of intermediaries. In the Old Babylonian period, only the recipient's name appeared on the envelope, since the sender could be identified by the legend on his seal (Figure 30). That practice differed from that of later periods, when, since the seals bore no legend, the sender's name was indicated on the envelope along with that of the recipient, as in this example: "To the deputy (governor), my lord: your servant Aššur-resiwa" (SAA 15 288 and its envelope 289: impression of the sender's seal and two lines of writing). Sometimes, the full incipit of the letter is reproduced on the envelope: "Letter of the temple steward to the temple steward. Good health to my brother! May the god Aššur and the temple Ešarra bless my brother!" (SAA 13 41 [the letter is no. 41]; Villard 2008, 187).

The sealed envelope's function as authentication is explicitly indicated by Shimatum, who asks her father, Zimri-Lim, for the gift of a seal: "May my lord, the Star, have a lapis lazuli seal brought to me in my name! When I send a message, no one will show contempt for me any longer, saying: 'There is no impression of her seal!'" (ARM 10 95 [LAPO 18 1225]: r. 7'–11').

Sometimes a letter in an envelope was opened by someone other than its recipient. One official, for example, thought he ought to alert the king of Mari that he had read a letter intended for Shumshu-liter because that colleague was away: "My lord sent a tablet here for Shumshu-liter regarding cereal-*burrum*. He was gone: I (therefore) opened that tablet and listened to it" (ARM 5 [LAPO 16 231]: 4–9).

FIGURE 30. Envelope of a letter from Zimri-Lim to Tish-ulme. On the obverse: "To Tish-ulme." The impression of the sender's cylinder seal is visible on the obverse and on the reverse (the edge of the matrix left a fairly deep groove), as well as along the edges. The seal contains a classic scene ("warrior with mace" opposite a patron goddess) and a six-line legend. (Courtesy of D. Charpin.)

By definition, envelopes were destroyed by the recipient when he sought to acquaint himself with the letter sent to him. That explains the rarity of envelopes preserved in full or in part. In Niniveh, a petition addressed to a Neo-Assyrian emperor was discovered in an unopened envelope. Its author complains that he had already written three times and had not had a reply. To judge by the fate reserved for his fourth missive, it is clear that his letters were not even read (*ABL* 382, 383 [*SAA* 15 288, 289]).

Seal impressions belonging to Zimri-Lim have been found on envelope fragments in the Mari palace (Charpin 1992b, 70–71) but also in that of Qaṭṭara (Hawkins in Dalley, Walker, and Hawkins 1976, 250, no. 5). We know there were several matrices of Zimri-Lim's seal, used by different agencies in the administration. By contrast, letters were sealed with a different matrix, of which only a single exemplar existed. That practice continued subsequently: in the Middle and Neo-Babylonian periods, the expression *kunuk šarrim ša šiprēti* designated such a "king's seal (for) letters"; it was sometimes specified that there was no duplicate and that the seal was not to be contested (Charpin 2002b, 180–181).

Once the tablet was placed in the envelope, it was too late to add anything, and if an additional piece of information needed to be brought to the king's attention, a new letter had to be composed. Buqaqum indicates this explicitly: "My tablet had just been placed in an envelope when couriers, four men from Asqur-Addu, arrived, saying . . ." (*ARM* 26/2 490: 4–7).

An altogether unique document shows how the royal chancellery stored the letters waiting to be sent. It is a label for a tablet basket with the following wording (Figure 31): "Four (tablets) that must be read to *[Iddiyatum]*, Yasim-El, Menirum, and Belshunu; they are ready" (Charpin 2001, 21 [M.8762]). These were letters drafted for individuals posted in the region of Jebel Sinjar: obviously, these four letters were to be sent together in a sack. Either a single messenger was to take them to each of the four individuals, in a sort of "tour" through Andarig and Karana, or the mail would

FIGURE 31. Tablet basket label in the shape of an olive; on the left are visible traces of the string used to close the receptacle. The inscription indicates that four letters were stored in the basket before being sent out. (Courtesy of D. Charpin.)

be sent by relay and the tablets ultimately delivered to each of the recipients.

When the king was traveling, it was not always easy to know where to send his mail. Witness this letter from Uṣur-awassu to Yasmah-Addu: "In addition, regarding the fact that, so far, I have not sent . . . any tablet to my lord, may my lord's heart not find fault in it. So far, those who brought me a tablet from my lord and know my lord's place of residence were not returning to where my lord is staying. I (thus) (could) not have sent any tablet from me to my lord. Now, ever since someone has learned my lord's place of residence in Qabara, may the news of the palace as well as my tablets reach my lord regularly" (*ARM* 26/2 291: 10–26).

How Letters Were Transported

A Rich Nomenclature

The conditions under which letters were sent to their recipients varied a great deal (B. Lafont 1997). The nuances of the various terms used to designate the people who transported the mail have not yet been completely elucidated. In the Mari archives, a first distinction is clear, however: on one hand, there are the true messengers *(mār šiprim)* and, on the other, mere "tablet bearers" *(wābil ṭuppim)*, whose immediate return was generally required. An unpublished text that recapitulates the enlistment of soldiers carried out in the gardens of Saggaratum at the end of year 9 of Zimri-Lim is important for two reasons. First, it contains the two categories mentioned above but under different terms, the "message-bearers" *(ša šipirātim)* and the "runners" *(lāsimum)*. Second, this document gives us the number of messengers mobilized when Zimri-Lim took his entire army to aid the king of Aleppo: there were no fewer than 100 *ša šipirātim* and sixty-four *lāsimum*. These are unexpected figures: heretofore we never would have believed that such a large number of messengers existed in the kingdom of Mari. These data can be confirmed by a document limited to the single district of Saggaratum, which attests the simultaneous existence in that region of nineteen "message-bearers" *(ša šipirātim)* and twenty-two "runners" *(lāsimum)*.

Personal Carriers and Relay Systems

Within the framework of international relations, diplomats often received a tablet upon their departure and took it to the king for whom the letter was intended, functioning more as ambassadors than as messengers. Nevertheless, from the moment the letter was put in writing, it was no longer necessary to entrust it to a single carrier who would travel the entire distance separating the sender from the recipient. In fact, the existence of regular relays is attested; they allowed correspondence to be delivered more quickly, since they involved a succession of couriers, not single messengers, who would have had to take a minimal time to rest *(ARM 26/1 29: 4–9)*. In a hymn, Shulgi, king of Ur, boasts of having perfected a relay network that covered the entire kingdom: "Because I am a powerful man who enjoys using his thighs, I, Šulgi, the mighty king, superior to all, strengthened (?) the roads, put in order the highways of the Land. I marked out the double-hour distances, built there lodging houses. I planted gardens by their side and established resting-places, and installed in those places experienced men. Whichever direction one comes from, one can refresh oneself when the time is cool; and travellers and wayfarers who arrive at night can seek haven there as a well-built city" (Šulgi A: 26–35, quoted from *Electronic Text Corpus of Sumerian Literature*). The vastness of the Assyrian empire in the first millennium compelled the administration to set in place a high-performance network (Villard 2006, 19–22). It was composed of a system of well-maintained roads, designated "king's highways" *(hūl šarri)* (Kessler 1980, 183–236). Stops where the messenger could change chariots if necessary were set up at regular intervals; drivers and fresh mounts were also available to him. These relays *(bēt mardēti)* were the responsibility of the provincial governors and had a dual objective. They were supposed to allow the carrier of a royal order *(ša qurbūte)* to arrive in person at his destination as soon as possible; but they also constituted a simple postal relay system, as attested in this letter from Mar-Issar to the king, reporting a breakdown: "Alongside the roadside the (personnel) of the post stations *(bēt mardēti)* pass my letters along from one to another and thus bring them to the king my lord. Yet for two or three times already, my letter has been returned from the towns of Kamanate, Ampihabi and [. . .] garešu. [Let a sealed order be s]ent to them that they should pass my letters along from one to another and thus bring them to the king my lord" (*SAA* 10 361: r. 3–11).

It is this system that the Achaemenids inherited, though Xenophon attributes its paternity to Cyrus:

> We have observed still another device of Cyrus to cope with the magnitude of his empire; by means of this institution he would speedily discover the condition of affairs, no matter how far distant they might be from him; he experimented to find out how great a distance a horse could cover in a day when ridden hard but so as not to break down, and then he erected post-stations at just such distances and equipped them with horses and men to take care of them; at each one of the stations he had the proper official appointed to receive the letters that were delivered and to forward them on, to take in the exhausted horses and riders and send on fresh ones.
>
> (Xenophon 1914, 8.6.17–18 [2:419])

The Obsession with Time

Officials were required to reply to the king by return mail: they often specified the time when they had received the letter to which they were replying, in some cases as an excuse for a tardy reply.

For example, Mukannishum added to the end of one of his letters: "My lord should not say: 'Mukannishum was negligent about those spears.' When my lord's tablet reached me, it was nighttime; the palace was bolted shut and I (could) not take out those spears" (*ARM* 13 8 [*LAPO* 16 104]).

Abnormal delays in sending the mail are also sometimes indicated (B. Lafont 1997, 326 [*ARM* 3 59]).

The Dangers of Transportation

Like any major undertaking, the sending of messengers was preceded by an oracular inquiry, especially during periods of hostilities. Asqudum indicates: "I took omens for the safety of the messengers: they are not good. I shall take them again. When the omens have become favorable, I shall send them" (*ARM* 26/1 87).

Messengers followed special routes in wartime. Many texts indicate so, such as this letter from Samsi-Addu: "The roads are dangerous and the messengers must travel incognito" (*ShA* 1 2: 39–40).

If there were bad omens and the situation was urgent, messengers could be accompanied by escorts, as Ishme-Dagan suggests: "When you send me that letter, give strict orders that (it) be protected in transit. Have oracles taken for the safety of the carriers of this letter, or have thirty of your servants escort them as far as the river and (then) return home" (*FM* 3 14: 18–25).

After an attack by Sutean nomads in the steppe, efforts were made to reassure the king of Mari about the mail sent to him from Qatna: "Our messengers the Qatneans and the tablets are in good condition; an escort [accompanied them] as far as Tadmor (Palmyra)" (Joannès 1997, 401, no. 2).

Despite these precautions, messengers were sometimes stopped by the enemy and the mail they were transporting intercepted. So it was that letters addressed to "my lord" were found in the Mari palace, but their intended recipient was not the king of Mari (see *ARM*

26/1 168–172). There is at least one example of Zimri-Lim explicitly giving an order to intercept the mail: "Regarding Asqur-Addu, my lord wrote me as follows: 'Why do the tablets [of Asqur-Addu] continue to get through and you do not seize [them]?' That is what my lord wrote me" (*ARM* 28 117: 5–8). We even possess a tablet that records the reward given to a person who had intercepted a letter.[16] Kings knew perfectly well the risk they ran in entrusting their messages to writing. To exonerate himself of accusations he judged slanderous, Shadum-Labua, king of Ashnakkum, listed the mistakes or reckless acts he might have committed: "Did I write to an enemy city, and were my tablets intercepted?" (*ARM* 28 103: 11–12).

Usually, the letters thus seized had been entrusted to messengers (B. Lafont 1992, 172). But in the interest of caution, mail could also be entrusted to merchants, who normally enjoyed immunity (Charpin 2010, chap. 8). In fact, however, they were sometimes searched and the letters they were carrying confiscated (Charpin and Durand 1997b, 378–379). Meptum, for example, had a caravan of merchants from Eshnunna stopped: "I searched them for tablets, telling myself: 'It is not impossible that they are smuggling tablets somewhere'" (A.16 [*LAPO* 18 912]: 25–27). The use of merchants to transport mail in wartime was common. One Old Assyrian merchant was stopped and accused of transporting a letter to the enemy; he had to pay a large sum of gold to avoid being executed (Günbatti 2001). In addition, in his epic, the Middle Assyrian king Tukulti-Ninurta accused merchants of collaborating with his enemies the Kassites (Foster 2005c, 303 ii: 1′–10′).

Mail Delivery

There are several known cases in which the delivery of mail gave rise to an error. The secretary of Samsi-Addu wrote to the king's son: "With the tablets they brought for the king (Samsu-Addu) from Qatna, the Qatnean messengers brought the king by mistake a tablet intended for my lord (Yasmah-Addu). Having opened it, I found that it was written to my lord and I therefore did not have the king listen to it. At present, I have just sent that tablet to my lord" (Charpin 1995a [A.2701: 5–19]). It was customary for messengers to receive a gratuity when they arrived at the recipient's home. After complaining of his state of destitution, the king of Ashlakka wrote to Zimri-Lim: "So I had borrowed two shekels of silver and (wanted) to give them to the messengers of my lord, but they did not accept, saying: 'It's too little!'" (ARM 28 49: 26–29). Even today, we are familiar with reactions of disdain at too small a tip, which is judged offensive.

How Letters Were Read

Letters could be read to rulers in various ways, depending on whether they dealt with internal affairs or with foreign relations. Letters were sometimes forwarded to a recipient not originally intended, or were recopied in part or in full. And a good portion of the messages sent in antiquity is at present unknown, since, for different reasons, no one wished to put them in writing.

Reading Royal Correspondence

How the king of Mari had the letters he received read to him depended on whether their authors were officials or other kings. In the case of administrative mail, messengers were not normally admitted to the monarch's presence: they left the letter "at the palace gate." It was only in emergencies that they were allowed access to the ruler. The royal secretary, who read his master's correspondence to him, therefore played an important role. Of these figures, the best known is Shu-nuhra-Halu, secretary to Zimri-Lim (Sasson 1988). Often senders attached to their letter for the king a second letter addressed to that secretary in which they summarized or recopied the first. In that way, Shu-nuhra-Halu could familiarize himself in advance with the content of the message he was to read and, if need be, draw the king's attention to one point or another. That type of missive often ended with an announcement that a present was being sent. In the Neo-Assyrian period, senders confined themselves to blessings: "Whoever you are, O scribe, who are reading (this letter), do not hide it from the king, your lord! Speak for me before the king, so Bel (and) Nabu may speak for you before the king" (*SAA* 16 32: r. 17–22).[17]

The practice of sending a tablet to the king and a duplicate to his secretary is also attested for others close to the king of Mari, such as Darish-libur: "Tell Mukannishum: thus (speaks) Darish-libur. I listened to the tablet from you that you sent me. The one you sent me for the king I communicated to him. He paid a great deal of attention to it. The king sent you a reply to the tablet with detailed instructions" (*ARM* 18 26 [*LAPO* 16 124]). Here it is Darish-libur who plays a role similar to that ordinarily fulfilled by Shu-nuhra-Halu. The king was undoubtedly traveling at the time, accompanied by Darish-libur, who is known to have been able to write. Thus he could serve as secretary to the king and read him the letters that were sent to him during his trip.[18] Darish-libur's role with respect to the king also appears in the letter Princess Tizpatum wrote to him: "Tell Darish-libur: thus (speaks) Tizpatum, your daughter. If you are really a father to me, do me a favor in the event. I have written the king regarding my wet nurse: my father must intervene in favor of my request. Intervene in favor of my request! Don't keep my nurse! Another thing: I am having several pounds of gingerbread taken to you for your table" (*ARM* 10 105 [*LAPO* 18 1238]). Accompanying a request with a present was customary among Shu-nuhra-Halu's correspondents.

Writing the sovereign and a high dignitary at the same time, in the hope that the dignitary would direct the king's attention to the letter, is a practice attested in the corpus of Tell al-'Amarna. When King Rib-Addi of Byblos wrote to the pharaoh to ask for aid in the form of grain (*EA* 85), he also sent a briefer missive to

Minister Amanappa (*EA* 86). Such actions are also attested in the Neo-Assyrian empire: efforts were made to use an intermediary close to the king, to whom a copy of the message for the ruler was sent, so that the aide could plead the case before the king. For example, a Babylonian dignitary wrote to King Sargon II: "To the king, my lord, your servant Bel-ibni: I would gladly die for the king, my lord! May Nabu and [Marduk] bless the king, my lord" (*SAA* 18 52: 1–4). We also possess a letter that is nearly identical but for its salutation: "To the chief eunuch *(rab ša-rēši)* my lord, your servant Bel-ibni. May Nabu and Marduk bless my lord!" (*SAA* 18 53: 1–2). And a final sentence closes that second missive: "I have grasped [the hand of the chief eunuch], my lord. May I not come to shame!" It is therefore very likely that the two tablets were delivered simultaneously to the chief eunuch, so that he would present the petition to the sovereign (Villard 2006, 22–23 and 29–30, nos. 14 and 15).

The existence of that practice can be deduced negatively from a petition by the chief exorcist Adad-shum-uṣur, in which he asks that his son Urad-Gula be reinstated: "None of those who serve in the palace likes me; there is not a single friend of mine among them to whom I could give a present, and who would accept it from me and speak for me" (*SAA* 10 226: r. 14–19). Nevertheless, how the mail of the Neo-Assyrian kings made its way to the palace and was finally read to the sovereign remains much less well understood than the procedure in the Mari palace (Luukko 2007, 231).

A letter from Ibal-Addu to Shu-nuhra-Halu shows us that messages for Zimri-Lim were to be brought to the attention of his secretary beforehand, even when they were transmitted orally and not in the form of a tablet: "So I transmitted a complete report by Ladin-Addu to you. Pay great attention to his report and send it to the king" (*ARM* 28 75: 4–9).

Some correspondents implicitly accused Shu-nuhra-Halu of "censoring" certain parts of the letters they had sent to the sovereign. General Yasim-Dagan, for example, threatened to come read his letter to the king in person (A.4215 [*LAPO* 16 65]). Conversely, others flattered Zimri-Lim's powerful secretary: "When I found myself in Mari with my lord, and you were my friend and fought on my side, I was able to observe your power. Everything you said before my lord was approved; nothing proceeded further without your decision" (*ARM* 28 109: 5–8).

In the case of letters exchanged between kings, the process was generally still the same in the age of Hammurabi: the sovereign gave his instructions *(ṭēmam wu"urum)* to those we call "messengers" *(mār šiprī)*, who were in reality diplomats (B. Lafont 1992). These men, having reached the recipient, set out the *ṭēmum*, whether by reading a tablet or by reciting an oral message learned by heart. In most cases, foreign "messengers" were brought in to the king during an audience. Some messengers emphasize how much attention their message received: "While Yanṣib-Addu was delivering the message of my lord, Hammurabi . . . the entire time he was delivering the message, never stopped listening to him and did not open his mouth; he remained very attentive until he had finished his message. When the message was completed, he spoke to us as follows: (. . .)" (*ARM* 26/2 449: 7–12).

In some cases the messengers, as a function of the situation they found on their arrival, somewhat distorted the words they were charged with expressing or added to the recipient's information: "I was brought a sealed tablet in the name of Ibal-Addu. The servant of Ibal-Addu gave me (in addition) this oral information" (*ARM* 13 144 [*LAPO* 16 304]: 19–21).

In a certain number of cases, the messages were not read during an open audience but in secret. Hence Iddiyatum, sent on a military mission to the king of Karana, told Zimri-Lim that messengers of the king of Kurda had come but that he was unable to attend the interview during which they delivered their message (*ARM* 26/2 521: 42–44). We also have the complaints of another envoy of the king of Mari, Yamṣum, who was no longer admitted to Haya-sumu's secret council and therefore did not hear the news that foreign messengers were bringing (*ARM* 26/2 307, 308, and 309). Yamṣum even explains that Haya-sumu refused to have the mail sent by Zimri-Lim read in Yamṣum's presence: "My lord sent a tablet to Haya-sumu. My lord wrote me this: 'Have the tablet opened before you and listen to it!' He (Haya-sumu) received the tablet, but I (could) not listen to the content of the tablet" (*ARM* 26/2 315: 4–7).

Archiving the Mail

When the king of Mari traveled, his secretary kept the tablets received by the sovereign in a chest, archiving them in the palace upon his return.[19] That explains why many of the letters found in Mari were actually addressed to the king while he was away from the palace: such is the case for the missives from the queens, from the steward Mukannishum, and so on. Sometimes in such cases we possess both the letter sent to the king and his reply.[20]

It is not known whether letters were archived with indications of the time when they were received, as is attested for Egypt. Several tablets found in Tell al-'Amarna include annotations in red ink in hieratic writing. This note appears at the end of the reverse side of a letter sent by King Tushratta to Pharaoh Amenhotep III: "Year 36, fourth month of the season-*peret*, day 1. One (the king) was in the north residence (the royal palace of Thebes), the house-of-jubilation (apartments associated with the jubilee ceremony) . . ." (*EA* 23; Abrahami and Coulon 2008, 14a). This was a special case, however, linked to the Egyptians' writing system: in Mesopotamia, as a general rule, clay tablets, once dry, could not be modified. We may therefore surmise that this type of specification was noted on labels; at present, however, none have come down to us.[21] It is clear, however, that the epistolary archives of Mari followed a certain chronological order: otherwise, it would not have been possible for Hammurabi's scribes to distinguish the "letters of the servants of Samsi-Addu" from the "letters of the servants of Zimri-Lim," to cite the labels on the tablet chests that have been unearthed (Charpin 1995b).

Forwarded Letters or Copies

Some letters were read several times. Hence Samsi-Addu sometimes transmitted to one of his sons a letter that had been sent to him, as in this example: "So I send you the tablet that Suprerah sent me: listen to it!" (*ARM* 1 16 [*LAPO* 16 301]: 5–8). Some officials believed it useful to forward the mail they had received to the king with an accompanying letter. Take the example of this missive from General Samid-ahum. While residing in Yabliya during wartime, he received a letter from the governor of Shitullum: "Anih-libbi sent me a tablet. But that tablet contains confidential information. I put it under seal and had it taken to my lord" (Unpublished A.705). That practice was obligatory when a provincial governor received a letter from a foreign king (Durand 1991, 28–29). The oath sworn by Sumu-hadu contained this clause: "I swear that no tablet—good or bad—has reached me from a foreign country or from a foreign king unless I showed it to Zimri-Lim, my lord; I also swear that I did not send or have sent a tablet to a foreign king or a foreign country!" (M.6182 [*LAPO* 16 51]: 8–16). The governor was supposed to listen to a letter from abroad, then transmit it to the king.

A letter from Zakir-Hammu, governor of Qaṭṭunan, offers a good example of such a course of action. After reproducing the content of a letter he had received from Qarni-Lim, king of Andarig, he added: "So I have just sent the messenger of Qarni-Lim to my lord. In addition, I sealed the tablet of Qarni-Lim that came to my house and had it taken to my lord" (*ARM* 27 69: 29–33). In this case, the tablet apparently circulated between Andarig and Qaṭṭunan with the seal of its sender, Qarni-Lim, then between

Qaṭṭunan and Mari, with the seal of its *recipient,* Zakira-Hammu, who forwarded the letter to a third party, in this instance the king of Mari, with an accompanying message.

If the person who forwarded a letter in that way was a king of the same rank, he could ask for its return, as this letter from Qarni-Lim to Zimri-Lim shows: "The tablets from Zaziya, Zībiya, and Mutu-Samsi that I sent to my brother, may my brother listen to them, then may he return them to me" (*ARM* 28 167: 6′–9′). And in fact, these three letters were not found in the archives of the Mari palace.

Sometimes the original was kept and its content recopied, in part or in full (Figure 32):[22] a large share of the correspondence that has not come down to us directly can thus be reconstituted, at least in part. The most extraordinary case I know of is that of *FM* 2 116. Turum-natki, king of Apum, had sent a letter to Zimri-Lim. Zimri-Lim then wrote to Sumu-hadu and attached Turum-natki's letter to his missive. Sumu-hadu, writing to the Benjaminites, quoted Turum-natki's words in his letter. And finally, Sumu-hadu reported to Zimri-Lim his mission through a letter in which he recopied the letter he had written to the Benjaminites. Naturally, we possess only that last tablet, but it allows us to learn about the other three.

Written Letters and Oral Messages

In some cases, to ward off the risk of the mail being intercepted, the messages were not set down in writing. Princess Atrakatum, sister of Zimri-Lim, revealed to her brother the existence of a conspiracy in the court of her husband, Sumu-dabi, the Benjaminite king of Samanum, which she hoped to set forth in detail during a meeting with Zimri-Lim: "Another thing: the Bedouin, a sheikh whom my lord once sent to Sumu-dabi and whom he (Sumu-dabi) offered clothing, one day in the middle of the night entered here and reported to Sumu-dabi all sorts of things. When I have an

FIGURE 32. Example of a copy of a letter within another letter. Following the address formula (lines 1–2: "Tell my lord: thus speaks Itur-Asdu your servant"), the sender announces (lines 3–4): "Here is a copy of the letter I sent: may my lord listen to it." After a double line are the words (lines 5–6): "Tell Turib-adal: thus speaks Itur-Asdu your brother." The rest is broken off. (Courtesy of D. Charpin.)

interview with my lord, I will repeat to him all the words of Sumu-dabi. If that is not so, and if it is an urgent matter for him, may he write me what ought to be: I will have the details of what that man said written on a tablet and will send it to my lord" (*ARM* 10 1 [*LAPO* 18 1186]: 3′–15′).

On several occasions, the notion is expressed that some things cannot be set down in writing. Samsi-Addu wrote as follows to Yasmah-Addu: "Regarding what Samsi-Dagan told you, this is what you wrote me: 'It is not suitable to write such things on a tablet.'

Why so? Do it and send it to me! Otherwise, (there is truly) a trusted man who can bring an oral message (literally, 'who will take the words in his mouth'). Give him instructions and send it to me, so that he will set out these things in front of me" (*ARM* 1 76 [*LAPO* 16 58]: 20–29). Yasmah-Addu's reluctance to write about certain subjects seems to have been a constant. Regarding a general who had caused trouble, Yasmah-Addu indicated that he would have to pay a visit to Samsi-Addu: "Dismissing a general is a serious matter. That will require a trip from me to the king! I told myself (in fact): 'How can one discuss with the king by (written) message a matter of dismissal?' The day I sent you that tablet from me, I left for the king's place. I shall send you all the details there" (*ARM* 5 18 [*LAPO* 17 458]).

Messengers who transmitted a purely oral message had to give proof of their mission, as this letter of accreditation sent by Haya-sumu to Zimri-Lim shows: "So I gave complete instructions to Aqbu-abum, my servant, and I have just sent him to you. Pay great attention to the instructions I gave him. . . . Give him instructions promptly and send him back to me. Other than him, there is no one in my service suitable for this type of mission" (*ARM* 28 85: 5–12, 15–20).

Some individuals emphasized their desire to receive a written reply to the mail they sent out. Hence this request in a letter to the king of Shusharra: "Let not your news come by oral message (lit. 'in a mouth'): send it to me by writing (lit. 'in a tablet')!" (*ShA* 1 50: 29–30). On one occasion, Samsi-Addu explicitly pointed out the danger of purely oral communication: was what an envoy from a besieged city had told him true or not? Samsi-Addu explains the different tests that allowed him to trust that envoy's words: "A *hullum* ring which I gave to Mutušu, the envoy, he told me as an indication, and the colleague of Mutušu, our Etellum, was ill in Arraphum, and he told me about the illness of this man. And he gave me all these indications, so that I trusted his message" (*ShA* 1 11: 25–34).

Sending messengers without a written tablet could be the source of problems. For example, messengers dispatched by Ishme-Dagan, king of Ekallatum, to Babylon were upset by the presence at the audience of envoys of Zimri-Lim, about whom their master wished to lodge grievances. Hammurabi, sensing that they were concealing a part of their report from him, attempted in vain to make them speak.

He then called in the Babylonian who had accompanied Ishme-Dagan's messengers from that king's capital: "After he had repeated the report that Ishme-Dagan's messengers had delivered, he completed it as follows: (. . .) (*ARM* 26/2 384: 52′–53′). They all must have learned by heart the message that Ishme-Dagan intended for Hammurabi, since the Babylonian began by repeating the same thing as the Ekallatean messengers, before completing their report.

A very interesting case in which the oral message was intentionally misleading, and where the truth had to be set in writing, is provided by a letter from the chief nomad Ibal-El: "When my lord sends a messenger to my house, may my lord send me orally the following message: 'May your people be gathered! Assuredly, I will go to Der (or wherever my lord wishes).' May he send me that message orally, but on a tablet may he say the real route that will be taken by my lord" (Unpublished A.836). The passage makes no sense unless, upon the arrival of a messenger, Ibal-El had to listen to the news delivered orally in the presence of a number of people. The ruse he suggested to the king also assumes that Ibal-El would then read (or have read to him) the true content of the tablet brought to him. It therefore appears that in this case, the messenger would personally have to travel the distance that separated the king from Ibal-El and that he would receive special instructions at his departure.

It sometimes happened that the king's order was transmitted only orally. The official for whom it was intended did not fail to underscore this, so as to be released of responsibility in the event of a later problem: "Iṣi-Ahu, the courier, a man from Zibnatum, arrived at my house, not being the bearer of a tablet from my lord. He said: 'By order of my lord, place the seals on the dwelling of Bannum and of Zakura-Abum'" (*FM* 2 49: 5–10). Often written confirmation was requested when rumors of an event had been heard. Witness this letter from a governor of Qaṭṭunan: "I learned only through public rumor about my lord coming to Qaṭṭunan. If my lord is coming, may a tablet from him arrive quickly so that I can be ready before his arrival" (*FM* 2 47: 4–11).

Sometimes an official explicitly expressed the desire to have a written order from the king before obeying. Hence Queen Shibtu wrote to Zimri-Lim: "Mukannishum arrived and told me this: 'It is to me that that gold was allocated.' I replied as follows: 'So long as a tablet from my lord has not arrived, I shall not hand over the gold.' Was the gold allocated to Mukannishum? May a tablet come from my lord if I must hand over (that) gold to him" (*ARM* 10 18 [*LAPO* 18 1132]: 5′–14′).

Conclusion

A very interesting passage from Thucydides speaks to the advantages of sending a written letter rather than an oral message:

(Nicias) had before sent frequent reports of events as they occurred, and felt it especially incumbent upon him to do so now, as he thought that [the troops] were in a critical position, and that unless speedily recalled or strongly reinforced from home, they had no hope of safety. He feared, however, that the messengers, either through inability to speak, or through failure of memory, or from a wish to please the multitude, might not report the truth, and so thought it best to write a letter, to ensure that the Athenians should know his own opinion without its being lost in transmission, and be able to decide the real facts of the case. His emissaries, accordingly, departed with the letter and the requisite verbal instructions.

(Thucydides 1950, 7.8 [491–492])

I have shown that Mesopotamian kings, however "barbarian" they may have been, understood the advantages of the written text well before the Greeks. The degree of sophistication that exchanges of correspondence had reached in the Near East in the early second millennium and the importance attached to written communication are obvious. It was not only the most powerful kings who had their messages written down: the nomad chiefs did the same, which allows us, for once, to know them otherwise than through the deforming prism of what the settled populations wrote about them. Women as well made use of the written text: of course, it was primarily those women belonging to the elite who are thus attested, but the corpus of their letters is substantial, whether from Mariot princesses, nuns-*nadītum* of Sippar, or the wives of Assyrian merchants. Finally, it is because certain prophets could not communicate the message of the gods directly to the king that several dozen prophecies are known to us from letters (Charpin 2002c).

We can understand the sentiment expressed by a woman in the age of Samsi-Addu, when she wrote that, thanks to the mail, distances were in some sense obliterated: "At present, I am afraid that Akatiya will say: 'Mari is far away.' It is not far away at all: the city of Mari, in relation to Assur, is like the suburbs of Assur. And the City (Assur) is near when it comes to the mail" (Durand 1985b, 410n155 [A.1248: 29–34]). A letter from Zagros found in Shemshara provides another example of the sense of proximity the ancients felt thanks to correspondence, which was a new phenomenon in these regions and in that era: "Bullattal brought me your greetings and I was very pleased. I felt as if you and I had met and embraced! And I myself am well! Be glad!" (*ShA* 1 65: 5–12). In reading this passage, we smile to think that many of our contemporaries had the same feeling when e-mail was invented.

The considerable expansion in the number of those able to read and write accounts for the radical transformation of correspondence during the four centuries between the fall of Ur (ca. 2000) and that of Babylon (ca. 1600). If we compare a letter written in Eshnunna in about 1950 (Whiting 1987) to a letter from Mari composed two centuries later, we can only be struck by the evolution: a rigid formula and laconic texts give way to what can sometimes be considered verbosity. One of the characteristics of the Old Babylonian epistolary genre is the importance given to quotations of conversations. It is clear that the ability to reproduce speeches was a very important dimension in the evolution of writing, which has too often been neglected until now.

Let me consider once again the epic *Enmerkar and the Lord of Aratta* with which I began this chapter. It is an etiological narrative of the birth of long-distance exchanges between kings, but also of their correlate, diplomatic correspondence.[23] I can therefore not share the point of view of H. L. J. Vanstiphout, who sought to make the ancients' ideas about the origin of writing coincide with our current conceptions: "Thus large-scale trade is seen to depend on writing, which simply implies Sumerian. And indeed, the very first cuneiform documents, without doubt written in Sumerian, are what we now call administrative and economic in nature. The scribes . . . hinted at the indubitable fact that writing was invented for economic, not intellectual, reasons" (Vanstiphout 2003a, 54). This comment contrasts, in an overly general way, "intellectual" and "economic" reasons, neglecting to take into account the precise nature of the texts. As it happens, the epistolary genre appeared rather late in the history of "cuneiform literature," since the most ancient letters that have come down to us date only from the late Early Dynastic period, about 2350 B.C., that is, more than eight centuries after the appearance of writing (Michalowski 1993, 2). This is no accident: it was only at that moment that writing had sufficiently evolved in its functioning to allow for the notation of texts of that kind. Michalowski has accurately described the "literary" texts from Fara and Abu Salabikh (ca. 2500 B.C.): "These texts were intended for someone who knew the compositions by heart and therefore they cannot be described as autonomous communicative devices" (Michalowski 2003). It is therefore clear that correspondence, because it seeks to *transmit to others* what were *speeches* originally conveyed orally, constitutes a derived, secondary use of writing—but one that largely became the most prevalent in the early second millennium, so much so that it was considered to have given birth to writing. And it is surely no accident that this period was also the one that saw the apogee of the phonetic notation of language.[24]

chapter four

Oral and Written, Part 2:
Oaths, Contracts, and Treaties

At first glance, given the place of the written text in Mesopotamian civilization, it is not surprising that a large portion of the archival documents is legal in nature. Nevertheless, contracts did not belong primarily to the realm of the written. On the contrary: an agreement between two persons, whether in the form of a fidelity oath by a "servant" to his king, a contract binding individuals, or an alliance between sovereigns, was characterized by the performance of symbolic gestures committing those who made them, and by the utterance of solemn words in the presence of witnesses, who committed to memory the affair concluded.

For a long time, jurists believed that the Code of Hammurabi considered only contracts set down in writing to be valid. That error is based on a misinterpretation of a few passages, especially section 128, relating to marriage: "If a man took a wife and did not arrange for her a marriage contract *(riksātum)*, that woman is not a wife" (Roth 1995). In this passage as elsewhere, *riksātum* designates a contract but not necessarily one that was in writing (Greengus 1969). What counted first and foremost was giving one's word; the punishment for perjury gave the oath binding force that was long judged sufficient. It was only gradually that the need was felt to set down the contracts on tablets. The care taken in preserving and transmitting legal documents (acts of purchase, adoption, inheritance, and so on) indicates the growing importance attached to the written text during the Old Babylonian period. From this standpoint, there was a temporal gap between the practices of private law and those of political life. Agreements concluded between sovereigns (treaties) were set in writing only later, in the second half of the second millennium.

Oaths and Symbolic Gestures

Fidelity Oaths

The Mari archives have preserved the oldest texts of fidelity oaths that officials had to swear to the king when they assumed their duties. The pledges varied depending on the nature of the position. Hence a diviner was obligated in the first place to conceal nothing from the sovereign, even in the event of a bad omen: "When making an oracular inquiry for Zimri-Lim, my lord, (or) when doing a ritual procedure (for my lord), as many as I see occur, or when making an oracular inquiry for a commoner, (or) when doing a ritual procedure (for a commoner), as many as I see occur: I will indeed tell Zimri-Lim, my lord, about every single evil or unfavorable sign that I see; I will not hide (them)" (*ARM* 26/1 1: 1–6; Lenzi 2008, 42–45). He was also required to practice professional confidentiality: "An evil and unfavorable sign that I see occur when making an oracular inquiry for Zimri-Lim, my lord, whether in an *izbum* or in an *izmum*, I will not tell (it) to any person at all" (*ARM* 26/1 1: 7–10).[1]

A provincial governor was not to take advantage of his situation to enrich himself unduly or to allow others to do so:

Of the booty and of anything over which my lord has installed me as arbitrator-*ebbum* and comptroller, (I swear) that I have taken nothing, that I will take nothing, that I will steal nothing, that I will sell nothing, that, having set it aside, I will give nothing to anyone as a favor or kindness. If someone takes more grain or wool than he has a right to and I see him, learn of it, or am told of it, (I swear that) I will not find any excuse for him, (that) very day I will tell Zimri-Lim, my lord, that I will write him of it and will not conceal it.

(Unpublished M.5719: rev. iii 1–13)

Assyrian emperors of the first millennium systematically used such oaths, called *adē,* to assure themselves of the fidelity of their people and to guarantee their own succession (Parpola and Watanabe 1988).

Concluding Contracts

I have analyzed elsewhere a few of the symbolic gestures used upon the conclusion of a contract (Charpin 2010, chap. 3) and would like to give a few additional examples here. When possession of a plot of land was transferred to an individual or to a group, it was the practice to "drive in a stake" *(sikkatam mahāṣum).* In the case of a field, we might immediately think of the need to survey the property, which was in fact done with rope and stakes. A letter from Mari indicates: "Verify (the boundaries of) that field and have the stakes driven in in your presence" (Charpin 1997a, 344 [A.2810: 10]). In addition, those in charge of the Crown lands in the provinces of the kingdom of Mari were called *ša sikkātim,* literally, "stakes (officials)," which is generally understood to mean "cadastral officials" (Lion 2001b, 150). Some texts show, however, that the act of driving in a stake was a symbolic gesture. It was the witnesses who did it, as indicated in this text from Mari, where the list of witnesses ends with the comment: "(Such are) the witnesses who drove in the stake" (Charpin forthcoming b [M.10556: 20]).[2] That interpretation is confirmed by several sales contracts for houses in Susa: they show that the acquisition of full title to the house was symbolized by a stake driven into its wall. The relinquishment clause was formulated as follows: "Should this house be claimed, a cone has been driven (into his property) in his town and in his country" (*CAD* S, 250b). And certain passages show what was done with that cone in the case of an unwarranted claim: it was driven into the mouth of the plaintiff, so that the punishment fit the crime. A text that relates a lawsuit regarding a field ends with this clause: "Anyone making a claim on the field . . . will have to pay 10 minas of silver to the palace and the stake (found) at the front boundary of the field will be driven into his mouth" (Charpin 1997a, 344 [*ARM* 8 85+]). It is therefore clear that the gesture of driving stakes into a field to measure it when a change of owners occurred ultimately took on a symbolic charge that far surpassed the practical need to survey the plot.

Another symbolic object was the "mace" *(ḫaṭṭum)* that the head of a family gave to the son he designated as his successor (Charpin 1994b). Inanna-mansum, chief lamenter of the goddess Annunitum in Sippar-Amnānum, chose to set aside his entire inheritance for Ur-Utu at the expense of his three brothers. He declared: "To them I will leave no inheritance. Ur-Utu is my son, the one who received my mace from me; it is to him that I will give everything" (Janssen 1992, 22–26 [DI 1194/IM 81943: 16–17]). Conversely, that mace was broken when the father disinherited his eldest son, as a document from Emar shows: "(The father) broke his (son's) mace, he took away his status as son" (Arnaud 1987b, 240, no. 17). And the father declared: "PN is no longer my son: his mace has been broken."

We cannot know whether these gestures were still actually performed or whether they had become simply figures of speech. A similar debate has occurred among jurists, regarding texts indicating, as the sanction for a crime, that a woman went away "naked": are we to take the expression literally, or was this a vivid way of saying "without her dowry or any property"? It appears we must opt for the view that it was a symbolic gesture (S. Lafont 1999, 86).

Note that the symbolic importance of all these gestures is never made explicit in the documents reporting their performance (Greengus 1969, 515n7; Kilmer 1974). Their interpretation by moderns has given rise to controversies, and certainty on the matter has not always been achieved. Such is the case for the symbolic gestures linked to a change in status from free to slave: part of the hair of the person reduced to slavery was shaved off, leaving only an *abuttum*, no doubt a lock hanging from the top of the skull. A slave could thus be immediately identified as such by his or her hairstyle. Conversely, the liberation of a slave consisted of shaving off that lock *(abuttam gullubum)*. Other symbolic gestures were sometimes performed on that occasion. A legal text reporting the emancipation of a slave indicates: "Her jar is shattered, her girdle(?) is broken" *(CT* 48 49; cf. *CAD* Š/II, 247b). It may be assumed that the former slave used a jar of that sort to fetch water; the role of the girdle (if that is how *qablītum* ought to be translated) is less clear.

Concluding Alliances

Symbolic gestures were not confined to the sphere of what we call private law: they were also performed within the framework of diplomatic relations. Alliances could be concluded during a meeting between the two parties, or they could come about long-distance, through special emissaries. The distinction between these two manners of proceeding is essential (Charpin 1990b; Durand 1997, 429–458; B. Lafont 2001, 262–293). When kings met to conclude an alliance, they began by agreeing on their reciprocal pledges; the ritual subsequently performed included the solemn utterance of the words of the oath that the parties to the alliance made to each other, and the immolation of a baby donkey *(hayāram qatālum)*. No text thus far has revealed the symbolism of that gesture, which is frequently attested. We may surmise that each party identified with the animal, agreeing in advance to have his throat cut in the event of perjury.

Upon the conclusion of an alliance by the Bedouin chief Ibal-El with various cities in his region, the modalities to be observed gave rise to a controversy among the participants: the delegates of the three cities proposed that a she-goat and a puppy be immolated, which scandalized Ibal-El. He saw to it that a baby donkey was sacrificed, to respect the customs of his king, Zimri-Lim. Unfortunately, the symbolism underlying these practices is nowhere made explicit. Ibal-El declares that he acted out of "reverence" for Zimri-Lim, which suggests that the donkey was considered a more noble animal (Charpin 1993, 168–170). We know, however, that Zimri-Lim used goats at the beginning of his reign (Charpin 2003).

Several texts allude to an alliance concluded "by blood" (Durand 1992, 116–117), and one of them mentions the act of rubbing oneself with blood (Eidem 2008, 313 [YTLR 185]): no doubt it was the blood of the sacrificed donkey. Other texts allude to the cup from which the kings forming an alliance drank, but without the nature of the liquid contained in that cup being specified. A vassal of the king of Mari wrote to Zimri-Lim to denounce the conduct of another vassal: "Once, that man sat before my lord and drank from the cup. Having elevated him, my lord counted him among the nobles, dressing him in a suit and placing a wig-*huburtum* on his head. But upon his return, he defecated into the cup from which he had drunk and become the enemy of my lord."[3] The alliance ceremony is described here as being the occasion for symbolic gestures:[4] the lord gave clothing and a wig to his vassal,[5] who drank from a cup. To demonstrate the breaking of the alliance, the vassal, once he had returned home, engaged in a gesture that was no less symbolic: he soiled the cup from which he had drunk during the ceremony, thus metaphorically, but very clearly, putting an end to the system of relations that had been previously established.[6]

When alliances were concluded long-distance, the two rulers swore their oaths separately, each performing the gesture of "throat-touching" *(lippit napištim)*[7] in the presence of his gods and those of his ally. Hence the king of Eshnunna swore an alliance

FIGURE 33. Example of a representation of a divine symbol on a cylinder seal: the bull surmounted by a bolt of lightning depicts Adad, the storm god. (©The Trustees of the British Museum.)

oath with the king of Mari: "During the 25th day of the month *kinūnum* (vii), the prince has just sworn an oath by the gods: may my lord be glad! Subsequent to my present tablet, I shall march at the head of my lord's gods, of the prince's gods and ambassadors. I shall join my lord and we shall have [my lord] swear the oath by the gods" (Charpin 1991, 163 [A.2028]). No text indicates in what form these gods were present: they were likely not statues but symbols, like the "great arms" to which an ambassador alludes in a letter to the king of Mari (Charpin 1991, 163n60 [A.3354+]) (Figure 33).

Bread, Cup, and Oil

The complementarity between solemn gestures and symbolic words is particularly clear in the case of oaths (Charpin 1997b, forthcoming b). Scribes usually used the expression "swear an oath" *(nīšam tamūm),* but we sometimes find the rather astonishing "eat an oath" *(nīšam akālum)*. That expression can be compared to the well-known formula "eat an *asakkum*" *(asakkum* is usually translated as "taboo"). But a contract from Mari provides an interesting variant, indicating that the parties to the contract "ate sweepings [*sar.meš*]"; in another contract, they "swore by sweepings" (Durand 2008, 580–582). It was therefore possible both to "swear" and to "eat" an oath-*nīšum*, an *asakkum,* or "sweepings" *(sar.meš).* These variants can be accounted for if we postulate that the utterance of an oath was accompanied by the ingestion of remnants of waste that bore a curse should the juror violate his oath.

The "materialization" of the curse that the parties to a contract called down upon themselves in the event of perjury could occur through different symbolic gestures, such as eating or drinking, or anointing themselves with oil. These acts are attested in different contracts from Mari and Terqa: "They ate bread, drank beer, and anointed themselves with oil." G. Boyer comments on the example in *ARM* 8 13, unique at the time: "That meal taken in common by the parties, alone or in the company of witnesses, surely had a legal significance. It can be seen as the symbol of a life in common being established between table companions and creating a bond of brotherhood" (Boyer 1958, 195; Veenhof 1966, 309b–310a). Durand has spoken of a "little feast" to conclude a real estate transaction (1982, 89). These festive rites, attested from the third millennium on (Gelb, Steinkeller, and Whiting 1991, 243–244; Steinkeller 1989, 143), may have had another dimension of a magical nature. They may have been self-imprecations pronounced while performing a symbolic gesture. A first example can be taken from nineteenth-century Anatolia. Within the context of an agreement being concluded between Assyrian merchants and a local prince, the contents of a goblet were spilled as the following formula was pronounced: "If we reject your oath-*māmītum,* may our blood be spilt like (the content of) the cup" (Çeçen and Hecker 1995). Similarly, the formula proffered during an oath in the Hittite world went as follows: "[Just as] you rub yourself down with oil, [thus also] let these oath-curses be rubbed down onto [you]! Just as you put on a garment, so also put on these oath-curses" (Kitz 2004, 316). And this significant passage appears in the curses for fidelity oaths sworn to the Neo-Assyrian king Esarhaddon: "Just as bread and wine enter into [your] intestines, [so] may they (the gods mentioned) make this oath enter into [your] intestines and into those of [your] so[ns] and your [daught]ers" (Parpola and Watanabe 1988, 52 § 72). And later on, "Just as oil enters your flesh, so may they cause this oath to enter into your flesh, the flesh of your brothers, your sons and your daughters" (Parpola and Watanabe 1988, 56 § 94).

The similarity between the Mari texts and the fidelity oaths to Esarhaddon no doubt extends even further, since the following curse also appears in the oaths: "May the great gods of heaven and earth turn water (and) oil [into a curse *(ikkibum)* for] you" (Parpola and Watanabe 1988, 51 § 61). As Veenhof has argued, "perhaps the meaning may be at the same time that water and oil drunk by the vassal in the oath ceremony may become his 'destruction,' may bring about his annihilation, because he infringed upon a 'tabu'" (1966, 313). If we replace *ikkibum* with *asakkum*—and the two words are known to have been synonyms—we obtain precisely the definition of *asakkum* proposed above. The idea would therefore be that, at the time of the oath, the juror swallowed a substance (sweepings, bread, beer, wine) that would be transformed into a destructive force in the event of perjury, the whole being described by the term *asakkum*.

Other comparisons are possible. Consider the ordeal by "bitter water" that the woman suspected of adultery is made to drink in Numbers 5:12–28 (Démare 1987, 49n1). Let me also mention the military oath among the Hittites, which contains many self-imprecations, such as: just as yeast makes a loaf of bread swell, so anyone who violates the oath will burst and will meet a deadly fate (Oettinger 1976, 8–9). Any comparative study would also have to include Saint Paul, who declares: "Whosoever shall eat this bread, and drink this cup of the Lord, unworthily, shall be guilty of the body and blood of the Lord. . . . For he that eateth and drinketh unworthily, eateth and drinketh damnation to himself" (1 Corinthians 11:27 and 29; KJV).

It is thus clear why the term *asakkum* was also used to designate goods set aside for the deity or king.[8] Whoever seized them fell victim to the destructive force dormant within them. Letter *ARM* 26/1 280 gives an excellent illustration. The three sons of Batahrum died suddenly on the same day and public rumor insinuated: "There is in that man's house [x minas] of silver, *asa[kkum* of the god?/king?]." It cannot be ruled out that the symbolic gesture to which the Mari contracts refer was accompanied by an imprecation of the same type as in Esarhaddon's treaties, but such a curse never seems to have been put in writing, with the exception, perhaps, of this passage, if the restoration of the lacunae is accurate: "This oath by my gods, which I swore to Zimri-Lim [*if I am not faithful*] to Zimri-Lim [my lord], may these gods, all those whose taboo [I have absorbed], make me perish" (Unpublished M.5719 rev. iv 11–15). Consider as well, in an Old Babylonian lawsuit, this phrase pronounced by the person swearing: "If anyone sees me in other dispositions, may they treat me (appropriately) for having held in contempt an oath by the king" (Anbar 1975, 121, no. 8, line 14). The process by which the *asakkum* that had been integrated into the juror's body became activated in the event of perjury is explicitly described in a curse from the Code of Hammurabi: "May the goddess Ninkarrak . . . cause a grievous malady to break out upon his limbs, an evil *asakkum,* a serious *simmum-*carbuncle" (Roth 1995, 139–140, lines 50ff.).

In other cases, the oath was pronounced in the presence of divine symbols (sometimes also called "divine weapons") (Dombradi 1996, 84–86). The "weapons" of the god Shamash included a net symbolizing the rays of the sun, which might seize hold of the evildoer, as an Old Babylonian document from Sippar indicates. The military authorities wanted Abi-ṣum and Ṣurarum to assume the service duties of a certain Shumum-libshi, who had recently died, but their aunt Lamassani asserted that he was not their father. For lack of witnesses, the matter could be decided only by an oath sworn by Shamash's "throw-net": "Warad-Kubi, the general of the troops of the Sippar countryside, the captains Qurrudum and Ina-palešu, Ibni-Sin, the military scribe, and the elders of his *arrum*, refused to approach the throw-net. But Lamassani, the *nadîtum* of Šamaš, declared as follows in the throw-net: 'Abi-ṣum and Ṣurarum were not born as sons of Šumum-libši; I am the one who has raised them.' This she declared" (Veenhof 2003b [BM 96998: 45–51]). These divine symbols had a dreaded religious power: the plaintiffs, a group of military men, did not dare pronounce the oath that the judges had demanded of them. It was the defendant who did so, thereby winning the case.

The Drafting of Agreements

The Case of "Treaties"

Strictly speaking, the term "treaty" should be avoided when describing alliances concluded in the first half of the second millennium. These were in fact merely personal pledges that did not endure beyond the lifetimes of the parties to the contract bound by an oath (Charpin forthcoming d). There was no difference in nature between the fidelity oath of an official to his king and a "treaty" between sovereigns. The fidelity oath that governors swore to the king of Mari included this pledge: "[From this day forward, when I swore this oath by my gods] to Zimri-Lim, (I swear) that so long as I live I shall not say: '[The oath by] my [gods] has become old, [(the solemn pledge) is no longer valid, (enough!)]" (Unpublished M.5719: rev. iv 1–7). The very same oath, formulated at greater length, is found in the text of a so-called treaty a few decades later, concluded by Hazip-Teššub, king of Razama, with Mutiya, king of Apum:

From this very day that I swore this oath of mine by the gods to Mutiya, son of Halum-pi-Umu, king of the country of Apum, his servants, his troops, his seasonal camp *(nawûm)*, and his kingdom, for as long as I live I shall not say thus: "My oath by the gods has become old and the treaty has become void! Enough! To Mutiya, son of Halum-pi-Umu, king of the country of Apum, his servants, his troops, his seasonal camp *(nawûm)*, and his kingdom I shall do evil." For as long as I live I shall not say thus. (Eidem 2008, 320 [L.T.-2: v. 24″–37″])

Alliances gave rise to written texts only when they were concluded long-distance. In that case, the two parties had to come to an agreement about each of their pledges before then swearing the oath. One of the best-known cases involves the negotiations between Hammurabi and Ṣilli-Sin, king of Eshnunna (Charpin 1988, 144–145). The two kings first had to exchange a "small tablet," which included only the clauses to which each proposed that the other subscribe (Figure 34). The accord was sometimes formulated in a very general way: to have the same enemies and the same friends, to come to the aid of whichever was attacked, not to conclude a separate peace. In some cases, the clauses were more detailed, as in the treaty proposal submitted by Ibal-pi-El II of Eshnunna to Zimri-Lim (Charpin 1991).

Once the terms of the accord were fixed, the kings had to exchange a "large tablet"; some examples have been uncovered and have been designated "treaties."[9] They begin with a list of deities guaranteeing the alliance, proceed to the clauses of the accord, and end with curses should these clauses not be respected. But the texts that have come down to us are only proposals, which were sometimes contested: it is still not known whether they were ratified as such, or even, in some cases, whether an oath was ultimately sworn (Charpin 1990b, 116–118; B. Lafont 2001, 283–293). Discussions had to do with the clauses in the agreement and sometimes with the

FIGURE 34. An example of a "small tablet" treaty: it includes the oath that Zimri-Lim wished Hammurabi of Babylon to swear to him at the conclusion of their alliance against Elam. (Courtesy of D. Charpin.)

list of gods by whom the oath was to be sworn;[10] Hammurabi registered surprise at the curses contained in the draft treaty that Itur-Asdu submitted to him in Zimri-Lim's name (Guichard 2004). When the kings met in person, that type of discussion took place orally.[11] The aim of these tablet exchanges was merely to finalize the text that was to be sworn (orally) by each of the kings pledging. It is therefore not appropriate to describe them as "treaties."

Beginning with the second half of the second millennium, alliances committed not only kings during their lifetimes but also the following generations. As a result, the text set in writing became a true treaty, whose formulation was in principle unalterable. The curses include indications that the gods "will punish anyone who alters the words of this tablet" (Beckman 1996, 153, no. 28A § 11). When Hattusili renewed with Benteshina of Amurru the treaty that had existed between Suppiluliuma and Aziru, and which his predecessor Muwattalli had not respected, he explicitly indicated that his treaty tablet was reproducing the terms of the former treaty (Beckman 1996, 96–97 § 7). And there are cases in which explicit reference is made to a treaty concluded between previous kings, whose clauses are obviously still in force. Hence Mursili II, needing to settle a matter with Tuppi-Tessub of Amurru relating to prisoners, cited a clause from the treaty that had been concluded between his father, Suppiluliuma, and Aziru, king of Amurru (Beckman 1996, 157, no. 3 § 10).

The transformation of treaties from protocols of oaths to true contracts is indicated by several markers. In the first place, the originals were henceforth sealed.[12] In the case of a treaty between a great king and his vassal, only the king apposed his seal, thereby demonstrating his pledge; the vassal for his part swore an oath. When it was a treaty between equals, each of the kings sealed the tablet that was to be sent to his partner. Tukulti-Ninurta I alludes to the treaty that bound him to the Babylonian king as an "inalterable tablet" bearing the seals of their predecessors (Foster 2005c, 307 iii: 30′). In the case of the treaty between Hattusili III and Ramses II, the copy received by the pharaoh bore Hittite seals, which are described in the Egyptian translation we possess: the seal of Hattusili on the obverse of the tablet and that of his wife Puduhepa on the reverse (Beckman 1996, 95; Edel 1997, 102n32).

The text became so valuable in itself that, if the tablet came to be lost, it had to be reconstituted. When the treaty between the Hittite king Mursili and Talmi-Sharrumma of Aleppo disappeared, Muwattalli executed a copy, which he sealed with his own seal: "My father Mursili made a treaty tablet for Talmi-Šarumma, King of Aleppo, but the tablet has been stolen. I, the Great King, have written another tablet [for him], have sealed it with my seal, and have given it to him" (Beckman 1996, 88, no. 14 § 2). The Ugarit palace has yielded an example of that kind: it is the proposal for an alliance made by Sharri-Kushuh, king of Karkemish, to Niqmaddu of Ugarit. The tablet we possess bears the seal of Ini-Tessub, grandson of Sharri-Kushuh, and ends as follows: "This tablet had been sealed in the time of the king's grandfather, but it was broken. At present, King Ini-Tessub has sealed a copy of it" (Nougayrol 1956, 54–55 [RS 17.334: 20–23]). This illustrates, in the realm of international law, a course of action that is documented for private law from the Old Babylonian period on: the reconstitution of a lost legal document. The aim was the same: to avoid future disputes, especially concerning territorial boundaries, whether these were the boundaries of a field or the borders of a country.[13]

Elsewhere, the document itself was solemnized and its text sometimes recopied on metal. It is known that the famous treaty between Hattusili III and Ramses II was inscribed in silver, though we have only a copy in clay. A bronze tablet of large dimensions, weighing 5 kilograms and reproducing the text of the treaty between the Hittite king Tudhaliya IV and Kurunta of Tarhuntassa, was found a few years ago in Hattusha (Beckman 1996, 108–117, no. 18C) (Figure 35). In some cases, the text of the treaty itself could be placed in a temple,[14] or even copied several times over[15] and placed in several temples.[16] In the Old Babylonian period, former "treaties" were sometimes preserved: but when Hammurabi consulted the tablets of alliances concluded by his predecessors, he did so for documentary reasons, not because the tablets were still valid at the time (Guichard 2004, 30).

The Use of Written Documents for Private Contracts

Some have been unable to resist the temptation to establish an opposition between the sphere of the oral, where local customs prevailed, and that of the written, seemingly characteristic of the central powers. That is why a few jurists believed that paragraphs from the Code of Hammurabi express the obligation imposed by the king to fix in written form contracts (relating to marriage, tenant

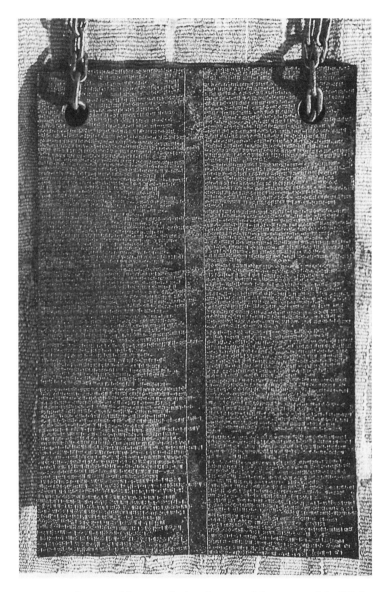

FIGURE 35. Bronze tablet reproducing the text of the treaty of the Hittite king Tudhaliya IV with Kurunta of Tarhuntassa, discovered in the Hittite capital of Hattusha. (From P. Neve, *Hattusa: Stadt de Gotter und Tempel* [Mainz, 1993], 21, fig. 38.)

farming, and so on), or risk having them invalidated. That interpretation has been abandoned: nowhere in Babylonian law does a contract have to be written down to be valid (Greengus 1969).

The case of marriage contracts demonstrates this clearly. There is no fixed model for that type of text, and all those in existence describe more or less unusual situations (polygamy, wives who were formerly slaves, and so on). The purpose of writing down the contract was therefore to protect the rights of those who were in a particularly vulnerable situation (Westbrook 1988).

A historian must be attentive to the fact that this type of text often provides only what was considered essential, without reflecting reality in its entirety. From this standpoint, documents dividing an inheritance are very characteristic. In no sense do they give a complete inventory of the deceased's property. Texts dating from after the inheritance was divided may show that certain property, such as fields, had remained jointly owned (Charpin 1980, 62–67), or that some categories of property were divided up among the heirs but not put in writing, as an inventory beginning as follows shows: "Sealed document of tools from Idin-Eshtar, which were not placed on the partition tablet" (Charpin and Durand 1981, no. 102a, line 3). Local customs differed in that regard. It was the scribes of Nippur who provided the most complete enumeration of the property divided up by heirs (Prang 1981).

Writing also made inroads as a result of the witnesses' mortality. In the case of an inheritance falling to someone who was adopted, years could go by between the act of adoption and the death of the adoptive parent; and it was precisely at that moment that the adoptee's right to the inheritance risked being contested, particularly by members of the adoptive family. The Babylonians understood that a written text had greater longevity than the witnesses. Clay tablets, after all, were sturdy, all the more so since they were protected by an envelope. Even when the witnesses were still alive, they could have forgotten essential details of the transaction they had witnessed. That was the case for the witnesses to the marriage of Geme-Asalluhi. When she wanted a divorce, they were questioned about the content of the dowry, and they admitted that they were unable to give a description of it: "We know that the dowry was given, but a great deal of time has elapsed, and we no longer know the amount" (Jursa 1997 [BM 16764]). Tablets could themselves be the object of symbolic manipulation, as shown in the following example. Economic life in the Old Babylonian period was punctuated by "redress" measures *(mīšarum)* taken by the sovereign, which consisted in particular of canceling debts. Following the proclamation of such an edict, creditors were obliged to take their debt contracts before a commission, and the tablets were solemnly broken. On one such occasion, in year 12 of Hammurabi, a creditor declared that she had lost her tablet. So that she could not subsequently enforce that contract against her debtors if she happened to find it again, a clod of dirt *(kirbānum)* was broken as a substitute for the lost tablet, whose value was rendered void as a result. But at the same time, in order to better protect the debtors, a text was delivered to them describing the ceremony and specifying that if the creditor subsequently found and attempted to enforce a tablet, it would be considered counterfeit and would be broken.[17] The two practices—performance of a symbolic act and drafting of a text—were thus not felt to be in any way exclusive of each other.

The Legal Value of the Written Text

The importance of the written document appears in judicial procedure in reference to the handling of evidence. In 1784, a nun-*nadītum* named Nish-inīshu purchased a plot of land from a certain Ishum-gamil. Fifty-two years later, Ishum-gamil's son, Ibbi-Shamash, took legal action against Nish-inīshu's heir, her niece Naramtani. His argument was simple: Nish-inīshu had taken possession of a piece of land larger than what she had actually purchased. The judges therefore sought to verify Naramtani's property deed. Naramtani produced the contract drawn up at the time of the sale fifty-two years earlier ("her old tablet"), and the judges confirmed her ownership of the land, whose dimensions were indicated in the contract:

> 5/6 *sar* 6 *gin* of bare land, next to the house of Mannatum, the *nadītum* of Shamash, daughter of Yasilum, and next to the house of Ishum-gamil; having on its first short side the main street and on its second short side the house of Ishum-gamil, which Nish-inīshu, *nadītum* of Shamash, daughter of Ubariya, purchased from Ishum-gamil, son of Ishum-naṣir, for ten shekels of silver in year 9 of Hammurabi—after fifty-two years had elapsed, in year 18 of Samsu-iluna, Ibbi-Shamash, son of Ishum-gamil, demanded that plot from Naramtani, *nadītum* of Shamash, saying: "Nish-inīshu, your father's sister, purchased a small plot from my father, Ishum-gamil, but she seized a great deal!" They went to find Sīn-ishmeshu, the governor *(šāpirum)* of Sippar, and the judges of Sippar. They examined their case. Since the envelope of the tablet was damaged, they extracted her tablet from it and, in conformity with her old tablet, they confirmed her ownership of 5/6 *sar* 6 *gin* of bare land. He shall not return thereto: Ibbi-Shamash, son of Ishum-gamil, shall not make any claim against Naramtani regarding the 5/6 *sar* 6 *gin* of bare land. They swore by Shamash, Aya, Marduk, and King Samsu-iluna.
>
> (Thureau-Dangin 1912; Charpin 2000a, 72, no. 32)

If in that case the judges did not question the witnesses, it was quite simply because of the amount of time that had passed: after half a century, none of them was still alive. The envelope itself had been damaged, and the judges had to extract the internal tablet to find the intact text of the sales contract. Once again, the written text had the advantage of longevity over the word of witnesses.

The role of the written text as evidence was not limited to legal texts. In many examples, a correspondent explicitly asked the recipient to preserve his letter to serve as his witness (Kraus 1985a): "Keep my note as witness for me *(ana šībūtiya)*" (*AbB* 12 130: 10 or 11 194). It is clear that the expression *ana šibūtim,* literally, "as witness," must be translated "as evidence," which a letter from Shamash-hazir confirms: "And Shamash-naṣir brought me his tablet as proof *(ana šībūtim)*" (*AbB* 9 19: 23–24). In some cases, the expression was even stronger: "You shall preserve my present tablet at the home of Lu-Enlila as an element of verification *(qīpum)* of my affair and evidence in my case" *(AbB* 10 148: 32–35).[18] It is interesting to analyze closely the terminology used in judicial contexts. The following comment appears frequently in the minutes: "The judges listened *(šemūm)* to the tablet" (Dombradi 1996, 86–89). Similarly, to refer to the content of a text, the expression used was "the mouth of the tablet" *(pī ṭuppim)* or "the word of the tablet" *(awāt ṭuppim).*[19] A written document was therefore considered a "frozen word" in some sense: a tablet had a mouth and its words could be listened to. As a result, it is evident that a letter could serve as a witness. Kraus aptly noted the "personification" of the tablet but neglected to pursue it any further (Kraus 1985a, 142). Yet it is clear that, for Mesopotamians, tablets were alive. They were sometimes "killed" *(dākum),* that is, rendered void (Veenhof 1987, 46), and even "brought back to life" *(buluṭum)* after they were lost (Charpin 1986b, 133–135; Veenhof 1987, 49). The Babylonians were able to adapt their law pragmatically to an evolution that was giving greater importance to the written text: since evidence was fundamentally conceived as testimony, they had only to engage in a sort of personification of the tablet to settle the problem. There could be no opposition between written evidence and testimonial evidence.

When both written evidence and testimonial evidence were lacking, the law turned to the procedure of the probatory oath. A trial that took place under Hammurabi provides a characteristic example. Because of military events, a resident from Isin who had a lawsuit with his brother had to take refuge with his family in another city (Charpin 2000a, 77–78, no. 36). The text explains: "He could bring neither tablet nor witnesses," which is understandable given his status as an exile: archives and witnesses had remained in Isin. The judges then decided to have him swear an oath by Shamash (god of justice) and by the deity of his city, namely, Gula. In this case, the oath was clearly considered a makeshift solution.

The Growing Importance of the Written Document

The importance attached to the preservation and transfer of property deeds shows, however, that it was no negligible matter to be able to take advantage of written evidence, and the preoccupation with such evidence seems to have increased throughout the Old Babylonian period.

We get a good sense of that evolution in analyzing the arrangements an individual made when a document was lost. A first attitude is documented in a lawsuit that occurred under the reign of Rim-Sin, king of Larsa. To exercise his right to an inheritance, a certain private individual was obliged to swear an oath as follows: "(I swear) that I am the son of Sin-magir, who adopted me, and that my sealed document was not destroyed" (Charpin 1980, 243, no. 58, lines 10–12). The aim of that last assertion was to eliminate the possibility that the adoption contract had been revoked, which would have found expression in a verbal repudiation and in the breaking of the tablet. The individual in question was obviously unable to bring in the tablet relating to his adoption by Sin-magir, no doubt because it was destroyed or lost. But he swore that the adoption was never invalidated: he gave his word as a substitute for the missing written text. About half a century later, however, there was a similar case in which an adoptee had lost his adoption tablet (Charpin 2000a, 74–76, no. 34). At that time, the municipality met and a procedure was set in place to reconstitute the lost document. This suggests that the possibility of simply resorting to an oath by the interested party or by the witnesses was no longer felt to provide sufficient guarantees.

In nineteenth-century Eshnunna, the practice of reconstituting a destroyed sales contract is attested: "A[n] . . . improved plot, its price (being) one third mina of silver, PN_2, wife of PN_3, had bought from PN; PN_4, the smith, had weighed the silver. The tablet was destroyed and PN_5, the *kakikkum*-official, renewed it" (*CAD* K, 43b–44a [Tell Asmar 1930, 542]). The *kakikkum* was responsible for overseeing the sales of urban lands (Charpin 1986a, 74–75, 138, 180). In this case he reconstituted the destroyed text; the beginning of the text was an exact reproduction of an ordinary sales contract. The situation in Eshnunna is rather special in that sixty sales contracts for houses or fields have been found at a single site in the palace, which suggests the existence of a sort of "title office" (Whiting 1977, 69).[20] The reconstitution of the destroyed tablet thus occurred within that framework and not at the request of the house's owner.

Also attesting to the growing authority of the written word was the universalization of deed transfers upon the deliverance of a property, whether in an exchange, an inheritance, or a sale. Those who received the property took the previous tablets relating to them at the same time (Charpin 2010, chap. 4). Consider the case of someone who purchased a house. He kept in his archives the document of purchase that had been handed over to him. Upon his death, the son who inherited the house received that tablet, and, if he sold the house, he transferred the previous purchase tablet to the buyer. The new owner thus had in his archives the two purchase deeds relating to the house. The aim of that practice was obviously to consolidate the rights of the new owner: in case of a lawsuit, the previous owner would be unable to make a claim based on his property deed, since he had had to surrender it. When the seller could not provide the buyer with the document(s) to the property transferred, a statement was drawn up stipulating that, should the tablets be found, they would belong by rights to the new buyer. "Because there is no purchase tablet or prior deed of property, if a purchase tablet or a prior deed of property is produced outside, it will belong to Beletum, the nun-*nadītum* of Shamash, daughter of Ipqusha" (Charpin 1994c, 80–81 [*BBVOT* 1 no. 111: 19–23]). That practice is also attested for the Neo-Babylonian period (Baker 2003, 248–249).

Many examples indicate the importance the Babylonians granted to written evidence. Hence, in a matter dealing with an aunt's inheritance, a nun-*nadītum* believed she had been wronged. She had received the property deeds from her aunt, but, as often happened, her archives were kept by her father. She therefore judged it wiser to await her father's arrival before undertaking a lawsuit: "My tablets are in the hands of my father: so long as my father does not come, I will not take legal action" (*AbB* 11 55). Such an example indicates the importance in the nun's mind of the written document for establishing her rights. The organization of the archives of Ur-Utu revealed during the excavation of his house can even be interpreted as being linked to the lawsuit that pitted him against his father's other heirs, which suggests that the texts were reread at that time (Tanret 2001).

Conclusion

The oral—who can be surprised?—came first: Mesopotamia was fundamentally a civilization based on giving one's spoken word. Writing was used only to document the agreements that had been concluded. But as time passed, it came to be recognized that not only did the written document serve to transmit information through space, it could also allow the spoken word to survive the person who had uttered it. That expansion of the use of writing also accounts for the proliferation of brief memorandums that have been found in the archives of merchants (Ulshöfer 1995), but that could also be penned by royal secretaries. Witness this brief note found in the Mari palace: "Regarding 4 minas of silver and 5 shekels of gold that must be taken to Tuttul for work on (the harp) Ningizibara: remind *(hussussum)* the king of it in Mari" (Joannès 1985, 111, no. 10; Ziegler 2007, 60). It is in this type of text that we best observe the function of writing as aide-mémoire.

chapter five

"Literary" Works and Libraries

A preoccupation with the sensational has sometimes stood in the way of a proper appreciation for archaeological discoveries. Just as the term "school" was often misused, so too that of "library" has not always been accurately employed. Let me therefore begin this chapter with a few definitions. The notion of "archive" and that of "library" are not always distinguished as they should be, even though they differ both in nature and in the objects they contain. Libraries are collections of works that have been categorized; archives are the accumulation of written traces left by the activities of a person, a collectivity, or an organization. Libraries manifest a desire for gathering together and organizing, which is not the case for archives.[1] Unfortunately, very few libraries and archives have been found in situ during modern excavations; the archaeological context of the vast majority of tablets currently in museums is therefore unknown. Hence the haziness of many assessments.

There has sometimes been an attempt to distinguish library tablets from archival documents by a material criterion, for example, whether or not they were baked. That is valid only for certain eras, such as the Middle Assyrian period, when library tablets were intentionally baked. Conversely, as J. Reade has indicated, the tablets of the famous "library of Ashurbanipal" were baked only when a fire destroyed Nineveh in 612 B.C. (1986, 219).[2] As a result, it is usually as a function of the content that the distinction is made: as soon as someone finds a group of tablets that are not archival documents, he designates them "literary texts" and a "library," not without some exaggeration. The library of Ashurbanipal, which I shall consider for its emblematic character, will provide me with an opportunity to dismiss a few preconceived ideas. I shall then analyze "private libraries": these are actually collections of manuscripts that were preserved by literati in their homes. I shall conclude with the libraries of temples, for which we have the good fortune to have available a recently excavated example.

A Preliminary: The Notion of "Work" and of "Author"

Generally Anonymous Works

As strange as it might seem, the names of the authors of most works of Mesopotamian literature are unknown—and will forever remain so (Foster 1991). The exceptions are rare, and in every case, they are a literary device. The author's name may be inserted into the work itself: such is the case for the hymn to Gula by Bullutsa-rabi and for the Epic of Erra. In the latter case, the scribe Kabti-ilani-Marduk claims he took down the poem with great care after a deity transmitted it to him in a dream. That was one way to portray divine inspiration in Mesopotamia, and it was not just valid for literature: dreams could also be premonitory. Acrostic poems are another example. If the first syllables of each line of the *Theodicy* are lined up, they spell out: "I, Saggil-kinam-ubbib, the incantation-priest, am adorant of the god and the king" (Lambert 1960, 63).

In a catalog from the library of Ashurbanipal, certain literary and scholarly works are associated with the name of a god or sage (Lambert 1957, 1962). Hence the corpus of the exorcists *(ašipūtu)* and that of the lamenters *(alūtu),* as well as many other texts, are attributed to the god Ea ("from the mouth of Ea"). Such a conception, which makes a god the author of a work, dates back at least to the third millennium: in the preamble to the *Hymn to the Temple of Kesh* (lines 1–12), it is said that the god Enlil chanted that hymn of praise for the temple and that the goddess Nisaba assembled its words like precious stones on a thread, by writing them on a tablet she held in her hand (Wilcke 2006). That hymn is purportedly not the work of human beings, then: it was the gods who created and transmitted it. This serves as a legitimation for a large portion of Sumerian literature: since the origin of time, setting hymns down in writing was the act of the gods. Some works are also attributed to legendary figures, such as Uanna-Adapa (Oannes). In all such cases, they were not really the authors: the texts were placed under the patronage of a god or of primordial sages, so as to emphasize their great age and indisputable authority. In certain incantations, the exorcist says explicitly: "The incantation is not mine, it is the incantation of the gods Ea and Asalluhi" (Lambert 1962, 73 [*KAR* 114 rev. 4]). Obviously, he hoped thereby to achieve greater efficacy.

Other works were associated with "historical" figures: "The Series of Gilgameš; by Sin-leqi-unninni the la[mentation priest]" (Lambert 1962, 66 [K.97117+: 10]; Beaulieu 2000, 3). Does that mean that Sin-leqi-unninni was the author of the Epic of Gilgamesh? The history of this text is actually very complex; Assyriologists have enough extant manuscripts from various eras to reconstitute it, which represents an obvious advantage over similar research on biblical writings or Homeric narratives (George 2003, 3–54; George 2007b). It is now believed that Sin-leqi-unninni was a scholar who lived in Uruk in the second half of the second millennium and who played an important role in establishing the recent version of the text. In our terminology, he worked more as an "editor" than as an "author."

Nevertheless, the notion of author cannot be eliminated altogether. Some texts have so much individuality in their language, style, and in the unity of their content that their attribution to a particular figure is beyond doubt. Such is the case for the Epic of Erra. A certain number of works allude to the conditions under which they came into being, evoking the circumstances of their creation, divine approbation, and the wish that the text will be transmitted to future generations. Other compositions are obviously the result of many transformations over the centuries, involving the intervention of several individuals. In that case, we may speak of multiple authors.

At a certain point, a choice was made among the different versions of a work: this is known as "canonization," a term that may give rise to misunderstandings (Rochberg-Halton 1984). There was in Mesopotamia no corpus of texts that received official recognition of any sort, nothing equivalent to the "sacred texts" that founded the Jewish, Christian, and Muslim religions. Assyriologists use the term "canonical" to designate the texts of the tradition that received a fixed form beginning in the mid-second millennium. The major collections were constituted into "series" *(iškarū)* divided into consecutively numbered tablets. Alongside them was "supplementary material" *(ahū),* which was complemented by the oral teachings of the masters, sometimes put down in writing with this comment: "According to the teaching [literally, 'the mouth'] of a master *(ša pī ummāni)."*

Defining the "Work"

The notion of a "work" was itself very different from what we understand by that term in the modern Western world. In the first place, there was no title: works were generally designated by their first words (known by the Latin term *incipit).* Hence the Epic of Gilgamesh was cited as *Ša nagba īmuru* ("He who saw the Abyss . . ."),[3] the *Babylonian Poem of the Creation,* as *Enūma eliš* ("When above . . ."), and so on. The Hebrew Bible adopted the same practice: *Bereshit* ("In the beginning . . .") is the name of the book that the Greek tradition designated as "Genesis." That practice has survived at the Vatican, where pontifical encyclicals, such as Paul VI's *Populorum progressio* of 1967 or Pius XI's *Mit brennender Sorge* thirty years earlier, are designated by their incipits. The incipit is one of the elements found in colophons (Hunger

FIGURE 36. Literary tablet with "firing holes." The lower half is occupied by the colophon, with widely spaced lines; it indicates that this tablet was copied for the palace of Ashurbanipal. (©The Trustees of the British Museum.)

1968). These short texts placed at the end of the tablets make it possible to identify the work, and they became much more widespread in the first millennium (Figure 36).

When the work occupied more than one tablet, the first line of the following tablet was indicated on the colophon, as well as its number in the series, the series "title," and the number of lines. Often the scribe specified the source from which he had made his copy of the text and gave the name of his patron along with his own name. Sometimes he mentioned the aim of his work: "to be read," "to learn from," "for his own instruction." Occasionally there are even anecdotal notations, such as this colophon by Nabu-zuqup-kena, which indicates that he wrote his tablet "quickly in order to read (it)." The colophon often ends with blessings and curses. When it includes the name of the scribe, that of his father and that of his ancestor, these provide valuable information for reconstituting the families of scribes.

Overview of "Library Texts"

Library works are often defined in negative terms, as texts that are neither archival documents nor commemorative inscriptions. That is obviously an unsatisfactory way of proceeding. But it must be admitted that finding the criteria that would allow one to define works often described as "literary and religious" is not easy. The reason is simple: the approach of the ancients was obviously not the same as our own, so that applying the various categories of Western scholarship to literary genres cannot be considered adequate (George 2007a).

"Reference works" were composed of two major categories: compilations and lists. The corpus for experts consisted of large compilations, invariably made up of a succession of paragraphs that are identical in structure. The first clause sets out a condition (called a "protasis"), the second its consequence ("apodosis"). In a compendium of omens taken from observations of abnormal births (teratology), we find: "If an anomaly *(izbu)* has two heads, (and) the second one is on its tail and it has four ears—there will be dissension in the land" (Leichty 1970, 105 [tablet 8:43']). A medical compendium similarly notes: "If he is ill one day and constantly places his hands on his belly, cries out in complaint, then constantly stretches out his hands: he will die" (Heeßel 2000, 172, 181 [*Sakikku* tablet 16:2]). They therefore consist of enumerations of particular situations, never formulations of general rules. That casuistic presentation holds in every field: "codes" of laws were composed on the same pattern. These anthologies can be grouped into a few major categories. The largest is the compilations of omens, with each divinatory technique having its own "manual(s)" (Bottéro 1974; Bottéro 1987, 157–169; Maul 2003a). The diviner who specialized in hepatoscopy referred to the *bārûtu* series, which described liver anomalies (Koch 2005), the astrologist to the *Enūma Anu Enlil* series (Reiner 2005), and so on. There were compilations devoted to dreams (Butler 1998; Bottéro 1987, 133–156), to abnormal births (Bottéro 1985, 1–28), and to medical symptoms (Geller 2005).[4] The major compendium *Šumma ālu* was dedicated to all auspicious omens and occasionally provides interesting insights into everyday life (Freedman 1998, 2006a). Physiognomy sought to predict the future of an individual based on his physical characteristics (Böck 2000). These compendia constitute the vast majority of "scholarly" texts that have been preserved. Modern anthologies generally do not include them: the texts are so monotonous that reading them usually brings on boredom. They were in fact not made to be read but to be consulted; future specialists copied them as a form of training in their discipline.

Another considerable portion of the literature consists of the conjurations of the exorcist *(āšipu),* who was charged with casting out the evil that afflicted his patients. Major rituals such as *Šurpu* or *Maqlū* take us into the world of magic and witchcraft (Abusch 2002a). *Namburbi* were used to ward off the threat predicted by an omen (Maul 1994b, 1999); hemerologies provided lists of auspicious and inauspicious days for one activity or another (Livingstone 1999).

"Lamenters" *(kalū)* were responsible for performing liturgical chants, often accompanied by musical instruments (Ziegler 2006). They inherited a corpus of texts in the Sumerian language, some of which were translated into Akkadian. This shows that these texts were still understood in the first millennium (M. E. Cohen 1988; Borger 1990). The nomenclature for hymns and prayers is very rich but often difficult to decipher (Seux 1976).

Mesopotamian scholars were very attuned to linguistic problems and developed philological practices unparalleled in antiquity. Lexical lists therefore constitute a large portion of library texts (Civil 1975). Bilingualism in Sumerian and Akkadian was not divorced from that phenomenon, of course, which did not exist in Egypt. In terms of our modern categories, Sumerian and Akkadian are totally unrelated languages, but that was not the ancients' sense of things. On the contrary: they believed there was a "harmonious relationship" between the two languages, at least according to the most recent interpretation of the controversial expression *lišān mithurti* (Klein 2000). A good share of commentaries elaborated in the first millennium is based on plays on the various meanings of cuneiform signs: the syllables of an Akkadian word could be read as so many Sumerian ideograms, thereby yielding a different sense (Finkel 2006; Freedman 2006b; Pearce 1998; Frahm, forthcoming).

Hence one scholar seeking to enter into Ashurbanipal's service claimed the ability to interpret omens. To demonstrate his skill, he cited an astrological omen and produced this explanation for it: "If Jupiter stands in Pisces: the Tigris and the Euphrates will be filled by silt. IDIM (means) 'silt,' (but) IDIM (also means) 'Spring,' SA$_5$ (means) 'to be full': (therefore) there will be prosperity and abundance in the land" (*SAA* 10 160: 14–16). On a first reading, the two great rivers filling with silt ought to have been considered an inauspicious omen. But the Akkadian word for "silt" that appears in the omen is *sakīku,* which can also be written with the Sumerian ideogram IDIM; and IDIM can also be read as *nagbu,* which means "spring." The author of the letter concludes that, despite appearances, the omen is actually favorable. The art of interpreting omens could thus coincide perfectly with the desire to please the ruler by reassuring him of the success of his reign.

When all is said and done, our notion of "literature" is a very restricted category (Foster 2007). Our only moderate interest in proverbs and admonitions must not conceal the fact that the most important category in the eyes of the ancients was surely made up of compendia of wisdom. We tend to take more interest in epics such as that of Gilgamesh, in mythological texts, or in folk tales. The problem lies in the conditions under which that literature was elaborated: the nature of our sources tells us more about the reception of the works than about the context of their creation. As A. R. George has rightly pointed out, apart from *Enūma eliš,* which was recited on two occasions during the cultic year in Babylon, "the realm of pedagogy is the only one proven context of the written literature"; George adds that in most cases that was obviously a secondary context (2007a, 41).

The Library of Ashurbanipal in Niniveh

The rediscovery, beginning in 1850, of the library of Ashurbanipal in Kouyunjik, one of the sites of ancient Niniveh (Figure 37), is held by many to mark the true birth of Assyriology (Larsen 1996). And it is true that the abundance of texts (more than 30,000 tablets and fragments inventoried) and their quality have made it possible to considerably broaden the corpus that was available before that time. Of that total, only a fifth is made up of archival documents (letters, administrative or legal texts, and so on), while the rest is constituted of "literary" texts.

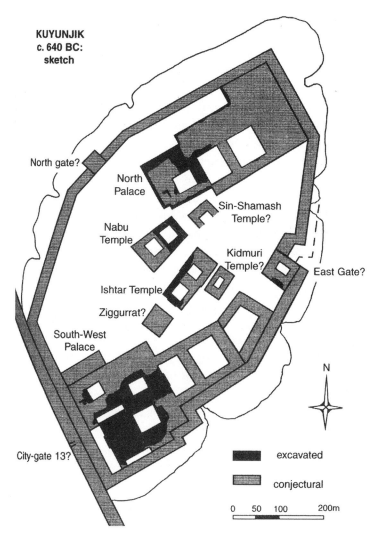

KUYUNJIK
c. 640 BC:
sketch

North gate?

North Palace

Nabu Temple

Sin-Shamash Temple?

Kidmuri Temple?

East Gate?

Ishtar Temple

Ziggurrat?

South-West Palace

N

City-gate 13?

excavated

conjectural

0   50   100   200m

FIGURE 37. Plan of the acropolis of Niniveh. The tablets of the "library" come primarily from the southwest palace and the north palace. (From J. Reade, "Ninive," in *Reallexikon der Assyriologie und Vorderasiatischen Archäologie*, vol. 9 [Berlin, 2000], 391.)

History of a Discovery

Nineteenth-century excavators were more concerned with the quantity of tablets reaped for the British Museum than with the details of their exact provenance; hence the information we possess about the original location of the tablets is meager. Some facts are certain, however (Walker 1987b; Reade 1998–2001). In the first place, perseverance proves to be an essential quality in archaeology: the first excavator of Niniveh was P. E. Botta in 1842, but since he did not find very much there, he moved on to Khorsabad, where he met with his celebrated success. But had he continued his initial work, the Louvre would have been the beneficiary of discoveries that are today the glory of the British Museum. The first group of tablets was discovered by Austen Henry Layard in May 1850 in rooms 40 and 41 and in corridor 49 of the southwest palace, which had been founded by Sennacherib but reoccupied by Ashurbanipal. That lot arrived in London in 1851. In 1853 Hormuzd Rassan discovered another group of tablets in the north palace of Ashurbanipal; it went to the British Museum in 1854. Unfortunately, these some 20,000 tablets and fragments were catalogued under less than optimal conditions, as a result of which the two lots obviously got mixed together. In both cases, it appears that archival documents as well as library texts were found at the site. It is generally believed that that situation resulted from the pillaging of Niniveh by the Medes, when they took and destroyed the city in 612. It has recently been proposed, however, that the confusion actually occurred when the tablets fell from rooms located upstairs in the southwest palace (Battini 1996).

A new phase occurred twenty years later, following the extraordinary discovery, by an assistant at the British Museum named George Smith, of a Babylonian account of the Flood. In taking inventory, Smith had set aside a series of tablet fragments with a mythological content. He was particularly interested in one of them:

On looking down the third column, my eye caught the statement that the ship rested on the mountains of Nizir, followed by the account of the sending forth of the dove, and its finding no resting-place and returning. I saw at once that I had here discovered a portion at least of the Chaldean (Babylonian) account of the Deluge. I then proceeded to read through the document, and found it was in the form of a speech from the hero of the Deluge to a person whose name appeared to be Izdubar *(now read "Gilgamesh")*. I recollected a legend belonging to the same hero Izdubar K. 231, which, on comparison, proved to belong to the same series, and then I commenced a search for any missing portions of the tablets. *(G. Smith describes the difficulties of the task.)* My search, however, proved successful. I found a fragment of another copy of the Deluge, containing again the sending forth of the birds, and gradually collected several other portions of this tablet, fitting them in one after another until I had completed the greater part of the second column. Portions of a third copy next turned up, which, when joined together, completed a considerable part of the first and sixth columns. I now had the account of the Deluge in the state in which I published it at the meeting of the Society of Biblical Archaeology, December 3rd, 1872. (*G. Smith then recounts the intervention of the owners of the* Daily Telegraph, *which allowed him to reopen the Kouyunjik excavation.*) Soon after I commenced excavating at Kouyunjik, on the site of the palace of Assurbanipal, I found a new fragment of the Chaldean account of the Deluge belonging to the first column of the tablet, relating the command to build and fill the ark, and nearly filling up the most considerable blank in the story.

(Smith 1876, 4–7)

At the time of his first undertaking in Kouyunjik, Smith found only 300 fragments, but the *Daily Telegraph* believed he had completed his mission. The British Museum allowed Smith to return in

1874, where 2,300 additional tablets were exhumed. Smith died in 1876, during a third mission. His work was taken up by Rassam in 1878–1880, and 3,000 more fragments were discovered at that time. During all those years, many tablets from Babylonia were also arriving in London, so that the work on the Kouyunjik texts advanced very little. It was only in 1887 that Carl Bezold began systematically to conduct an inventory; between 1889 and 1899, he published a five-volume catalog, a masterpiece that remains of great utility (Bezold 1889–1899). At the time, it comprised 14,230 "K" entries, plus other smaller collections.

In 1903 Leonard W. King and Reginald Campbell Thompson were sent to Niniveh, from whence they brought back another 850 tablets, which were inventoried in a first supplement to Bezold's *Catalogue,* along with fragments that Bezold had omitted (King 1914).

Campbell Thompson returned to Niniveh in 1927–1932, hoping to unearth the library of the temple of Nabu, whose existence appeared to be confirmed by many colophons of tablets already discovered. He found the foundations of that building, but extracted only three tablets explicitly described as having been part of the collection of the temple of Nabu. The rest of the 1,200 texts or fragments that he brought back to London came from various locations. An inventory of them was published only in 1968 (Lambert and Millard 1968). The unexpected discovery, in a cupboard of the British Museum, of nearly 5,000 fragments was the object of the third and last supplement to Bezold's *Catalogue* (Lambert 1992). In 1997 the highest numbered item was K.22247; the total for the other collections rose to 9,102 (Reade 1998–2001, 421). The British Museum is in the process of making photographs available online of all these tablets and fragments.

That set of fragments, then, was in an extreme state of disorder, attributable both to the original conditions of their preservation and to the circumstances of their discovery.

The Library as Seen through the Colophons of Ashurbanipal

To learn more, we must turn to the texts themselves. Descriptions of that "library" are found primarily in the colophons of tablets discovered in Kouyunjik (Hunger 1968; Lieberman 1990, 317–320). There are more than twenty different types of these colophons. The briefest is simply a property mark, sometimes stamped on the tablets with a matrix: "Palace of Ashurbanipal, king of the universe, king of Assyria" (Hunger 1968, 97, no. 317 [Asb. Typ a]). Others enumerate the sovereign's epithets and genealogy and insist on the king's devotion to Nabu, god of writing: "Palace of Ashurbanipal, king of Assyria, son of Esarhaddon, king of the universe, king of Assyria, governor of Babylon, king of the land of Sumer and Akkad, king of the kings of Kush and Muṣur (Nubia and Egypt), king of the four shores of the earth, son of Sennacherib, king of the universe, king of Assyria—who trusts in Assur and Mulissu, Nabu and Tashmetu. Whoever trusts in you will know no shame, O Nabu!" (Hunger 1968, 100, no. 322 [Asb. Typ h]). Some colophons point out the role the king played in constituting his library: "Palace of Ashurbanipal, great king, powerful king, king of the universe, king of Assyria, whose eyes rival those of Marduk, the king of gods, to whom Nabu and Tashmetu have shown compassion and whom they raised like a father and a mother. He wrote (this tablet), collated it, and placed it inside his palace to refer to it and to read it. Whoever trusts in you will know no shame, O Nabu!" (Hunger 1968, 100, no. 323 [Asb. Typ i–k]).

Colophons of this type begin by indicating that the tablets belong to the "palace of Ashurbanipal" and may specify that the king placed them inside his palace for his own reading. Ashurbanipal specifies "for my royal reading" *(ana tāmarti šarrūtiya),* "to read (it) (and) have (it) read to me" *(ana tāmarti šitassiya),* "so that I may examine (it)" *(ana tamrirtiya),* or, in the third person, "to refer to it (upon) his reading" *(ana tahsisti šitassišu).* The conclusion is therefore clear: this was the *private* library of Ashurbanipal, who, to be sure, did not forget he was king of Assyria but who presented himself as an erudite scholar of his time like any other. Nowhere is a "library" *(girginakku)* of the royal palace precisely in question: that term is used only for the tablets placed in the temple of Nabu.

The Aim: To Control the Views of His Entourage and Protect the King

According to A. L. Oppenheim's definition, that library was primarily intended to provide exorcists, diviners, and medical doctors of the royal entourage with the means to perform their duties, that is, to see that no evil would strike the royal person. The knowledge that was to be gathered together was thus for the most part of a religious nature.

That orientation is perceptible in the very composition of the library (Oppenheim 1964, 15–23). In reality, attempts to estimate its size are complicated by several factors. In the first place, it is necessary to assess how much was found compared to what existed in antiquity. Luckily, the scribes of "literary" texts did not yet use papyrus or parchment as a support at that time, so there is no loss to regret on that account, unlike contemporary archives of documents. Conversely, we know that many texts were preserved on wood or ivory writing boards covered with wax, which have of course disappeared (Figure 38). The mutilated state in which the clay tablets were found is also unfortunate; many were broken into numerous fragments (up to sixty or so in some cases). That mass of fragments is constantly being pieced back together: 5,351 joins have been made thus far, but the work is still far from complete. A few trends can be identified, however: about a quarter of the tablets belonged to the realm of divination with its different "series" (astrology, auspicious omens, teratology, and so on); 20 percent bore rituals, incantations, and prayers; 20 percent were

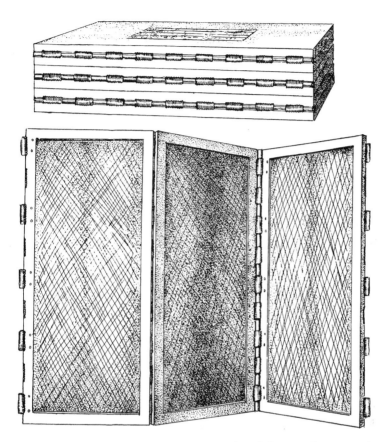

FIGURE 38. Drawing reconstituting a writing board discovered in Nimrud (Kalhu). Remarkably, intact elements of this polyptych in ivory were recovered from a well, where the moisture preserved the polyptych. Engraved on the outside of the first panel: "Palace of Sargon." The text that was inscribed in the wax belongs to the astrological series *Enūma Anu Enlil*. (Courtesy of the British Institute for the Study of Iraq [BISI].)

devoted to lexicography. The texts that have made for the fame of that library, such as the Epic of Gilgamesh with its account of the Flood, represented in all only about forty tablets. In fact, even the texts we consider "literary works" sometimes had a practical aim:

hence excerpts from the myth of Erra were sometimes inscribed on amulets intended to protect their bearers from the plague (Reiner 1960).[5]

It is clear that the king had no encyclopedic aspirations, as is indicated by a few letters that tell us how that library was constituted. One scribe wrote: "Let me read the tablets in the presence of the king, my lord, and let me put down on them whatever is agreeable to the king; whatever is not acceptable to the king, I shall remove from them. The tablets I am speaking about are worth preserving until far-off days" (*ABL* 334 [*SAA* 10 373]: 4–13; Frame and George 2005, 278–279). It is clear that a choice is being made, but the criteria for such a selection are not made explicit. The sovereign, however, wrote his own instructions to an official living in the Babylonian city of Borsippa:

> The command of the king to Šadunu: I am well, you should be happy. The day you read this tablet, take in your company Šumay son of Šum-ukin, his brother Bel-eṭir, Aplay son of Arkat-ili, and the scholars of Borsippa whom you know, and collect whatever tablets are in their houses and whatever tablets are kept in Ezida. Search out for me: amulet tablets for the king . . . , sets of four stone amulets for the head of the king's bed and the foot of the king's (bed), (the ritual) Wand of *e'ru*-wood, for the head of the king's bed, the incantation "Let Ea and Asalluhi use wisdom in full for me!" . . . and any texts that might be needed in the palace, as many as they are, also rare tablets that are known to you but do not exist in Assyria, and send them to me. Now, I have written to the temple-steward and the governor: in the houses where you set to work nobody will withhold tablets from you (sing.). And if, furthermore, you (pl.) come across any tablet or ritual which myself have not mentioned to you (pl.) and it is beneficial to my governance, take it too and send it to me.
>
> (*CT* 22 1; Frame and George 2005, 280–281)[6]

Remarkably, we have the reply that the scholars of Borsippa made to that request of the king (or to another similar one):

Further: The dutiful Borsippans will send back to the king their lord the instruction that he wrote as follows, "Write out all the scribal learning in the property of Nabu and send it to me. Complete the instructions!" Maybe the king says to himself, we *(are ones)* who, like the citizens of Babylon, will shirk (it) by (using) confusing language. Now, we shall not shirk the king's command. We shall strain and toil day and night to complete the instruction for our lord the king. We shall write on boards of sissoo-wood, we shall respond *immediately.* And regarding the board in Sumerian, the glossary about which you sent word, there is none but that in Esagil. Let enquiries now be made before our lord the king. [You should] send word to the citizens of Babylon.

(Frame and George 2005, 267–269 [BM 45642: 8–14])

It is not known whether the scholars of Borsippa were feigning to misunderstand the orders received: in their response, they speak of sending copies of the texts, not the originals, as the letter from the king commands. In addition, the text reveals a sort of rivalry between the scholars of Borsippa and their colleagues from Babylon. Another text, a copy of a letter sent by Ashurbanipal at the start of his reign, shows that at the time, he had asked the scholars of Babylon to copy many texts on his behalf. He also indicates that he sent a very large sum of money for that purpose (Frame and George 2005, 272–275 [BM 28825]).

The Catalogs

Catalogs are one of the features of a library properly speaking. In the case of Niniveh, we at least know of "acquisition records," to use a modern term. They confirm the information from the letter cited above: the king quite simply decided to gather together in his capital tablets taken from libraries that already existed in the residences of scholars in his kingdom (Parpola 1983; Fales and Postgate 1992, nos. 49–56).

These three catalogs inventory a total of about 2,000 tablets and 300 writing boards *(lē'u)*. They confirm the incidental place occupied by "belles lettres" (myths, epics, and so on), since only ten tablets belong to that genre. The texts most widely represented belong to the areas of exorcism, astrology, teratology, divination by auspicious omens, medicine, oneiromancy, and hepatoscopy. It seems that most of the tablets thus enumerated were from Babylonia. And in fact, the library of Niniveh held many tablets whose Babylonian origin can be immediately detected based on the difference existing at the time between Babylonian and Assyrian cuneiform writing (Fincke 2003–2004).

These tablets were catalogued in twenty-three sections, each representing the tablets and writing boards from the library of one scholar: between 2 and 435 depending on the case. It is clear that it was not the entire libraries of these literati that were taken from them: the scholars could continue their activities. But since the majority of those cited were Babylonians and the date of the catalog was 647 B.C., the situation is clear: this was war booty in the wake of Ashurbanipal's victory over the rebel Babylonians. Nevertheless, tablets from Assyrian libraries, such as those that the scribe Nabu-zuqup-kena had copied in Kalhu between 716 and 683, also became part of the royal library. The king's son Adad-shum-uṣur "gave" his father, more or less voluntarily, a portion of these tablets, while the rest remained in Kalhu, where they were found during the excavations of the site.

Copying New Manuscripts

Ashurbanipal was not content merely to concentrate all these tablets in his capital: he also set up a vast copying operation. Witness the colophons of certain tablets, which show they were copied for the royal library:

> Palace of Ashurbanipal, king of the universe, king of Assyria, to whom the gods Nabu and Tashmetu have given vast understanding (literally, "broad ears"), who possesses a clear eye. That which is essential in the art of the scribe, a task that none of the kings who preceded me learned, remedies concerning the body from the forehead to the nails, supplements to the series, precious teaching, medicine of the gods Ninurta and Gula, everything that exists—I have written it on tablets, verified and collated; to read them and to have them read to me, I have installed them inside my palace.
>
> (Hunger 1968, 103, no. 329 [Asb. Typ q])

Given the obligatory rhetoric of the time, it is to be understood that the king *had* these tablets copied. (If we are to believe the royal inscriptions, it was the sovereign in person who dug the canals through the mountains to feed water into Nineveh, and so on.)

In addition, there was not among Mesopotamian scribes any sentiment comparable to modern "bibliophilia": when they discovered an interesting ancient tablet, they recopied its content but were little concerned with the original. So it was that Asharedu wrote to Ashurbanipal: "The tablet used by the king is damaged and incomplete. Now I have written down and brought back from Babylon an ancient tablet used by King Hammurabi and an inscription prior to King Hammurabi" (*SAA* 10 155: 5–13). What counts is the text, not the support: Asharedu brought back to Niniveh not the "ancient tablet" but the transcription he made of it on site. In another letter, Akkulanu reports that he wrote tablets on the basis of Babylonian and Assyrian texts on writing boards (*SAA* 10 101: 7–10). It is remarkable that the scribes to whom Ashurbanipal entrusted the constitution of his library were not content to recopy the originals exactly as they were when the scribes received them. Their work as *editors* is particularly evident in the omen texts. It was only at that time that the "divination" *(bārûtu)* series was constituted as such; supplementary omens were added to them, in which the king is presented as just and glorious (Jeyes 1997).

The Tablets of the Temple of Nabu

Some colophons show that, in addition to the palace library, there was another library located in the temple of Nabu:

> I wrote on tablets, verified and collated the wisdom of Ea, the science of the exorcist, the secret of the sages, which is perfectly suited to appease the hearts of the great gods, based on exemplars from Assyria and Babylonia, and I placed them in the library *(girginakku)* of Ezida, temple of the god Nabu, my lord, in Niniveh. O Nabu, king of the whole heaven and earth, look favorably therefore on this library and give your blessing every day to Ashurbanipal, your servant who reveres your divinity, so that I may ceaselessly praise your divinity.
>
> (Hunger 1968, 102, no. 329 [Ash. Typ o])

Hence that library ultimately functioned at two levels. Concretely, it provided the scholars in the royal entourage with the reference tools needed to accomplish their task with maximum efficiency. But symbolically, it constituted a votive offering to the god Nabu, who in return would ensure religious protection for the sovereign.

Ashurbanipal was not a precursor to the "enlightened rulers" from the Age of Enlightenment, and the library he constituted in his capital was not the result of a desire for encyclopedic knowledge. No doubt that king boasted in several of his inscriptions of being a fine scholar; it is also certain that he received an advanced education before being designated crown prince, and that subsequently he always took an interest in every aspect of the "art of the scribe." But his assertion had a symbolic value as well: no domain was alien to the king, not even that of writing. The sovereign was an accomplished scribe as well as an expert warrior, as he says in an inscription that recalls the training he received when he was chosen by his father as heir to the crown of Assyria: "Amid joy and gladness, I entered the House of the Administration *(bīt redūti),* a place built with skill, bond of the kingdom, where Sennacherib, father of the father who sired me, exercised power as crown prince, then as king; where Esarhaddon, my own father, was born, grew up, and exercised power over Assyria . . . ; and where I myself, Ashurbanipal, learned the wisdom of Nabu, the art of the scribe in its totality; I followed the teachings of all the masters, as many as there are. I learned to draw a bow, to ride horseback, to drive a chariot, and to hold the reins" (Prism A [i 23–34]; Borger 1996, 16, 208–209 [Prism A § 3]). Ashurbanipal is therefore not a "patron of arts and letters" who decided to found a center uniting the total knowledge of the age in Niniveh. Rather, he wanted to have at his disposal a reference tool that would allow him to verify personally what the diviners and other scholars in his service wrote to him. That interest by a sovereign in divination was not new: even in the early second millennium, kings such as Samsi-Addu and his son Ishme-Dagan discussed the interpretation of omens.[7] But with Ashurbanipal, that interest reached an unparalleled level, as he himself liked to point out.

The Precursors

Ashurbanipal was not the first Neo-Assyrian king who sought to constitute a library. A writing board has been found in Kalhu containing the text of an astrological omen, whose ivory frame bears the inscription: "Palace of Sargon" (Figure 38). That suggests that a "library" already existed in the palace of the Assyrian capital of that time. Letters from the age of Esarhaddon also indicate that that king gathered together manuscripts (Reade 1998–2001, 423b).

The examples of royal libraries prior to the first millennium that are usually cited are either poorly documented or erroneous. Some mention a library supposedly founded by Shulgi, king of Ur. The idea is particularly appealing in that Shulgi was the first of the Mesopotamian sovereigns to claim to be literate: Ashurbanipal thus supposedly imitated him in both respects. That library *(gìr.gin.na),* it is believed, was primarily the place where the tablets of hymns were deposited for the use of musicians (George 2005, 133). But a different translation of the term *gìr.gin.na* has recently been proposed, and it rules out any allusion to a library founded by Shulgi (Richardson 2006).

We must therefore look outside Mesopotamia to find the first royal library whose existence cannot be called into question. In the heart of Anatolia, the capital of Hattusha, the Hittite kings had both royal archives and a library (Pedersén 1998, 44–55). The library was obviously constituted primarily for religious reasons: rituals held a preponderant place there. The existence of a royal library in Assyria, predating that of Ashurbanipal by several centuries, was postulated by Ernst F. Weidner in 1953; the reality of that "library of Tiglath-pileser I (1114–1076)" is currently in doubt. About 160 tablets have been identified as belonging to that hypothetical collection; many were written by the children of a royal scribe, others by various specialists (diviners, exorcists, and so on), and it is possible that this was actually the manuscript collection of a family (Maul 2003b).

Manuscript Collections in the Houses of Scholars

Is it possible to speak of "private libraries" in Mesopotamia? If we limit ourselves to the definition given above, it must be admitted that nowhere is there any "collection of categorized works." Twenty years ago, I proposed introducing into studies on Mesopotamia the more accurate notion of *manuscript collections,* which a medievalist defines as "very similar to that of an archival collection: a manuscript collection is the set of hand-written books or documents concerning the intellectual history—understood in the broadest sense—of the collectivity, the family, or the individual who copied them, had them copied, received them in tribute, or gathered them together" (Ouy 1961, 1091). In a sense, the "library" of Ashurbanipal fits that definition, and the fact that the manuscripts seem to have been mixed in with archival documents might confirm such a conclusion. In any case, that is the situation for almost all the "private libraries" discovered thus far.

The Old Babylonian Period

I shall not revisit here the case of Ur in the Old Babylonian period: the houses inhabited by members of the temple staff of Nanna/Sin have yielded both their archives and their manuscript collections, dating from the eighteenth century (Charpin 1986a). The same is true for Nippur. Other exceptional discoveries have been made (Figure 39). One of the most interesting occurred recently along the Diyala in Tell Hadad, the ancient Me-Turan (Cavigneaux 1999b). Whereas "literary" texts were discovered in many places at the site, magical texts were found exclusively in a zone designated "Area II," which seems to have been a private house. An exorcist may have resided there, but he cannot be identified until an in-depth analysis has been conducted of the many archival documents discovered in the house. For the moment, questions remain: "During Old Babylonian times magical texts were relatively rare at southern sites,

FIGURE 39. Discovery in the house of the chief lamenter of Isin of a jar containing a tablet of love incantations (Old Babylonian period). (Hirmer Verlag, Munich.)

but here, at Meturan, we find them in the same house with the 'belles-lettres.' Is it possible that the Meturan collection was the first attested professional reference library?" (Michalowski 2003). It is not yet possible to reply, but let us note the almost exclusive presence of texts in Sumerian, which says a great deal about the influence of "classical" culture far from the Sumer region.

Libraries from the Second Half of the Second Millennium

Babylonia has yielded almost nothing in the way of libraries dating from the second half of the second millennium. That fact, obviously attributable to the randomness of finds, is particularly worthy of mention in that scholars seem to have been very active at the time: many series began to be constituted during that era.

Paradoxically, examples of libraries are found much more often in the west, in Syria. There are several in Ugarit, such as those of Rap'anu and Urtenu (Arnaud 2007). And among the discoveries made between 1972 and 1976 on the Euphrates in Emar (Arnaud 1980 and 1987a; Dietrich 1990), building M_1 yielded many "library" texts (Fleming 2000, 13–47). The nature of the building in which these tablets were discovered is in dispute; the excavator called it a "temple of the diviner," which is a concept totally alien to both Syrian and properly Mesopotamian realities. It has been noted that, from a strictly architectural point of view, this was simply a house. Both the archives of a family of diviners and a manuscript collection linked to their activities have been found there (d'Alfonso et al. 2008).

Libraries from the First Millennium

In the mid-ninth century, when King Assurnazirpal II transferred his capital to Kalhu (Nimrud), Assur lost its political role, but it remained an important religious metropolis until its destruction by the Medes in 614. The house of a family of exorcists who lived in the seventh century has been found; it held a large manuscript collection belonging to Kiṣir-Assur, to his son, and to one of his nephews. In all, nearly 1,200 tablets and fragments were uncovered, during old excavations but also in the 1990s (Maul 2003c). These are primarily rituals, incantations, and medical compendia: in other words, texts with a direct relation to the profession of their owners. But there were also prayers as well as historical, literary, lexical, and other types of texts. In addition, the library of Qurdi-Nergal was discovered by an Anglo-Turkish team in 1951 in Sultantepe, the ancient Huṣirina.[8] Babylonia has also yielded manuscript collections in the residences of scholars: note the case of Ninurta-ahhe-bulliṭ in Nippur from the Achaemenid period (Joannès 1992), and that of exorcists and lamenters in Uruk in the Seleucid period (Hunger 1976; von Weiher 1983–1998). The most recent case is that of families of lamenters living in Babylon between 137 and 86 B.C., in whose houses hymns and lamentations composed in the Sumerian dialect of *emesal* were preserved (Maul 2005). Some colophons indicate that they were copied "to be chanted" *(ana zamāri):* these tablets therefore served a practical purpose.

Nevertheless, these manuscript collections are in large part made up of copies made by their owners during their apprenticeships. When their specialization can be identified, it is evident that they copied texts directly connected to their art but also many others: let us not forget that, for the ancients, all these disciplines formed a single one, that of "wisdom," the domain of the gods Ea and Nabu (Parpola 1993b). Subsequently, they may have been led to consult only a portion of the tablets they kept at home. That is why Ashurbanipal had no difficulty confiscating part of the manuscript collections of Babylonian scholars: only the tablets corresponding to disciplines not directly within their area of competence were taken from them (Parpola 1983, 9).

The Libraries of Temples

Many difficulties arise when attempting to evaluate the role temples played in the elaboration and preservation of the written tradition in Mesopotamia. The chief one is that there are only a few rare cases in which tablets were found in their original context. And these cases indicate that, most often, tablets did not have a specific colophon indicating they belonged to the library of one temple or another. As a result, it is not possible to attribute with certainty the tablets found out of context to a particular place.

The Pseudo-Libraries of Temples in the Second Millennium

Here and there it has been claimed that temple libraries existed in Babylonia in the Old Babylonian period, especially in Nippur or

Shaduppum. All the cases cited thus far are based on errors in interpretation. The most famous example in the annals of Assyriology concerns the excavations of Nippur. H. V. Hilprecht claimed he had discovered the library of the temple of Enlil from the early second millennium (Hilprecht 1910). The importance of the discoveries he made accounts for the enthusiasm perceptible in his writings. But subsequent research has shown that the part of the site that was so rich that, from the start of its exploration, it was designated "Tablet Hill," was actually occupied by a residential neighborhood. The many "literary" tablets were simply exercises by apprentice scribes found in the dwellings of the clergy members who, under Samsu-iluna, offered training in their homes (Robson 2001). The consequences of that state of affairs are great: it is clear that there was never any desire to "save Sumerian literature from oblivion." That literature was *essentially* oral in nature (Civil 1999–2000). In addition, the entire corpus of Sumerian literature is known only through school copies: we have yet to find any manuscript of a quality high enough to be considered a "master's model." The modern editions of Sumerian texts cannot therefore establish stemmata as has been done for copies of works from Greco-Roman antiquity. The examples we possess are not generally copies of other manuscripts, but notations of works learned by heart, written directly by the student or dictated by the master. The situation changed subsequently.

The claim is often made that there was a sort of library in Shaduppum, in the temple of Nisaba and Haya.[9] In fact, however, the building in which some of these tablets were found was the main temple of the city, devoted to its poliad deity, named Belgasher (Charpin 1986a, 354–355).

The Temples of Nabu: Libraries or Votive Deposits?

Sumerian scribes had a tutelary deity, the goddess Nisaba, described as the one who bestowed wisdom and attributed a beautiful "hand" to the scribe. It fairly often happened that an apprentice, having finished copying the text that his master had assigned him as an exercise, added at the end a short doxology: ᵈnisaba zà.mí, "praise to Nisaba." Sometimes these doxologies associated the god Haya with his consort. It was only in the second half of the Old Babylonian period that, in certain families of scribes, devotion arose for the god Nabu, son of Marduk and god of Borsippa, who subsequently became the patron god of scribes (Charpin 1990b). In the salutation of a letter to a scribe appears this formula: "To Nabiummalik, the gentleman whose calamus is guided by the gods Marduk and Nabu" (*AbB* 3 33: 1–4). From the Kassite period on, the god Nabu was represented in the form of a stylus, the attribute of his function. Apprentice scribes adopted the habit of dedicating tablets to him, just as their predecessors had done for Nisaba and Haya (Figure 40).[10]

The Temple of Nabu in Kalhu (Nimrud). The excavations of the temple of Nabu in Kalhu (Nimrud) took place between 1955 and 1957, then again in 1985–1986. Facing the "cellas" of Nabu and Tashmetu, on the other side of the courtyard, was a row of rooms (TN11, TN12, and TN13): it is there that many "literary" tablets were found. It seems that the library was originally located in TN12, a room measuring about 26 × 13 feet (8 × 4 m), exactly opposite the entrance to the cella of Nabu. It was undoubtedly created when Adad-nirari III renovated the Ezida temple in Kalhu in about 800. It was destroyed a first time during the sack of Kalhu, between 616 and 612. Unfortunately, pits were dug at the site during the Achaemenid period: what was then still a fine Neo-Assyrian library buried under the debris of the building that had housed it became a heap of fragments, more or less gravely damaged. These were found primarily in room TN12 but also in the surrounding area. As a result, we have no sense of the way the tablets were originally preserved. That situation is the reverse of the one existing at the temple of Nabu in Dur-Sharrukin (Khorsabad): there, in two

FIGURE 40. Neo-Babylonian copy of an inscription of Hammurabi. The colophon (on the back) indicates that the copy was made in Babylon by the scribe Rimut-Gula from an original found in the Enamtila temple. He dedicated his copy to the god Nabu and placed it in the Ezida of Borsippa, where Rassam discovered it in the nineteenth century. (©The Trustees of the British Museum.)

rooms, niches in which tablets had been kept were unearthed, but the niches were unfortunately empty (Loud and Altman 1938, 46 and pl. 19c [H 5] and 24d [H 15]) (Figure 41).

The content of that library is nothing if not classic (Wiseman and Black 1996; Lambert 1999–2000). As might be expected, divination makes up the lion's share: astronomical (nos. 1–30) and teratological omens (nos. 31–35) and those drawn from daily life (nos. 36–49); hemerologies and menologies (nos. 50–60); extispicy (nos. 61–63); miscellanea (nos. 64–69); "medical" omens, physiognomy (nos. 70–79); and unidentified texts (nos. 80–89). There are also magical and medical texts (nos. 90–164); prayers and hymns (nos. 165–184); and rituals (nos. 185–190), among other things. The "literary" texts (nos. 197–207) are few, especially when compared to the situation in the "library" of Sultantepe, which has nearly

FIGURE 41. Niches in the library of the temple of Nabu of Khorsabad (U.S. excavations of 1936). (Courtesy of the Oriental Institute of the University of Chicago.)

the same number of tablets. There is also an abundance of lexical lists (nos. 208–245). None of the tablets includes a colophon that would indicate it belonged to the temple of Nabu; those colophons that have been preserved refer to exorcists or scribes, some of them members of the family of Nabu-zuqup-kena.

The Ša Harē *Temple of Nabu in Babylon.* Apart from votive tablets, the *ša harē* temple in Babylon was found empty, with one exception: in a kiln of room 15, a fragment of the New Year's ritual and a prayer to the god Ea were uncovered (Cavigneaux 1999a, 388). These tablets are very different from the thousands of exercises unearthed in the building: they are likely the only vestiges of the library that was located in the temple, of which nothing else has come down to us (Figure 42).

FIGURE 42. The *ša harē* temple of Nabu in Babylon. The school tablets discovered there were found incorporated into the renovations of the building done during the reign of Nebuchadnezzar. (Courtesy of D. Charpin.)

The Library of the Temple of Shamash in Sippar

There might be a tendency to think that libraries existed only in the temples of Nabu, a protector of scribes. That would be a mistake: some colophons reveal the existence of a library of Eshtar in Uruk. But the most famous example is that of the temple of Shamash in Sippar, which was discovered by a mission of the University of Baghdad in 1985–1987 (Al-Jadir 1998). The room measured only about 14½ × 8¾ feet (4.40 × 2.70 m). A structure for holding the tablets was found there, similar to those discovered by the U.S. excavations of Khorsabad (Charpin 2007c). The niches for housing the tablets formed a sort of cabinet along the back wall (six niches wide) and the side walls (four niches wide); depending on the location, the cabinet was between two and four niches in height. The niches measured 17 × 30 × 70 cm (6¾ × 11⅞ × 27⅝ in.). The tablets did not stand on the shelves like books in a modern library, but rather lay on their sides and were arranged like files in a file cabinet, with as many as sixty tablets to a niche. Unfortunately, not all the niches were filled, so that only 800 tablets could be exhumed.[11]

All in all, little new was discovered. Many lexical lists, the usual divinatory series, hymns, and prayers: nothing of that is original. The few "literary" texts are also unsurprising: there are tablets from *Atra-hasis,* from *Lugal.e,* and from *Enūma eliš.* What is more unusual, but also characteristic of the era, was the interest taken in the past. Copies of authentic documents were found, generally with the writing modernized. These are primarily Old Babylonian royal inscriptions: a dedication by Zabaya, the king of Larsa, the prologue to the Code of Hammurabi and two other inscriptions by that king, an inscription by Ammiditana. Bilingual letters from Kurigalzu and Nebuchadnezzar I were also identified, as well as a few apocryphal documents. The copy of the so-called Weidner chronicle is interesting in one respect: the scribe not only indicated that he had copied it from a damaged exemplar but even reproduced the broken-off passages by drawing hatching and triangles (Al-Rawi 1990). The texts that seem to be new are very limited in number: a prayer, a hymn, two lamentations. It cannot be ruled out that we will some day find duplicates of them in the storerooms of some museum, as happened with the *Tale of the Poor Man of Nippur,* originally discovered in the library of Sultantepe.

Thus far, that is the only case corresponding to a true library. It is obviously regrettable that we have no information on the use that was made of it. There is no dearth of questions: who had access to it? For what purpose? How was a consultation of the tablets arranged? At present we have no answers for any of them.

Other temple libraries have existed, but they were not discovered during scientifically conducted excavations. That is true for the most part of the library of Bīt Rēsh in Uruk from the Seleucid period (van Dijk and Mayer 1980). The remains of the library of Esagil from a late period were purchased in the nineteenth century and are currently in the British Museum (Beaulieu 2006; Clancier 2005).

The Problem of Readers

Were all these tablets consulted after being copied? The question that arose regarding archival documents must be raised anew for the library texts. Oddly, the problem of readers has almost never been considered, though I find it crucial. Many colophons curse anyone who carries off a tablet.[12] The threat is often a terrible one for a scribe, namely, blindness: "Anyone who carries off this tablet, may Shamash carry off his eyes!" In other cases, the guilty party is even threatened with death: "May Nabu promptly kill anyone who carries off this tablet!" We may conclude that no thought was given to lending tablets, as books and other materials are lent in modern libraries. That impression may be confirmed by this recommendation from a Seleucid colophon on a tablet from the sanctuary of Bīt Rēsh in Uruk: "He who venerates Anu and Antu must venerate (this tablet) and respect it. He must not steal it by carrying it off or borrow it inadvertently; (otherwise) he must bring it back the next day to its owner's home!" (Hunger 1968, 42, no. 96, line 4). A colophon from Sultantepe yields this injunction: "Do not mistreat the tablet, do not disorganize the library!" (STT 38 iv 12; Hunger 1968, 111, no. 354).[13] The recommendation recalls the attitude of some librarians of today, who have developed an aversion for readers, accusing them of damaging "their" books.[14] But I am dubious about the accuracy of that interpretation. These curses must be situated in their context: similar ones exist with reference to all sorts of votive objects, tablets being only one particular category of these. In the colophon that follows, it is quite simply forbidden to interfere with the property of the Eanna, the temple of Eshtar in Uruk: "The scholar who does not change a line and puts (this tablet back) in the library *(girginakku),* may Eshtar look favorably on him! But he who takes (it) out of the Eanna, may Eshtar assail him in anger!" (Hunger 1968, 46, no. 106). The status of the tablet as votive offering safeguarded by the gods is confirmed by a colophon of Ashurbanipal. This text is suggestive of "classic" commemorative inscriptions in its motif of the feat never before accomplished, and it ends with a curse similar to what could be found at the end of a stela:

Palace of Ashurbanipal, king of the universe, king of Assyria, who trusts in Assur and Mulissu, to whom Nabu and Tashmetu have given great understanding, who has acquired a clear eye, the highest level of the art of the scribe, which none of the kings who preceded me learned. The wisdom of Nabu, cuneiform signs, as many as exist, I have written on tablets, verified and collated, and have installed them in my palace to read them (and) have them read to me. Whoever trusts in you will know no shame, O king of gods, Assur! Whoever would carry off (this tablet) or inscribe his name in place of my own, may Assur and

Mulissu curse him furiously (and) with rage, and may his name (and) his posterity (literally, "seed") disappear from the land! (Hunger 1968, 97–98, no. 318 [Asb. Typ c–e])

Note, finally, that there is no description of a specialist going to a library to consult a work.

Conclusion

Two things must be pointed out. First, Assyria was clearly very dependent culturally on Babylon. There were two particularly significant moments. In the thirteenth century, after the victory of Tukulti-Ninurta I over Babylon, he brought back many tablets to Assur as part of the booty.[15] The second crucial phase took place under Ashurbanipal. Political domination can coexist with cultural dependence. Recall the famous passage from Horace: *Graecia capta ferum victorem cepit et artes intulit agresti Latio,* which, freely translated, renders: "Vanquished Greece vanquished its fierce victor and brought civilization to the Latin peasants." The comparison, as always, does not imply that the situations were identical, but it is nevertheless suggestive.

Second, let me point out a phenomenon that most specialists are not always aware of: beginning in the twelfth century, Mesopotamian culture gradually became ossified. It took more than a millennium to die out completely; the only real area of progress in knowledge was in mathematical astronomy, which came into being in Achaemenid Babylonia. But in the first millennium, the geographical influence of cuneiform narrowed: only a few traces remained west of the Euphrates, directly linked to the political presence of the Assyrian and then the Babylonian kings. But there was no center reminiscent of Ebla in the third millennium. The literati gradually came to focus on a closed corpus. The lexical lists assumed their definitive form at the end of the second millennium, and it is precisely at that moment that the first commentaries were drafted. However fascinating that literary genre, which appeared for the first time in the history of civilizations, it was nonetheless the sign of the end.

It is also striking that all the libraries contain nearly the same texts. This phenomenon elicited surprise when the library of Sultantepe was exhumed in 1951–1952 and its content was compared to that of the library of Ashurbanipal; it was recently confirmed by the discovery of the library of the temple of Shamash in Sippar. It is a boon for efforts to reconstitute the texts: each new discovery provides additional manuscripts for works already known and makes it possible to fill in certain gaps. In fact, *no* text of Mesopotamian literature has as yet been reconstituted in its entirety.[16] Nevertheless, let me insist on how much that situation differs from that attested for the first half of the second millennium. In that case, Akkadian literary texts are often known by only a single manuscript: the process of "canonization" had not yet begun.[17] Paradoxically, it is the most creative periods that are the least well known. In the late first millennium, Mesopotamian culture was dying out in the sanctuaries where it had taken refuge. That does not mean that the last generations of scribes were not active: but activity must not be confused with vitality.

chapter six

Messages for the Gods and for Posterity

The texts examined thus far had for the most part a practical aim: they were associated with the activities of administrators responsible for managing storehouses or lands, or of merchants keeping track of their transactions; or they were the property titles of individuals that were kept in their homes; or finally, they were letters. The so-called literary texts were actually the product of the training that apprentice scribes received and were only very rarely conserved in libraries. There is one last category of sources, generally called "historiographical": these were written by the ancients to perpetuate the name of the person who commissioned them,[1] with the idea that the texts would transmit a message beyond the present world, that they would communicate with the gods or with posterity.

Dedications and Foundation Inscriptions

Dedications and foundation documents are generally studied together under the rubric "commemorative inscriptions," which is undoubtedly not very accurate. The term "inscription," often used to distinguish such texts from business documents, has little meaning in the case of Mesopotamian civilization. In most cultures, the writing support in everyday use is soft: papyrus, parchment, or paper, and the writing is in ink. Inscriptions, by contrast, are texts engraved on a hard surface (stone or metal, for example) and intended to last. In Mesopotamia, however, cuneiform writing, being three-dimensional, was always inscribed. The difference lay solely in the nature of the material support: clay was used for the most common texts, with stone (and metal) explicitly reserved for those on which one wished to confer a particular solemnity, those that were supposed to endure as long as possible. At the end of the *Lugal.e* myth, the god Ninurta details the fate of all sorts of stones. He speaks directly to diorite, the raw material for most statues: "Any king who wants to establish his renown for a life in far-off days and to make a representation of himself for distant days, will have you stand in the Eninnu, the temple full of splendor, at the place of libation, where you will be placed in keeping with (your) fate (as a statue)" (Radner 2005, 116–117). One example shows that Mesopotamians were aware of the enduring quality of stone when compared to clay: a stone *kudurru* dating from the reign of Merodach-baladan I tells how the beneficiary of a donation from Nazi-Marutash had the royal deed transcribed onto a clay monument *(narū ša haṣbi),* which he placed in a temple. About a century and a half later, the temple wall collapsed, destroying the monument. The first beneficiary's heir then had a new copy of the royal deed engraved in stone.[2]

Dedications

It is necessary to distinguish between ex-votos proper and votive objects, though items in both categories were inscribed with a dedication to a god or goddess.

True Ex-Votos. The mechanism, so to speak, is well known: a god is promised a present if he helps the petitioner obtain what he desires. Once that aim is achieved, the petitioner must keep his promise, and the object offered is an ex-voto in the strict sense of the term.

Such wishes were formulated under various circumstances. Individuals sometimes wanted to be healed or to have success in a commercial enterprise; but most familiar to us are the requests for victory made by sovereigns. So it was that Samsi-Addu offered a throne to Itur-Mer, the principal deity of Mari, to thank him for having delivered up the city to him: "When the god Itur-Mer heard my prayers and petitions and entrusted to me the entire land of Mari, the Bank-of-the-Euphrates, and its domains, I dedicated, devoted, and offered to him for his divine splendour a great throne of ebony which was perfectly made with everything pertaining to the goldsmith's art" (Grayson 1987, 57, no. 5).

The king's intimates made vows of the same type: "[To the goddess Eštar], who . . . , who listens to prayers, her lady, Izamu, the musician[3] who makes the prayer of her lord Yasmah-Addu find favour, when the goddess Eštar, my lady, heard my prayers and granted my request, I dedicated her statue to her. I dedicated to her a statue that was perfectly (fashioned) by the craftsmen" (Frayne 1990, 617–618, no. 4).

If necessary, the gods demanded their due. Hence the god Shamash intervened with King Zimri-Lim on behalf of other deities, through the intermediary of a prophet: "The god Nergal, lord of Hubshalum, in the course of the defeat (of the enemies), stood by your side and by your army's side. Have everything you promised him made, as well as a large bronze sword, and bring them to Nergal, lord of Hubshalum" (*ARM* 26/1 194: 24–31).

The objects dedicated to the different deities were generally related to their "specialty." Nergal, a war god, would be offered a sword or a mace. It was different for Gula, the goddess of medicine. As in the case of other healer deities in antiquity, her fetish animal was the dog, so people offered Gula dogs as ex-votos to thank her for healing them.[4]

An ex-voto was not necessarily a statue or even an object: it could sometimes be a living being. After a victory, for example, the king would offer the gods a share of the booty, which might consist of slaves (Charpin 2006a, 151). Then there is the case of kings who consecrated one of their daughters as a priestess or nun to a deity who had expressed the desire for one. This was not uncommon. We even possess the letter that the god Shamash sent to Zimri-Lim to ask for a throne but also for his daughter: "Thus [speaks] Shamash. I am master of the land. Have a large throne sent quickly to Sippar, city of life, for the dwelling of my plenitude, and your daughter, which I demanded of you" (*ARM* 26/1 194: 3–7).

In fact, we have several letters that this daughter sent after she became the *nadītum* of the god Shamash (Durand 2000, 390–402). These nuns were considered secondary wives to the god, whose consort, the goddess Aya, was the principal wife *(kallatum).*

Making a vow could prove dangerous, if one forgot to keep one's promise. Witness a letter to Yasmah-Addu from the diviner Asqudum (*ARM* 26/1 84): after the son of an important man fell ill, Asqudum consulted an oracle regarding the cause of the ailment and received as his answer, "promise to the god Sin." The question arose whether it was Yasmah-Addu or his father, Samsi-Addu, who had forgotten to keep his vow, thereby inciting divine wrath. Another example comes from Shubat-Enlil. When Till-Abnu became king there, a certain Ea-malik issued a warning, reminding him of the conduct of his predecessor, who had met an untimely end: "Previously Mutiya, before he ascended his throne, several times made the following vow: 'If I were allowed to ascend my throne, I would donate silver, gold, cups of silver, cups of gold, and clever maids to Belet-Nagar, my Lady.' This vow he made several times, (but) when this man ascended his throne, he did not send greetings to the goddess, and he never saw the face of the goddess" (Sasson 1997; Eidem 2000). Ea-malik therefore advised the new king to accede to the demands that the goddess had just made of him.

Votive Objects. In contrast to ex-votos in the strict sense, certain dedications followed a different procedure: an object or a statue representing the dedicator, bearing an inscription of a prayer to the deity, was brought into the temple. The dedication of a statue offered by the son and successor of the famous Gudea provides a good example (Figure 43): "For Ningišzida, his god, Ur-Ningirsu,

FIGURE 43. Statue of Ur-Ningirsu with dedication to the god Ningizzida. The head belongs to the Metropolitan Museum and the body to the Musée du Louvre: the reconstituted statue alternates between New York and Paris. (Erich Lessing / Art Resource, New York.)

ruler of Lagaš, son of Gudea, ruler of Lagaš, who had built Nin-girsu's Eninu, fashioned his (own) statue. 'I am the one beloved by his god; let my life be long'—(this is how) he named that statue for his (Ningirsu's) sake, and he brought it to him into his House" (Edzard 1997b, 185, no. 6).

Sometimes it was not the statue of the king himself that was introduced into the temple but rather one of his predecessors. An inscription by Sin-iddinam, king of Larsa, provides the key to this procedure: he had a statue fashioned of his father, Nur-Adad, which he arranged to be placed in the courtyard of the temple of Shamash and "consecrated for his own life." That meant having the statue intercede with the god, as the words Sin-iddinam addressed to it show: "You, statue of the just shepherd, stand daily in the sanctuary of the Ebabbar to lengthen the days of my life!" (VS 17 41: 173–177; van Dijk 1965).

The objects dedicated to the gods were usually statues, but they could also be weapons, thrones, and even curios such as shells. Ordinary individuals could also offer objects to the deities; their dedications usually included a prayer for their sovereign. A good example is provided by the famous votive dog discovered in Tello, dedicated to Ninisina, one of the incarnations of the goddess Gula (Figure 44): "For the goddess Ninisina, lady, good . . . , wise physician, his lady, for the life of Sumu-El, king of Ur, Abba-duga, the *lú.mah* priest, son of Urukagina, chief cantor of Girsu, dedicated to her with praise (this figurine) named: 'Faithful dog, a stand for a pot of life-giving medication'" (Frayne 1990, 134, no. 2001).[5] The act of dedicating votive objects for the life of the new king may also be evidence that the populations whose former sovereign had been defeated had accepted their fate. Such is the case for a bronze figurine known as the "adorant of Larsa" (Figure 45).[6] The dedication is as follows: "For the god Amurrum, his god, for the life of Hammu-rabi, king of Babylon, Lu-Nanna, . . . , son of Sin-le'i, fashioned for him, for his life, a suppliant statue of copper, its face plated with gold. He dedicated it to him as his servant" (Frayne

FIGURE 44. Statuette dedicated to Ninisina (alias Gula) for the life of King Sumu-El. On the back of the dog is a little vase of sorts that was supposed to hold a medicinal preparation with a plant base (the "pot of life-giving medication" mentioned in the inscription). (Réunion des Musées Nationaux / Art Resource, New York.)

1990, 360, no. 2002). This, then, truly entailed the intercession of an individual with the god Ammurum in behalf of the king. It is interesting to note that the person in question was an inhabitant of the former kingdom of Larsa, annexed by Hammurabi: this may therefore have been a demonstration of loyalty to the new king.

Sometimes it was not politics but family that was the object of concern. Touchingly, a wife of Rim-Sin, king of Larsa, offered a diorite bowl to the goddess Inanna to ask that her daughter be healed: "In order to save Liriš-gamlum from the hand of evil-doers or brigands, to hand over the *asakkum* and *ašbur* diseases that are in her body to [a demon] who fears nothing, to expel the . . . , something that is in her eye, to protect her life, I, the servant who respects her (the goddess Inanna), dedicated (this vessel) for the life of Liriš-gamlum, my daughter, and for my own life" (Frayne 1990, 302–303 [Rim-Sin 23: 30–39]).

FIGURE 45. The so-called adorant of Larsa: the dedicator is represented with his right knee on the ground, his right hand raised to his mouth; his face and hands are gold-plated. On the base, a relief depicts an individual in the same posture, before a deity seated on a throne. The statuette is therefore in a sense "staged." (Réunion des Musées Nationaux / Art Resource, New York.)

How was the inscription that appeared on these objects composed? There is evidence that kings were intent on being closely associated with the formulation of the text (Charpin 2006a, 153–154; Frahm 1997, 281). When Zimri-Lim had a statue of himself taken to Aleppo for the temple of the storm god, he wrote to his steward: "Thus, as for the votive inscription to have written [on the statue], have the votive inscription that (So-and-So) made taken quickly to me as well as that made by Nab-Eshtar, so that I may see (read) them,[7] and so that I may have the votive inscription that I choose taken [to your house]" (*ARM* 18 16+ [*LAPO* 16 92]). Once the text was selected by the king, it was transmitted to artisans to be engraved on the votive object. Paradoxically, the texts that were inscribed on tablets found in the palace are obviously the drafts that were not accepted: in order to interpret them correctly, it is very important to be aware of that.

Apotropaic Inscriptions. Some texts generally included within the corpora of "royal inscriptions" are not dedications at all but inscriptions that could be called "apotropaic." That is particularly true of the inscriptions planned for a pair of lions that were to stand on either side of the entry gate to the temple of Eshtar in Mari: "The name of this lion is: 'He who strangles the enemy of Samsi-Addu on the order of the goddess Eshtar.' The name of this lion is: 'He who drinks the blood of the enemy of Samsi-Addu on the order of the goddess Eshtar'" (Frayne 1990, 65–66, nos. 2001 and 2002; Charpin 2006a, 147 about no. 331). The practice of giving a name to such apotropaic animals is attested as late as the first millennium, as indicated by the one of the two lions that Shamshi-ilu installed at the gate of Kar-Shalmaneser (Til Barsip): "The name of the first is: 'The lion who . . . , angry demon, unrivalled attack, who overwhelms the insubmissive, who brings success.' The name of the second, which stands before the gate, is: 'Who charges through the battle, who flattens the enemy land, who expels criminals and brings in good people'" (Grayson 1996, 231–233, no. 2010: 21–24).

This was an essential aspect of writing for ancient Mesopotamians: its performative character, which bestowed reality and life on what was written, as many amulets attest. What we call "magical" texts must be understood as a function of the principle that "what is written is real" (Maul 1994b, 189; Abusch and van der Toorn 1999). But once again, the written text merely echoes spoken words, since it was primarily at the time of their utterance that incantations had the power to act on reality.

Foundation Documents

The line of demarcation between votive inscriptions and foundation documents is somewhat blurry: all things considered, temples were only a particular type of votive offering. An inscription of Shalmaneser I, king of Assyria in the thirteenth century, demonstrates this in an altogether explicit manner: "To the god Aššur, his lord—(I), Shalmaneser, appointee of the god Enlil, vice-regent of Aššur, son of Adad-nirari [I], vice-regent of Aššur, son of Arik-din-ili (who was) also vice-regent of Aššur, I have entirely rebuilt the temple of the god Aššur, my lord, from top to bottom; I have made it larger than before. I have dedicated (this temple)[8] to the god Aššur my lord, for my life, the safe-keeping of my seed, and the well-being of Assyria" (Grayson 1987, 209–210, no. 20). The projects thus commemorated were, in the first place, buildings, usually temples, but also palaces, ramparts, and so on. They might include the foundation of a new city, which the king often named after himself. Another important theme was the digging of canals, which were essential for the prosperity of a country where agriculture depended on irrigation (Charpin 2002d). These construction projects were generally given a name (Radner 2005, 37–42). Temples bore a Sumerian name: the temple of Marduk in Babylon was Esagil, "Temple Whose Top Is High." The palace built by Sennacherib in Niniveh was designated the "Palace without Equal." The wall that Hammurabi built around Sippar was called "On the Order of Shamash, May Hammurabi Have No Rival!" Different canals were named "The-God-Nabium-(Brings)-Plenty" and "Samsu-iluna-Is-the-Source-of-Plenty."

The supports for these inscriptions varied widely. Some were bricks that had been inscribed or stamped and then incorporated into the construction. A single text was sometimes mechanically reproduced by means of stamping (Figure 46); such texts must be distinguished from those that were unique exemplars copied by hand, which could result in variants. Found in foundation deposits were tablets (in stone or metal) or copper figurines (R. Ellis 1968; van Driel 1973). Door sockets, in which the axes of the leaves of doors pivoted, often bore an inscription. Baked clay objects frequently served as supports: small "cones"

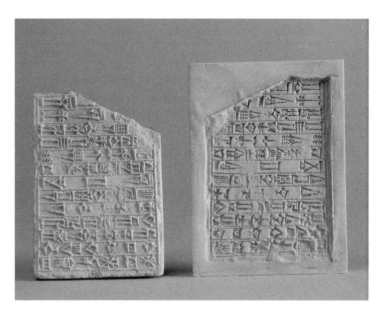

FIGURE 46. Brick matrix and its impression, an inscription of Sin-iddinam, king of Larsa, commemorating his construction work in the temple of Shamash (Frayne 1990, 162, no. 4). The matrix comes from the excavations of A. Parrot in Larsa. Subsequently, bricks were found bearing the impression of that inscription (the impression at right is modern). (Réunion des Musées Nationaux / Art Resource, New York.)

in the third millennium (Figure 47), large-headed "nails" in the second.[9]

These foundation documents generally consist of four parts (Sollberger and Kupper 1971, 24–36). They begin with the name and epithets of the deity to whom the building (or the object) is dedicated; the name and epithets of the donor, usually a king, follow. A third, optional section gives a more or less brief description of the events contemporary to that offering; the object and modalities of the offering are indicated in the fourth section. The entire text may be followed by curses against anyone who does

FIGURE 47. Example of a foundation inscription on a small cone; the text is by Gudea, prince of Lagash (twenty-second century B.C.). (Courtesy of D. Charpin.)

not respect the object of the dedication and/or the inscription. All sorts of variants of that pattern exist.[10]

All these inscriptions were primarily intended for the deities: they were supposed to demonstrate to them the piety of kings and other dedicators, and the object itself was supposed to intercede with the god in favor of the one who had offered it: "Thou, foundation stela of Sennacherib, king of Assyria . . . speak to the god Aššur and the temple of Ešarra, may his offspring prosper, may his sons and grandsons abide among the human race for ever and ever" (Luckenbill 1924, 146, lines 30–32).

The Development of Narration

Gradually, the commemorative function of royal inscriptions took on greater scope, giving rise to new literary genres of a narrative nature: the annals in Assyria, the chronicles in Babylonia (Grayson 1980). Some authors have objected to the term "commemorative texts," preferring that of *res gestae* (Fales 1999–

2001, 130). But it seems preferable to me to use a comprehensible term, even if one must explain its precise connotations, rather than resort to a Latin terminology whose advantage is not really clear.

The First Forms of Commemoration

A form of commemoration attested from the Akkadian period on was the system of year names, used in Babylonia especially. At the end of each year, the chancellery sent the different provincial cities a tablet containing the name of the new year (Horsnell 1999, 1:chap. 13).[11] These formulas could be long and so were sometimes abridged in everyday use. Hence, the complete wording for year 7 of Samsu-iluna was: "Year when King Samsu-iluna dedicated to Marduk a powerful 'weapon,' a magnificent emblem, a brilliant object plated with red gold and silver, an ornament worthy of a temple, and made it shine in the Esagil like a star in the sky" (Horsnell 1999, 2:187). In practice, scribes usually dated the tablets of that year with a very abridged formula: "Year (of) the weapon, emblem." Some year names are known only through the abridged version; we do not possess the complete wording. In addition, it sometimes happened that certain scribes did not use the official formula: hence the existence of parallel, often interesting formulas that can be difficult to locate in the chronology.

These year names had to do with different aspects of royal deeds. Military events, of course, occupied a place of choice. Hence year 28 of Samsu-iluna was titled: "Year in which King Samsu-iluna, on the order of the god Enlil and thanks to the wisdom and the strength that Marduk gave him, defeated Yadih-abum and Muti-Hurshana, kings who had been hostile to him, and crushed them with his violent weapon" (Horsnell 1999, 2:220). Such formulas therefore constitute an essential source for reconstituting the sequence of political-military events (Horsnell 2004): they mention battles won over enemies, the taking or destruction of cities, and more rarely, diplomatic events such as dynastic marriages. But kings also judged other events worthy of being commemorated, such as public works projects: the digging of canals, construction of walls, or erection of temples; or offerings made to the gods, such as statues, precious furnishings, and so on; or the appointment of religious staff, such as the "high priestesses" *(entum)*, and their assumption of duties. As a result, a victory was not always commemorated by a year name. For example, Gungunum, king of Larsa, did not dedicate any year name to the taking of Ur, which he had seized from the king of Isin.

Thus far, a set of two letters found in Mari constitutes our only explicit evidence about the way a year name was chosen. These letters show that a formula commemorating an offering to a deity could be chosen even when a major political event had taken place that year. The first missive was written to Zimri-Lim by his "minister of finance": "Another thing: the year that has begun must be named as follows: 'Year when Zimri-Lim came to the aid of Babylon for the second time, in the land of Larsa'" (*ARM* 13 27 [*LAPO* 16 157]). The same person wrote a more detailed letter to the king's secretary at the same time: "Tell Shu-nuhra-Halu: thus (speaks) Yasim-Sumu. As for the designation of the year, regarding which you wrote me as follows: 'Year when Zimri-Lim offered a great throne to Dagan.' But that throne has not yet been offered. So I have just sent a tablet to the king. The designation is: 'Year when Zimri-Lim came to the aid of Babylon for the second time, in the land of Larsa.' Draw the king's attention to that tablet and write me one way or the other" (*ARM* 13 47 [*LAPO* 16 90]). We know that the year was designated by the formula that Shu-nuhra-Halu proposed, namely: "Year when Zimri-Lim offered a great throne to Dagan." Fortunately for modern historians, the campaign conducted by Mariot armies in the region of Larsa is abundantly documented elsewhere. But the conclusion is clear: it is not possible to write the political history of a kingdom based solely on the year names of its successive sovereigns. Conversely, historians most often encounter an insurmountable handicap when they do not have available the guidelines that the year names provide: hence the political history of Eshnunna remains much less well known for the Old Babylonian period than that of Babylon, Isin, or Larsa.

In Assur, time was computed in a slightly different way: years bore the name of a person, the *limmum,* a term we translate as "eponym." In order that the chronological order of these eponyms could be recovered subsequently, lists had to be kept of them. Some of these lists were accompanied by commentary (Birot 1985; Durand 2003) summarizing the noteworthy political events of each eponymy: "During (the eponymy of) Sharrum-Adad, the sovereign of Elam achieved a victory over Ipiq-Adad, and King Samsi-Addu came (to the throne of) his father's house" (Birot 1985, 229, no. 8 [S.115–126: 9′–12′]).

The inscriptions of the Old Assyrian kings are laconic; they usually commemorate construction projects in the king's capital. It was only with Adad-nirari I (1305–1274) that they became more substantial (Lackenbacher 1990; Charpin 2006a, 133n14; Galter 1997). The notation of events that sometimes appeared at the end of the construction accounts became longer and longer at that time, giving rise to the annals genre in the late second millennium, under the reign of Tiglat-pileser I.

The Annals of the Assyrian Kings

The annals contain accounts of one or several military campaigns; they are written in the first person and arranged in chronological order. The king is the supposed author of the narrative (Fales 1999–2001). We know this task was entrusted to his "chief scribe" (Luukko 2007, 228n5), but his name never appears.[12] The fairly significant differences among the different annals of the Sargonid rulers doubtless reflect in part the individual personalities of the scribes (Tadmor 1997, 328).

The typology of these texts is quite rich. Some accounts are limited to one campaign, engraved on a rock or stela in the region where the king fought. But there are also collections of several campaigns inscribed on cylinders or prisms buried in the foundations of buildings (Figure 48), or engraved on paving stones in public view. Such collections were edited at several moments during the reign, with the account of the first campaigns becoming more and more abridged as time went on. The second part of that kind of inscription commemorated the king's construction projects, especially the creation or beautification of the capital by Neo-Assyrian sovereigns. The irrigation projects of Niniveh and the acclimation of exotic plant or animal species by Sennacherib are particularly interesting examples. Alongside these annals, texts that are sometimes called "summary inscriptions" organized the campaigns by geographical sector. Such documents are much more difficult for the historian to exploit, since we cannot situate the campaign accounts chronologically without consulting other sources, which are often lacking.

For a long time, these texts were given a literal reading. Consider this judgment by J. V. Scheil regarding the annals of Tukulti-Ninurta II: "In terms of historical documents, what more can we dream of than written accounts such of this: 'In the month of Nisan, 28th day, under the eponymy of Nadilou, I left Assur and camped out on the plain; from the plain, I left and crossed the Tartar, I set up camp, etc.' For historical science, this is obviously the ideal document" (Scheil 1937, 37). We have a tendency to smile at such naïve positivism today. We have learned in the meantime to do a critical reading of these sources, to consider the events less in themselves than in the way they are narrated (Liverani 1973). Hence the first-person viewpoint must not fool us: in certain cases, we have the correspondence between the king and the officers who actually conducted the campaign in the field (Fincke 2003–2004, 120b).

FIGURE 48. Prism of Ashurbanipal. Most of this version of the annals is devoted to the account of the sack of Susa (648). (Réunion des Musées Nationaux / Art Resource, New York.)

We must not conclude, however, that royal inscriptions are "deceptive" or "misleading." The manifestation of such a phenomenon tells us something essential about the nature of kingship: the sovereign held ultimate responsibility for everything that happened in his kingdom, which led him, if necessary, to attribute to himself actions that had been performed by subordinates on his instructions. The phenomenon of successive editions is also very important: we can compare accounts written at different times during a single reign and analyze the technique for condensing the text implemented by the author(s). That is particularly important in the case of kings for whom we have only annals dating from the end of their reigns, in which the narratives of events for the first years are greatly abridged. Finally, we must take into account the essentially theological vision of history at work in these texts, in which the irruption of the marvelous is common. For example, the fate of the rebellious Arabs as it is described in the annals of Esarhaddon corresponds almost exactly to the curses that appear at the end of the treaties they had concluded but not respected.

A critical approach to the texts should not lead to generalized skepticism, however (Charpin forthcoming f). Hypercriticism has sometimes resulted in positions that have turned out to be untenable. For example, it has been possible to recover the original account from which certain texts previously dismissed as "legendary"—such as the famous *Insurrection against Naram-Sin* (Charpin 1997c)—were directly derived. In addition, to consider royal inscriptions as a literary genre that must be studied as such does not rule out using them *as well* to write a political history (Charpin 2006a, 150). That can be demonstrated by comparing the accounts of the campaign against Qabra given both by Dadusha, king of Eshnunna, and by Samsi-Addu, which each king commemorated on a stela, to the data drawn from the sets of letters discovered in Mari and Shemshara (Charpin 2004b). The oft-used term "sources" can be illusory, as can "data": historians in fact *construct* the object of their study.[13] But that construction must take into account all the texts, *including* those of a narrative nature (Charpin 2004a, 39–56).

The Babylonian Chronicles

Chronicles are typical of first-millennium Babylonia, whose kings left no annals but only inscriptions, most commemorating their work projects on temples (Da Riva 2008). These chronicles cover the period extending between the eighth and the third centuries; but within that half-millennium, there are more lacunae than data, given the chronological limitations of the individual tablets and the poor condition of preservation of some of them. These texts share the same typology, having a similar, very dry style of composition: the events are recounted laconically. The taking of Jerusalem by Nebuchadnezzar in 597 is reported as follows: "The seventh year, in the month of Kislev, the king of Akkad (Babylon) mustered his troops, marched on Hatti (Levant), and set up his quarters facing the city of Yehud (Juda, or Jerusalem). In the month of Adar, the second day, he took the city and captured the king. He installed there a king of his choice. He collected its massive tribute and went back to Babylon" (Glassner 2004, 230–231). These chronicles are not written in the first person and clearly do not come from the sovereign's entourage: it is not unusual for them to mention defeats. In the absence of precise indications, it is difficult to say who the authors were and with what aim in view they wrote them. But it is at least clear that the historian must resist the temptation to see these authors as very ancient colleagues.[14]

Inscriptions Made to Be Read

The case of the victory stelas is perfectly evident: the sovereigns who had them erected wanted them to be visible and to demonstrate the kings' dominance (Morandi 1988). The reliefs engraved in the mountain rocks bordering Mesopotamia were also intended to make the local populations understand the supremacy of the sovereign, who is depicted as the victor. In many cases, iconography complemented the text, giving everyone, literate or not, access to its meaning (Russell 1999). The famous Stela of Vultures includes on the front a depiction of the god Ningirsu, holding a net in which the defeated enemies are captured (Figure 49). That was a way of saying that the deity had given the victory to Eannatum, as the inscription explicitly indicates. The efficacy of that type of representation is demonstrated by the relief of Anum-hirbi on Mount Adalur, which is described in an inscription of Shalmaneser III, about eight centuries later. The figure of Anum-hirbi must have been accompanied by an Akkadian inscription in cuneiform, which allowed the Assyrian king to identify it. He then placed his own representation next to it.

Other stelas did not commemorate victories but served to underscore the role of the sovereign, especially in matters of justice. In Susa, therefore, a stela standing on the marketplace indicated the price of foodstuffs, day wages, and so on: "Atta-hushu, shepherd of the god Inshushinak, son of the sister of Silhala, made a stela of justice; he installed it in the marketplace. He who does not know the right price, let Shamash inform him of it!" (Malbran-Labat 1995, 32–33, no. 12; Charpin 2010, chap. 5). The stela of the Code of Hammurbai must be understood in that context. The king invited his subjects to come read it, as the epilogue indicates:[15] "May the wronged man who faces trial come before the representation of me as king of justice, may he read my inscribed stela, may he listen to my precious words, may my stela show him his case so that he may see the verdict concerning him and be reassured" (Roth 1995, 134 [xlviii 3–17]). The traditional translation of the passage is "may he have my stela read to him," but the text actually says, "may he read." What follows shows that the king is imagining someone reading out loud to himself ("may he

FIGURE 49. Stela of Vultures, front. The god Ningirsu is represented with a net, in which he catches the enemies of Eannatum, king of Lagash. Tello, Protodynastic III period (about 2400 B.C.). (Erich Lessing / Art Resource, New York.)

listen . . ."). No doubt this is a vain wish: how could a simple subject of Hammurabi's have found his case among the some 275 laws of the code? It would have been particularly difficult in that the layout of the stela offers no guidelines (Figure 50). But the way the stela of the code was, as it were, "staged" in this passage must not elicit skepticism from the outset: access to the courtyard of temples was not reserved for members of their staff. Apprentice scribes, for example, could enter the courtyard of the temple of Enlil in Nippur to recopy the inscriptions of stelas or statues located there. And we must not conclude that the people of the kingdom were unable to read that stela because they were illiterate. That is indicated in a letter from the "chief accountant" Yasim-Sumu to King Zimri-Lim: "I have just sent my lord the inscription for the chariot of the god Nergal and the inscription for the palanquin of the god Itur-Mer. Should the inscription of Nergal be written on the front or on the back of the chariot? May my lord reflect on the fact that the inscription should be inscribed on the back of the chariot, where the coat of arms is located, so that whoever will [see]? it and the reader can read it. Also, should the inscription on the palanquin . . . be written on the front or on the back? May my lord write me one way or the other, so that before my lord's departure these inscriptions shall be engraved" (*FM* 2 17). The advantage of that letter from Mari is that it is less suspect of ideology and, at the same time, more realistic than the passage from the Code of Hammurabi, written within a few years of it. It seems clear that, for Yasim-Sumu, some of the people assembled on the procession route could have been able to read these inscriptions (Wilcke 2000, 24).

Some authors (such as Radner 2005, 130) have maintained that the value of commemorative inscriptions did not depend on their having readers, since indisputably a good part of them were out of sight.[16] I find that view doubtful for two reasons. In the first place, many curses explicitly mention that burying an inscription was a crime. That was above all, but not exclusively, the case for the *ku-*

FIGURE 50. The stela of the Code of Hammurabi: the layout offers few guidelines to someone wanting to consult it. The Code "was not made to be read, it was made to be there." (Réunion des Musées Nationaux / Art Resource, New York.)

durrus, which curse "whoever throws this stela into a well, destroys it with a stone, burns it in fire, buries it in the earth, or hides it where it cannot be seen" (*BBSt* no. 7 ii 11; see *CAD* T, 336a). Some inscriptions, like the one on the chariot of Nergal in Mari and like the Code of Hammurabi, were meant to be in public view.

Moreover, even when inscriptions were intentionally buried, they were intended to be read: by the gods (who were not bothered by the underground location) and by posterity, who might read the texts when they renovated the building after it had fallen into ruins.

Messages for Posterity

Beginning in the early second millennium, sovereigns habitually considered foundation inscriptions the best means to ensure the survival of their name; new supports, such as nails and cylinders, appeared at that time. The most ancient explicit evidence comes from Larsa, as on this cone of King Rim-Sin discovered in the temple of Ninshubur in Girsu: "I put there for ever my foundation inscription proclaiming my royal name" (Frayne 1990, 290 [Rim-Sin I, no. 13: 36–37]). Shortly thereafter, the same practice was adopted in the north. An inscription of Samsi-Addu found in the temple of Assur bears this injunction: "When the temple becomes dilapidated: may whoever among the kings, my sons, renovates the temple anoint my foundation inscriptions *(temmennum)* and my monumental inscriptions *(narūm)* with oil, make a sacrifice, and return them to their places" (Grayson 1987, 50 [Šamši-Adad, no. 1: 88–98]). And there are earlier examples of such acts. Hence, in the foundations of the temple of Shamash in Mari, Yahdun-Lim deposited different items that clearly date back to the Early Dynastic period, as well as his own inscribed bricks (Parrot 1954, 160–162; R. Ellis 1968, 69–70).

Samsi-Addu was the first king to have explicitly described that behavior. He indicated that while restoring the temple of Eshtar, he discovered foundation inscriptions of Manishtushu, king of Akkad,[17] adding:

> The monumental inscriptions and foundation inscriptions of Maništušu I swear I did not remove but restored to their places.

I deposited my monumental inscriptions and foundation inscriptions beside his monumental inscriptions and foundation inscriptions. Therefore the goddess Eštar, my mistress, has given me a term of rule which is constantly renewed. In the future when the temple becomes old, when Ekituškuga which I built has become dilapidated, and the king whom the god Enlil appoints restores (it): May he not remove my monumental inscriptions and foundations inscriptions as I did not remove the monumental inscriptions and foundation inscriptions of Maništušu but restore them to their places.

(Grayson 1987, 54–54 [Šamši-Adad I, no. 2, ii 21–iii 10])

There is no dearth of examples of rulers who followed these instructions (Radner 2005, 209–224). Most date from the first millennium, and the most extensive use of that practice was made by King Nabonidus, who is sometimes called for that reason—in scare quotes to mark the anachronism—the "archaeologist king" (Schaudig 2003) (Figure 51).

The temple of Shamash in Larsa had already been restored by Nebuchadnezzar, but only partially, and the monarch had not found any inscription prior to the Kassite king Burnaburiash. Nabonidus managed to go him one better, thanks to a sort of "cosmic vacuum cleaner" that present-day archaeologists would like to have available to clear away the spoil earth from their excavations:

On the order of Marduk, the great lord, the winds rose up from the four cardinal points into a great tempest, and the sand that covered the city and that temple were removed. Of the Ebabbar, an imposing temple, dwelling of chants (of joy), habitation of Shamash and Aya, and the ziggurat, its august high temple, eternal cella, chamber of their delight, the foundations could again be seen and the plan for them once again discerned. I saw there an inscription in the name of Hammurabi, ancient

FIGURE 51. Tablet dating from Nabonidus, king of Babylon (r. 555–539), bearing on the obverse a copy (probably cast) of a stone inscription of Shar-kali-sharri, king of Agade (2217–2193). (Courtesy of the Penn Museum.)

king who, seven hundred years before Burnaburiash, rebuilt for Shamash the Ebabbar and the ziggurat on the ancient foundations. (After making oracular inquiries, Nabonidus launched the project.) The Ebabbar, for Shamash and Aya my lords, like (the one from) past times, I reconstructed exactly and I restored it. The alabaster tablet inscribed in the name of Hammurabi, ancient king, that I had seen inside, I placed with my own inscription and deposited them forever.

(Schaudig 2002, 397–409 ii 10–iii 31)

In this case, Nabonidus cannot be suspected of exaggeration: the excavations of Larsa have allowed us to find all the inscriptions he mentions and to note the superimposition of strata from the Kassite to the Neo-Babylonian period (Huot 1987).

Enmerkar, king of Uruk, was believed to have invented writing to serve the needs of long-distance communication (in letters). But another text criticizes him for not having used writing to communicate with future kings, that is, for not having left any commemorative inscriptions. The criticism comes in a passage from the *Legend of Kutha,* an apocryphal text supposedly written by Naram-Sin, which declares: "(Enmerkar) on a stela *(narūm)* he did not write (and) did not leave (it) to me, myself, he did not make a name for himself so that I could not pray for him" (J. G. Westenholz 1993, 306–307, lines 29–30). Conversely, Naram-Sin is supposed to have left an account of his exploits, which was to serve as an example for future kings, as indicated in the conclusion of the work:

You, whoever you are, be it governor or prince or anyone else,
whom the gods will call to perform kingship
I made a tablet-box for you and inscribed a stela for you.
In Kutha, in the Emeslam,
in the cella of Nergal, I left (it) for you.
Read this stela!

(J. G. Westenholz 1993, 326–327, lines 149–154)

The notion of "stela, commemorative inscription" *(narūm)* ultimately came to designate apocryphal texts. These pseudo-"autobiographies" belonged to wisdom literature and were intended for the edification of future kings (Radner 2005, 155–161). The exact nature of some inscriptions of this type is at times unclear. It has been argued, for example, that the famous "Statue of Idrimi" is in reality a forgery from the thirteenth or twelfth century, but the most recent studies have called into doubt that hypercritical position (Sasson 1981; Liverani 2001, 306).

Exchanges of Messages with the Gods

Dedications and foundation inscriptions were intended to be read, in the first place, by the gods. But there were other ways for human beings to communicate with gods in writing. The easiest was quite simply to send them a letter. Zimri-Lim thus sent the "river god" a message, for which we possess a draft: "To the river god, my lord, say: thus (speaks) Zimri-Lim, your servant. At present, I have just sent my lord a gold vase. Previously I had sent a report to my lord and my lord had given me a sign: may my lord allow me to obtain without reservation the sign that he showed me! May my lord not neglect anything pertaining to the protection of my life! May my lord not turn his face away! May my lord not direct his kindnesses anywhere but toward me!" (*ARM* 26/1 191; Charpin and Ziegler 2003, 202n384). Formally, this letter is just like one a king might send to a more powerful sovereign. That is also true for its content: sending a present and requesting protection were part of the rhetoric in use at the time in that kind of epistolary exchange. If we take into account the fact that the river god's principal city was Hit, the meaning of the king of Mari's action becomes clear: he wanted to hold on to Hit despite Hammurabi of Babylon's claims on that city and thus asked the god of Hit to send an omen ("sign") favoring the return of his city to the kingdom of Mari.

No text describes how such a letter could be brought to the attention of the deity, but it is very likely that someone read it before his statue, just as the royal secretary read mail to the king. The account of the famous eighth campaign of Sargon, for instance, was read in the temple of Assur in 714 B.C.: it has been preserved in the form of a letter from the Assyrian king to his god (Oppenheim 1960; Fales 1991; Chamaza 1992; and for the letter of Esarhaddon, Eph'al and Tadmor 2006). The god could himself demand such a report. For example, a subject of the king of Mari had a dream in the temple of Terqa, and the god Dagan told him: "The messengers of Zimri-Lim, why are there none constantly before me, and why does he not place before me his complete report *(ṭēmum gamrum)?* Have I not for a long time given the kings of the Benjaminites fully over to the power of Zimri-Lim? Now go! You are my messenger. This is what you will say to Zimri-Lim: 'Send your messengers to me and place before me your complete report, so that I may make the kings of the Benjaminites swarm into the fisherman's sack and may place them before you'" *(ARM* 26/1 233: 24–39). Letters of that kind were also sent to the gods by private individuals (Böck 1996).

There are also precise indications of the various ways that the gods wrote to men. In certain cases, these were replies to inquiries made to them. Oracular inquiries were made through a diviner, who formulated the question *(tāwītum)* while sacrificing a lamb. The diviner prayed to Shamash and Adad, patron gods of divination, to inscribe an unambiguous reply on the liver of the sacrificed animal: the liver was in fact described as the "tablet of the gods" (Fincke 2006–2007, 147n109). A prayer to Shamash said explicitly: "You write on the flesh inside the sheep (in its viscera), you set an oracular decision there" (Rochberg 2006, 339n14 [*OECT* 6, pl. 30 K 2824: 12]). The question arises whether there was not more than a superficial analogy between the livers of lambs and the clay tablet, the support for written signs. J.-M. Durand, positing as his premise that reading comes before writing, wondered whether divinatory practices, aimed at deciphering signs, were not at the origin of the intellectual revolution that led to the invention of writing (Durand 1988b).

The text of certain oracular inquiries by Hammurabi and several of his successors was put in writing and recopied as a model up to the Neo-Assyrian period (Lambert 2007). The questions could even deal with the details of the tactic to be followed: "Hadanshu-likshud, son of Sin-nerari, who occupies the post of head of the infantry, must he take the lead or must he follow in the center (literally, 'in the navel')?" (Lambert 2007, 24, lines 9–12). It is clear in reading these texts why diviners were compelled to practice professional confidentiality, as indicated by this excerpt from the oath they had to swear: "And the guarded matter that Zimri-Lim, my lord, tells me in order to do an oracular inquiry, or, he tells my diviner colleague, and I hear, or even (if) I see the sign when my diviner colleague is doing an oracular inquiry, that matter I will indeed guard" (*ARM* 26/1: 11–16). Questioning the gods about what one was planning to undertake amounted to revealing one's plans, whether to make war or to conclude a treaty. As a general wrote, "Apart from the secret report of the diviners, what other secret is there?" (*ARM* 26/1 104: 14–15).

The gods could take the initiative in matters of communication by sending messages in the sky, through lunar or solar eclipses or other astronomical phenomena (Brown 2000; Rochberg 2004). It was the task of astrologists to decipher the meaning of that "heavenly writing" *(šiṭir šamê)* (Radner 2005, 18; Rochberg 2006, 338–339), and the role they played with respect to the rulers became significant in the first millennium. Diviners established a link between the two types of "writing," as the divinatory series "If the liver is the mirror image of the sky" shows. Gods wrote to men both by inscribing their marks on a lamb's liver and by making a comet appear in the sky.

But the gods could also send their messages in the form of cuneiform tablets. An altogether privileged case is attested in the

Mari archives: it tells us who the human intermediary between the deity and the king was. A prophet asked that someone send him a scribe to whom he could dictate the letter that the god Shamash intended for King Zimri-Lim (*ARM* 26/2 414; Charpin 2002c, 14–15). Remarkably, we possess the letter that was actually sent to Mari (*ARM* 26 194). A few letters from deities date to the Neo-Assyrian period. In particular, these are replies from the god Assur to letters that kings had sent him (*SAA* 3 41–45). A letter from the god Ninurta shows that, as in Mari, this type of communication belonged to the realm of prophecy (Pongratz-Leisten 1999, 227–231). It begins with a note from the messenger: "The great lord, the king of the gods, Ninurta, has sent me" (*SAA* 3 47: 1, 2–5). We do not know to what category of prophet this messenger belonged, but the formula is also found in prophetic declarations of Mari, such as *ARM* 26/ 210: 11, "Dagan sent me." Then the letter proper begins with this salutation: "Say to the prince, my outstretched hand, to the one who has received sceptre, throne, and regnal insignia, to the governor appointed by my own hand: thus speaks Ninurta, the great lord, the son of Illil." The letter is known through a copy that a colophon allows us to link to the library of Ashurbanipal, but that does not necessarily mean it is a "literary" letter: originally, it may well have been an "authentic" letter similar to *ARM* 26 194, that is, dictated by a prophet on behalf of a deity.

Conclusion

Mesopotamian history has been written in good part on the basis of the sovereigns' commemorative inscriptions. In the first phase, modern "histories" were little more than a paraphrase of these texts: consider the case of A. T. Olmstead's famous *History of Assyria,* published in 1923. But to check the tendency of Assyriologists toward collective self-flagellation, I should point out that Gustave Glotz's *Histoire grecque (Greek History),* published in

1925, was scarcely different in its methods. Since then, the progress of historical criticism has made it possible to "decode" these inscriptions. They nevertheless constitute the basis for reconstituting many periods, though historians also add data from documentary sources such as treaties, correspondence, and so on (Van De Mieroop 1999; Charpin 2006b, 108–111). It is therefore incumbent upon us to properly understand the different literary genres to which they belong so as not to misinterpret them, even while avoiding the excesses of hypercriticism.

Conclusion

A basic question remains to be answered: did the practice of reading and writing in Mesopotamia lead to a fundamental change in the relation to the world (Frake 1983)? The speed at which such a transformation was able to come about must not be exaggerated. There are still disagreements about whether the advent of writing made possible the emergence of the state or whether it was simply an enabling factor (Larsen 1988, 187). It was primarily in administration that the written document played a central role, even becoming paralyzing at times: "The maintenance of such a large and expanding bureaucracy may have become, at particular moments in history, an intolerable burden. We can, in fact, observe that the major collapses of Mesopotamian society in the third millennium, in the ED IIIa, Sargonic, Ur III, and perhaps in the Late Uruk periods, all coincide with the maximum production of tablets and the highest number of scribes" (Visicato 2000, 243). That conclusion must be qualified by an observation, however: in the archives, the great mass of texts date from the period immediately preceding the catastrophe that put an end to the archaeological stratum in which they are located. We may therefore be dealing, at least in part, with a documentary illusion.

In any event, the large volume of cuneiform texts that have come down to us (more than 500,000 inventoried) must not conceal the truth from us: the transmission of information and knowledge in Mesopotamian civilization was for a long time primarily an oral affair. Hence rituals were only very rarely put in writing before the first millennium. One of the central rituals of Mesopotamian religion was that of "washing" (or "opening") the mouth of divine statues, which allowed the gods to take control of what had been until then merely the work of artisans (Dick 1999). There are mentions of the ritual from the third millennium on, with certain incantations dating back to that era as well (Charpin 1986a, 488). But it was only in the library of Ashurbanipal that the ritual in its entirety was set down in writing (Walker and Dick 2001). The most explicit texts do not predate the Seleucid period;[1] that interest in saving the rituals from oblivion was probably not unrelated to the contact with Greek culture.

The different traditions relating to the transmission of the diviners' knowledge are enlightening in this respect. Mesopotamian ideology, which Berossos echoed in the Hellenistic period, denied men any discoveries: at the dawn of time, knowledge was bequeathed to men by Oannes, the sage from before the Flood. Berossos explains: "Since that time nothing further has been discovered" (Verbrugghe and Wickersham 1996, 44). The problem therefore arises as to how knowledge could have been transmitted at the time of the Flood, which ought to have entailed a rupture. A text explains that the secret knowledge of divination was originally entrusted by Shamash and Adad—patron gods of that discipline— to Enmeduranki, king of Sippar from before the Flood. He in turn transmitted these mysteries to men of Nippur, Sippar, and Babylon, who subsequently passed them on from father to son. The master who communicated his most secret knowledge to one of his sons was thus simply the last link in that long chain, which, in the last instance, went back to the gods themselves (Lambert 1967). Reflecting that view is a medical text that ends as follows: "Proven and tested salves and bandages which are suitable for use(?). According to the old sages from before the flood, which, in Šuruppak, in the second year of Enlil-bani, king of Isin (1859 B.C.), Enlil-muballiṭ, sage *(apkallu)* of Nippur, transmitted" (*AMT* 105 iv 21– 24; Lambert 1957, 8; and Reiner 1961, 10). The Epic of Erra explains for its part that the city of Sippar was spared by the Flood, which permits us to understand why the oral tradition was not interrupted: "Sippar, eternal city, on the territory of which the Lord of the earth did not make the Flood come" (*Erra* 4.50). Berossos provides another version in his account of the Flood: "Kronos (Enki) appeared to Xisouthros (Zisudra) in a dream and revealed that on the fifteenth of the month Daisios mankind would be destroyed by a great flood. He then ordered him to bury together all the tablets, the first, the middle and the last, and hide them in Sippar, the city of the sun" (Verbrugghe and Wickersham 1996, 49–50). After the Flood, when the ark touched down on the highest summit of the Armenian mountains, and Xisouthros was taken up into heaven, a voice ordered his companions to pay tribute to the gods: "The voice then instructed them to return to Babylonia to go to the city of Sippar, as it was fated for them to do, to dig up the tablets that were buried there and to return them over to mankind." There is thus a shift from the idea of the oral communication of knowledge to that of a tradition in writing. Significantly, this passage was written in the Hellenistic period.

The growing importance of the written document is also marked by several "pious frauds" committed by the clergy from the sixth century on. Consider first the example of the famous "cruciform monument of Manishtushu." It looks like an authentic inscription from the twenty-third century B.C. and contains the text of a royal donation to the great temple of Ebabbar in Sippar (Sollberger 1968). In reality, it is a pastiche, perhaps produced in the early part of the reign of Nabonidus (sixth century B.C.) and almost certainly commissioned by the clergy of Sippar to obtain the king's aid for their sanctuary.[2] In the Hellenistic period, the clergy of Uruk also engaged in a pious fraud, but this time in a more disinterested manner (Beaulieu 1993). A pseudo-prophecy was made at the time the cults of Uruk were reorganized, when Anu took precedence over Eshtar and a new temple, the Bīt Rēsh, was built. A tablet indicates that the new rites were "rediscovered" in Elam.[3] That was obviously a way to ensure that the innovations would be accepted, by passing them off as the reestablishment of a forgotten ancient situation.

It is likely no coincidence that this process of putting the tradition in writing occurred at a time when alphabetical writing systems were emerging and developing, in the late second and in the first millennium. It seems to me that Mesopotamian scholars understood that cuneiform writing could not rival alphabetical systems, particularly Aramaic. Instead of trying to simplify cuneiform, they made it even more difficult, adding more values to the signs and playing on their different readings: the decipherment of an omen text from the Old Babylonian period is much easier than that of the same text as it was written by scholars of the first millennium.[4] That play on the different values of signs produced a literature of commentaries similar to what the Kabbalah later developed (Frahm, forthcoming). The process led to the notion of a secret knowledge that was to be transmitted from initiate to initiate. True sages were those who were acquainted with the most secret knowledge.

Gilgamesh is presented as such a sage at the beginning of the epic devoted to his quest for immortality: "He saw the secret and uncovered hidden, he brought back a message from the antediluvian age" (George 2003, 538 I: 6–8). Prior to that time, writing was used primarily to set down the oral and thereby allow for its transmission, either in time (in administrative and legal texts and in commemorative inscriptions) or in space (in letters): it thus consisted above all of communicating. Even texts explicitly concerned with the future did not have the aim of transmitting knowledge: hymns and commemorative inscriptions sought to preserve the name of the king (Jonker 1995; Radner 2005). Hymn B to Lipit-Eshtar, which underscores the abilities of that king of Isin as a scribe, ends with this doxology:

> Your praise shall never disappear from the clay in the Edubba;
> May every scribe therefore sing of this bliss
> And glorify (you) greatly,
> So that your laudation in the Edubba shall not cease.
>
> (Vanstiphout 1978, 39, lines 59–62)

And this text was recopied dozens and dozens of times, since it was among the elementary texts used to train young scribes. Hence, as soon as they began to write, apprentices were perpetuating praise of the sovereign.

The beginning of the later version of the Epic of Gilgamesh shows us how that legendary king of Uruk's vain quest for immortality finally led him to entrust the account of his adventures to writing (George 2003, 538–539). Cuneiform writing was no longer used for communication at that time—Aramaic sufficed for that; rather, its function was to transmit the secret knowledge dating back to the sages from before the Flood.

Abbreviations

A	siglum for tablets from the royal archives of Mari (now in the Museum of Dēr ez-Zor, Syria)
AbB	*Altbabylonische Briefe*
ABL	*Assyrian and Babylonian Letters*
AfO	*Archiv für Orientforschung*
AMT	R. C. Thompson, *Assyrian Medical Texts* (London, 1923)
AO	siglum for tablets in the Louvre Museum, Paris
AoF	*Altorientalische Forschungen*
ARM	*Archives royales de Mari*
ASJ	*Acta sumerologica*
AuOr	*Aula Orientalis*
BaM	*Baghdader Mitteilungen*
BBSt	L. W. King, *Babylonian Boundary-Stones and Memorial-Tablets in the British Museum* (London, 1912)
BBVOT 1	D. Arnaud, *Altbabylonische Rechts- und Verwaltungsurkunden* (Berlin, 1989)
BIN	Babylonian Inscriptions in the Collection of James B. Nies
BiOr	*Bibliotheca Orientalis*
BM	siglum for tablets in the British Museum
CAD	*Chicago Assyrian Dictionary*
CCT	*Cuneiform Texts from Cappadocian Tablets in the British Museum*
CDLJ	*Cuneiform Digital Library Journal*
CRAIBL	*Comptes rendus de l'Académie des Inscriptions et Belles Lettres*
CT	*Cuneiform Texts*
CTMMA	*Cuneiform Texts in the Metropolitan Museum of Art*
CTN	*Cuneiform Texts from Nimrud*
DI	siglum for tablets from Tell ed-Dēr (Iraq)
EA	W. L. Moran, *The Amarna Letters* (Baltimore, 1992)
FM	*Florilegium Marianum*
IM	siglum for tablets in the Iraq Museum, Baghdad
JAOS	*Journal of the American Oriental Society*
JCS	*Journal of Cuneiform Studies*
JEOL	*Jaarbericht van het vooraziatisch-egyptisch Genootschap* Ex Oriente (Lux)
JESHO	*Journal of the Economic and Social History of the Orient*

JNES	*Journal of Near Eastern Studies*
KAJ	E. Ebeling, *Keilschrifttexte aus Assur Juristischen Inhalts* (Leipzig, 1927)
KAR	E. Ebeling, *Keilschrifttexte aus Assur Religiösen Inhalts* (Leipzig, 1919–1920)
KTT	siglum for tablets from Tell Bi'a
LAPO	
16, 17, 18	Durand 1997–2000
M	siglum for tablets from Mari (Syria)
MARI	*Mari: Annales de Recherches Interdisciplinaires*
MDP	*Mémoires de la Délégation en Perse*
MHET	*Mesopotamian History and Environment Texts*
NABU	*Nouvelles Assyriologiques brèves et utilitaires*
NAPR	*Northern Akkad Project Reports*
NL	siglum for Nimrud Letters
OECT	*Oxford Edition of Cuneiform Texts*
PRU 6	J. Nougayrol, *Textes en cunéiformes babyloniens des archives du grand palais et du palais sud d'Ugarit* (Paris, 1970)
RA	*Revue d'Assyriologie et d'Archéologie orientale*
RlA	*Reallexikon der Assyriologie und vorderasiatischen Archäologie*
RS	siglum for tablets from Ras Shamra (Ugarit)
SAA	*State Archives of Assyria*
SAAB	*State Archives of Assyria Bulletin*
SCCNH	*Studies on the Civilization and Culture of Nuzi and the Hurrians*
ShA 1	J. Eidem and J. Laessoe, *The Shemshara Archives, vol. 1: The Letters* (Copenhagen, 2001)
SMEA	*Studi Micenei ed Egeo-Anatolici*
SpTU I	H. Hunger, *Spätbabylonische Texte aus Uruk,* vol. 1 (Berlin, 1976)
STT	siglum for tablets from Sultantepe (Turkey)
TCL	*Textes cunéiformes du Louvre*
TIM	Texts in the Iraqi Museum
UF	*Ugarit-Forschungen*
VS	siglum for tablets in the Vorderasiatisches Museum (Berlin)
WZKM	*Wiener Zeitschrift für die Kunde des Morgenlandes*
YOS	Yale Oriental Series. Babylonian Texts
YTLR	Yale Tell Leilan Research
ZA	*Zeitschrift für Assyriologie und Vorderasiatische Archäologie*

Notes

1. [When an English-language source is indicated for a quotation, the quoted passage is taken from that edition. All other quotations are my translation—Trans.]

2. Note that the modern point of view on the question is different: we are very aware of the visual dimension of the original protocuneiform writing, which only gradually became phonetic. See esp. Green 1981.

3. For an analysis of lines 318–324 of this epic as the account of an invention under divine inspiration, see Foster 2005a.

4. This was an inscription of King Tiglath-pileser I: see Grayson 1991, 7–31, no. 1.

5. Note that our alphabetical transcription is the least economical, comprising twenty-one characters.

1. APPRENTICESHIPS IN THE ART OF THE SCRIBE

1. See the collective entry on "Sumer" in the *Supplément au Dictionnaire de la Bible* 72–73 (1999–2002): 78–359, as well as Bauer, Englund, and Krebernik 1998.

2. Colophons are the indications given by the copyist at the end of the tablet, such as his name, the title of the text, and the modalities of the copy.

3. See the inventory of H. Waetzoldt in Gesche 2001, 15–16. These texts are to be published in their entirety by G. Rubio (cf. Rubio 2000).

4. That also explains, at least in part, why we possess almost no private archives for the Ur III period.

5. Note, however, that the reformation of writing occurred during the reign of Ur-Nammu (Waetzoldt 1991, 638); and it is Ur-Nammu, not Shulgi, to whom we ought definitively to attribute what is now known as the "Code of Ur-Nammu." It is therefore possible that too much has been attributed to his son, simply because it is for the middle part of Shulgi's reign that the administrative documentation begins to be abundant.

6. The Sumerian term *é.dub.ba.a* is generally translated as "house of tablets" because of its Akkadian equivalent, *bīt ṭuppim,* but the ending in

.a is problematic. The expressions "house that ascribes tablets" and "house in which tablets are ascribed" have recently been suggested (Volk 2000, 3).

7. This quotation and the two following ones from "Shulgi E" are taken from the Sumerian text provided by the *Electronic Text Corpus of Sumerian Literature* (www.etcsl.orinst.ox.ac.uk).

8. Translation of these texts by H. Vanstiphout (1997).

9. This title, like all the others, is a modern invention: the Mesopotamian tradition was to cite a work by its first words (incipit).

10. Charpin 2001, 30n56. This argument supplements others of an architectural order (Margueron 1982, 345–349; Margueron 1986, 144).

11. Many examples have been collected in K. Radner (2005, 244–250). For the earlier period, cf. Klein 1986.

12. For the current state of the question and bibliography, see Svenbro 1997 and Gavrilov 1997; the latter contains a vigorous argument for the view that silent reading existed well before Saint Augustine's time.

13. For many Old Babylonian references to *amārum* in the sense of "to read," see *CAD* A/II, 18.

14. See the examples collected in *CAD* T, 111b.

15. References in *CAD* Š/II, 166b (with a different translation).

16. "The book from which you will learn to read Latin is the psalter; but only those who know how to read French perfectly will be placed in that class" (J.-B. de La Salle, *Conduites des écoles chrétiennes* [Avignon, 1720], chap. 3, eighth article "on reading Latin").

17. Civil, Gurney, and Kennedy 1986, 45–69; Gurney 1989, nos. 103–141; Maul 1991, 858–860.

18. The tablets published by P. Gesche (2001) are held at the British Museum and are acquisitions made in the nineteenth century. Their precise origin, and especially, their archaeological context are unknown; most seem to have come from Babylon and Sippar. Note the discovery in the recent excavations at Nippur of school texts from the second half of the eighth century (Cole 1996): lists of signs and lexical lists (nos. 114–123), lists of proper names with a scholastic aim (nos. 124–127), a copy of "Advice to a Prince" (no. 128).

19. Letter *SAA* 10 160:49 contains a list of five professions listed in the following order: scribes *(ṭupšarrū)*, lamenters *(kalū)*, exorcists *(āšipū)*, diviners *(bārū)*, and doctors *(asū)*. Medicine is not generally singled out

as a particular domain, however, though a distinction is sometimes made between "medicine" *(asūtu)* and "exorcism" *(āšipūtu).*

20. See the commentary in Rochberg 2000, 361–362. For the dating of that letter to the reign of Esarhaddon, see Fincke 2003–2004, 118n56.

21. *SAA* 16 65. Giving one's child the name of the reigning king or of one of his predecessors was also forbidden (Kataja 1987).

22. That oath is totally different in nature from the oath taken by the diviners in the Old Babylonian period (at that time, professional confidentiality was at issue, that is, the obligation not to divulge anything regarding the content of oracular inquiries).

23. This prologue already existed in the version copied in Ugarit in the thirteenth century (George 2007c).

24. Note the existence of an exercise in paleography: one fragment is from Niniveh, and another was discovered in Nimrud (*CTN* 4 229).

25. Seidl 2007; more precisely, it is the type of calamus used to write on a wax tablet, which no doubt represented the most prestigious type of support at the time.

26. Consider this comment by P. A. Beaulieu: "In short, the author of the Verse Account accuses Nabonidus of having imposed a 'knowledge' and 'wisdom' alien to Babylonian culture, and of having claimed that they were superior to the oldest and most sacred writings of Mesopotamia" (1989, 218). Let me add that the author of the Verse Account denies Nabonidus not the art of the scribe in general *(ṭupšarrūtu)* but, precisely, "the art of writing in cuneiform [literally, "striking of the stylus," *mihiṣ qān ṭuppī*]." In the Neo-Babylonian period, in fact, Aramaic writing was very widespread in Mesopotamia, but the scholarly texts continued to be written in cuneiform. To confess that one had not mastered that writing system amounted to admitting one did not have direct access to the Mesopotamian religious tradition.

27. The first author to my knowledge to have made that claim is J. Renger (1971, 33).

28. By way of comparison, during the same era, the correspondence of a highly skilled scribe such as Mar-Issar contained a repertoire of 225 signs (170 syllabic signs and 55 logograms).

29. Wilcke 2000, 32. New data have become available since his study. Among the school tablets from the house of Ur-Utu, Tanret has identified a small group of obviously more ancient date (2002). They must

have belonged to the nun-*nadītum* who lived in that house before Ur-Utu's father moved in: that is the first evidence of a scribal apprenticeship by a woman of that status.

30. Such is the case for the woman scribe named Shima-ilat in *ARM* 22 322: 58 (inventory of Shimatum's dowry). Princess Kiru may also have had a woman scribe in her entourage (Durand 1984, 167n41).

31. The woman, named Attar-palṭi, lent money belonging to the goddess Mulissu in two contracts dating from a postcanonical eponymy, between 648 and 612 (*CTN* 3 39; 4 and env. 5, as well as 40:3).

32. Praise of the craft of scribe published by Sjöberg 1972, which expresses no disdain for other statuses.

33. *Ṭupšarrūtam wuddi lamdāni* (*CCT* 4 63: 5, cited in *CAD* Ṭ, 163a).

34. ᵈNÀ *bānu šiṭri ṭupšarrūti*, cf. *CAD* Ṭ, 162b; such a use of the word *šiṭrum* is unusual, however.

2. THE ARCHIVAL DOCUMENTS

1. See Charpin 2002a, in an issue of the *Bibliothèque de l'École des chartes* devoted to the "exports of diplomatics." That study is republished in English translation in Charpin 2010, chap. 2. Note that K. R. Veenhof—who writes in English—in seeking to point out the need for such an approach, uses the German term *Urkundenlehre* (1986b, 15), which was also adopted unchanged by M. Brosius (2003b). Although diplomatics was very well developed in Germany in the nineteenth century, it was founded by the Frenchman Jean Mabillon (*De re diplomatica*, 1681).

2. The most recent datable tablet is an astronomical text from A.D. 75 (Sachs 1976).

3. It is striking that references to clay *(ṭidu)* as a support for writing are very rare in the Akkadian texts, occupying a scant quarter-page in the *CAD* Ṭ, 109.

4. Bonneterre 1988. That technique has been used especially by specialists on the Creto-Mycenaean world (bibliography in Palaima 2003, 174).

5. See the conclusive argument of Margueron 1995. F. Joannès (1990, 25) believed he had found a mention in a late text of a tablet "deposited in the kiln (to be baked)," but the text simply says that the tablet "is in the kitchen *(bīt tinūri)*"; Baker 2003, 243, must also be corrected.

6. I am speaking here only of archival documents, not of commemorative inscriptions, which were sometimes engraved in stone or metal.

7. Otten 1988. English translation in Beckman 1996, 108–117 (no. 18C) (with bibliography).

8. Marazzi 1994. The question has arisen what writing system and language were notated on the diptych with vestiges of wax discovered in the famous shipwreck of Ulu Burun off the coast of Turkey; see the series of articles published in *Anatolian Studies* 41 (1992). A single mention of a "wax tablet" *(ṭuppa ša iškuri)* can be found in the Ugarit archives *(PRU* 6 18:23).

9. Donbaz and Stolper 1997, 101, no. 27, line 8 (eight scrolls were part of a loan that included land, water, and animals).

10. The *CAD* M/I gives only one reference for *magallatu,* but there are others, indicated in a brief note, *RA* 72 (1978): 96.

11. The tablets written in Aramaic are an exception in this respect (Fales 2007, 103).

12. Another question, still the object of debate, has to do with the orientation of the writing. J. Marzahn has done some interesting experiments, which he explained in a still-unpublished paper given at a colloquium in Baghdad in March 2001.

13. B. Kienast maintains that the tablet was covered with a fine layer of flour before the envelope was formed (1996, 2), but I confess I do not know whether analyses have been conducted on the fine white dust sometimes seen when an envelope is opened.

14. Note that the text of the envelope almost always appears upside down in relation to that of the internal tablet. This makes it possible, in cases where only half a document has been preserved, to have a complete text.

15. This phenomenon is well known, for example, in the case of C. H. Johns's collection of Neo-Assyrian documents and the tablets from the Ur III period published by N. Schneider.

16. The same is true for M. J. Steve's book on the Elamite syllabary (1992): all the usefulness of this volume lies in the fact that it confines itself to one geographically and culturally well-delimited region.

17. For the Old Babylonian period, see A. Goetze's introduction to his book on divinatory texts (1947). This study has not yet been superseded, despite inaccuracies that would now have to be corrected. For the Sumerian literary texts of the same period, see Mittermayer 2006.

18. See http://www.cdp.bham.ac.uk.

19. For a similar example dating from the Ur III period, see Hallo 1977.

20. For an example, see Charpin and Beyer 1990. The oldest impressions of Yasim-Sumu's seal mention only the title "scribe" for that official in the Mari palace, whereas the most recent include his title as "bookkeeper-archivist."

21. For the Ur III period, see, for example, the observations of I. Winter, confirmed by H. Waetzoldt (1991, 640b).

22. Unpublished A.4344 in Charpin forthcoming c. The text distinguishes the "engraving" *(naqārum)*, which refers to the iconography, from the "inscription" *(šaṭārum)*, which refers to the legend.

23. For that practice, see the observations of Voet and Van Lerberghe 1994. These authors have identified chronological differences: at the start of the Old Babylonian period, the notations were made under the impression, perpendicular to the figure, and in the same ductus as the main text; in the late Old Babylonian period, notations were inscribed on the impressions themselves, vertically between the figures, and in a smaller ductus.

24. Nevertheless, prosopography often allows one to identify the seal's owner: see the examples of Sippar studied by Voet and Van Lerberghe 1993.

25. Note that in the unpublished AO 11152, Damiq-ilishu, once again the seller, used his own seal.

26. Charpin and Durand 1981, no. 107A, lines 12–13 and 107, lines 15–16.

27. The seal impression in BIN 7 64 occupies three lines, but there are only two lines in the unpublished AO 11147. That confirms what other similar examples have already shown, namely, that stamps of the *bur.gul* type were fashioned at the time the contract was drawn up and were then destroyed (Charpin 1980, 14 and note d).

28. In a sense, then, the cylinder seal can be considered a "status symbol"; see Gorelick and Gwinett 1990.

29. See in particular the writings of D. Beyer, F. Blocher, G. Colbow, C. Reichel, D. Stein, and B. Teissier and the recent collection of studies edited by Hallo and Winter (2001).

30. I shall limit myself here to a few significant situations. For an analysis of other examples, see Sanders 2006.

31. See, for example, the study limited to the sales contracts from the region between Sippar and Eshnunna in the early Old Babylonian period (Skaist 1990).

32. See Wilhelm 1970. It is common in the history of writing for both the writing system and the language it notated to be borrowed. The adapta-

tion of the writing system to the language of the borrowing people generally occurs only at a second stage. The Hurrians do not seem to have felt the need for that writing in their documents, as opposed to their correspondence.

33. Wilhelm 1991. This letter must be supplemented by the famous "Mitannian letter" sent to the pharaoh by the Mitannian king Tushratta and discovered in the Egyptian capital of the time, Tell al-'Amarna (see G. Wilhelm's translation in Moran 1992, 63–71 [EA 24]).

34. The hypothesis that the second scribe is drawing on a sheet of papyrus or leather is not accepted by M. Fales (2007, 107).

35. NL 86 (Iraq 28: 181), quoted in M. Fales (2007, 109).

36. The number of extant clay tablets written in Aramaic continues to grow, however. New examples have recently been discovered in Tell Shioukh Fawqnai near Karkemish and in Tell Sheikh Hamad on the Lower Habur; see Lemaire 2001.

37. SAA 17 2. See commentary of Fales 2007, 104n47.

38. In letter NL (Iraq 17: 130), an official has translated into Akkadian a letter for the king written in Aramaic. Fales has shown that one word from that letter was not translated into Akkadian but simply reproduced in Aramaic (2007, 110), which indicates the extensive Aramaization of elites at that time.

39. See esp., for the pre-Sargonic and Sargonic periods (twenty-fifth to twenty-third centuries B.C.), Visicato 2000. Note as well the studies limited to geographically and chronologically restricted corpora, such as Negri Scafa 1999 (Nuzi), Ikeda 1999 (Emar), and van Soldt 2001b (Ugarit).

40. Charpin 1992a; new translation in Durand 1997, 103–110 and Foster 2005c, 221–223. For the Neo-Assyrian period, see Parpola 1987.

41. See Lieberman 1992, 130 and no. 18. Lieberman's untimely death kept him from publishing the Manual of Sumerian Legal Forms he was preparing. For a recently published example, see Hallo 2002 and Klein and Sharlach 2007.

42. See esp. the collection of studies published in Veenhof 1986a, and, for the most recent periods, Pedersén 1998. See also Brosius 2003a. For Assur, see Pedersén 1985–1986; for Babylon, Pedersén 2005.

43. Think, for example, of the tablets illegally exhumed in Meskene (about 250 have currently been published) after the salvage excavations at the site—which had uncovered about 450 tablets—had come to an end in 1976. But the situation of greatest concern is Iraq since the Gulf War.

44. For a similar enumeration in an Old Assyrian letter, see *CTMMA* 1 no. 84a.
45. Sigrist 1984, 19 ("between fifty and seventy years"). I have taken into account the observations by Kraus (1985b, 530) but have corrected his calculations. He arrived at 140 years, no doubt by confusing Lipit-Enlil with Lipit-Eshtar.
46. There are exceptions, of course, as demonstrated by the archives of Ur-Utu found in his house in Tel ed-Dēr, in ancient Sippar-Amnānum; see Janssen 1992, 30–32. Another case is provided by Cole 1996.
47. The treaties found prior to that time correspond to draft agreements, not to the text of the treaties actually concluded (Charpin forthcoming d).
48. Cf. Charpin 1984, 1985a, and 1985b. K. R. Veenhof makes reference to my writings on the question in his introduction (1986b, 8), but without adopting the term "dead archives," which I define in Charpin 1985a, 255 and Charpin 1985b, 461. In a study that has been too long overlooked, G. Goossens saw the importance of dead archives but did not use the term (1952, 105).
49. I find it regrettable that Brosius did not understand its importance (2003b, 8). The concept of "silent archives" introduced by C. Castel is unfortunate (1995, 131). By that term she designates archives whose status cannot be established; there are thus in reality only two types of archives, not three.
50. For contemporary archives, the term "dead archives" designates superannuated documents that must nevertheless be preserved. In Mesopotamian antiquity, discarded documents were preserved only accidentally, as a result of the nature of the clay support. What I call "dead archives" consist of outdated tablets that were intentionally thrown away (and not simply moved elsewhere).
51. Italics in quoted passages indicate that the translation is uncertain.
52. For other references and a published example of a (dated) copy of a text held in the archives of the capital, see Stol 2001.
53. Garfinkle 2004, 20; I am not in agreement with Garfinkle, however, when he maintains that only the debt tablets preserved in sealed envelopes kept their value (21).

3. ORAL AND WRITTEN, PART 1

1. It is a letter from a king of Isin (Damiq-ilishu, or, according to C. Wilcke, Enlil-bani) to a king whose identity is unclear, either Apil-Sin of Babylon or Rim-Sin of Larsa.

2. The corpus is published in the *Archives royales de Mari* and the *Florilegium marianum* series; more than 1,200 letters have been edited and translated into French in Durand 1997, 1998, and 2000. English-language collection in Heimpel 2003 (see Charpin 2005–2006b).

3. A project to resume study of these letters has recently been undertaken by M. Jursa; see Hackl 2007 (corpus assembled 4–6).

4. Observations about "scribe's hands" also apply to the shape of the tablets: in this case, it does seem to have been the scribe himself who fashioned his tablet.

5. A photograph of a letter in an envelope with its "supplement" appears in Michel 2008, 140.

6. *ARM* 4 86 (*LAPO* 17 772).

7. *ARM* 1 18 (*LAPO* 16 43).

8. See the unpublished A.3611 quoted in Charpin 2010, chap. 1.

9. Apparently the procedure Hammurabi followed was not dictation: he "told" Shu-nuhra-Halu about the matter, and the scribe would then put it in writing.

10. *ARM* 26/1 1.

11. Note the parallel between the art of the scribe (*ṭušarrūtum*) and that of the diviner (*bārūtum*) found in the unpublished A.2583 (see Charpin 2010, introduction). For the oath of a "chief scribe" to the Hittite king Suppiluliuma II, see Singer 2003, 346n35.

12. A.1101 (*LAPO* 16 230); see Sasson 1998, 462.

13. I am not referring here to the letters sent by the king while traveling, to an official or a member of his family residing in the Mari palace, which, logically, were discovered in that building.

14. That is the case, for example, of the "*pro domo* defense" of Yasmah-Addu (Durand 1987, 175) or in *ARM* 1 109 (*LAPO* 16 70).

15. The letters written *by them* are comparatively much rarer: 41 for Yasmah-Addu (versus 483 received, that is, 8.5 percent) and 86 for Zimri-Lim (versus 1,625 received, that is, 4.7 percent). These figures do not take into account the letters not yet published.

16. Unpublished M.11368. This is a letter sent by Samiya; on this subject see Charpin and Ziegler 2003, 167.

17. For the Neo-Assyrian king's secretary, see Radner 2005, 7.
18. Note, however, that Darish-libur does not explicitly write that he read *(šušmūm)* the tablet to the king; he says that he brought *(ṭuhhūm)* it to him. I know of no parallel to this passage: are we to understand that Zimri-Lim himself read the letter?
19. There are exceptions, of course: a letter received from Yasmah-Addu in Tuttul (Tell Bi'a) remained there instead of being brought back to be archived in Mari (Krebernik 2001, KTT 375).
20. For examples, see *ARM* 10 16 and 10 136 *(LAPO* 18 1158 and 1157); 10 131 *(LAPO* 18 1154) and 26/1 242. See also A.1285 and *ARM* 13 10 *(LAPO* 16 136 and 134).
21. But note the existence in the Old Assyrian archives of labels used to identify a single very precise tablet (Michel 2008, 124n23).
22. See, for example, *ARM* 1 24+ *(LAPO* 16 330): 3–8 and *ARM* 26/1 25.
23. It is striking to observe that Old Babylonian scribes considered the invention of envelopes to be linked to correspondence as well. In reality, the most ancient envelopes we possess are for contracts.
24. Note Michalowski's important remark on this question: "It is not surprising that the first letters are in Semitic 'Eblaite,' documented from the Syrian mound of Tell Mardikh, ancient Ebla. By this time cuneiform had been adapted to the writing of Semitic, using a fairly complete syllabary. Letters, by definition, are aimed at absent addressees, and the message has to be fully comprehensible and autonomous" (2003).

4. ORAL AND WRITTEN, PART 2

1. That oath was entirely different from the one the apprentice diviner had to swear in the first millennium.
2. In *ARM* 8 12+19: 32–33, the *māhiṣ sikkātim* is the last witness, that is, the scribe. In *ARM* 22 328 rev. iv: 4, we find the name of an individual followed by the comment: "That is the one who drove in the stakes."
3. *FM* 2 122: 39–44 (adopting the translation of J. Sasson in B. Lafont 2001, 250n162). See Guichard 1994. For the role of the cup in alliance ceremonies, see B. Lafont 2001, 267.
4. For other examples, see Charpin 2004a, 299.
5. Note the keen intuition of E. Cassin: "The headpiece, the turban, and the wig represent the individual, whose physical appearance they exalt

and whose influence they enhance. They are therefore objects ready-made for investiture procedures" (1987, 279).

6. We may wonder whether this was a vivid way of expressing himself (Guichard 1994, 240 note h) or the inversion of a symbolic gesture (cf. Michalowski 1994b, 35–37). See, more generally, Guichard 1997.

7. B. Lafont 2001, 271–276. J.-M. Durand has proposed that *napištum* is a term designating blood (Durand 2000–2001).

8. *ARM* 1 101: 6; *ARM* 7 105: 2; *ARM* 22 196: 2; *ARM* 22 234: 7.

9. Nine texts have been preserved: four in Mari and five in Tell Leilan (for detailed references, see B. Lafont 2001, 283–289). For the texts of Tell Leilan, see Eidem 2008.

10. See *ARM* 26/2 372: 56–57.

11. A good example is given in *ARM* 26/2 404.

12. Note that no Old Babylonian treaty is sealed, despite what is indicated in Frayne 1990, 753, 755 (Charpin 1992c, 89).

13. This is indicated in the treaty of Hattusili III with Ulmi-Tessub of Tarhuntassa (Beckman 1996, 107, no. 18B § 14).

14. Some texts of treaties include a clause relating to an obligation to reread its content on a regular basis. See, for example, Beckman 1996, 76, no. 11 § 28 (restored); 86, no. 13 § 16 (three times a year in that case).

15. Seven copies with the seal of the gods (Beckman 1996, 117, no. 18C § 28).

16. These elements of solemnization (copying the act on a more prestigious support than clay, placing that copy in a temple) are somewhat reminiscent of how, in the same era, acts of royal donations were treated in Babylonia. The original tablets, sealed by the king, were recopied on stone, with the addition of curses and iconography, thus becoming *kudurrus*. This evolution does not seem to have affected royal donations in Syria or the Hittite world (Charpin 2002b, 174nn38 [Hattusha and Ugarit] and 181 [Terqa]); but it may very well be that the dissymmetry of sources is to be attributed to the randomness governing finds and that we shall some day also discover copies on stone or metal in Syria or the Hittite world.

17. See my annotated translation of this text in Charpin 2000a, 89–90, no. 45. Another example of a clod of dirt destroyed in place of a tablet appears in TIM IV 40 (Leemans 1991, 327); see also Goddeeris 2002, 149 (*CT* 6 47a [*MHET* II/1 44]).

18. Commentary on the term *qīpum* by Kraus (1985a, 142), who is right to criticize the dictionaries for not having recognized that meaning.

19. This is particularly interesting in that "mouth" and "tablet" were used elsewhere as antonyms to distinguish a message transmitted orally from a written letter.

20. The only other example of an institution of that kind is the "Central Archives" of the Ugarit palace, called the "royal notary's office" by Nougayrol (1955, xxiv).

5. "LITERARY" WORKS AND LIBRARIES

1. Let me clarify that, for the archives of modern institutions such as the French "Archives nationales," there is a will to gather together and to classify. In that case, the term "archives" refers to the *collections* that such organizations have assembled and preserved.

2. Some "library" tablets contain what are often considered to be firing holes, which were intended to promote the evaporation of water from the core of the tablet (see Figure 36); that interpretation is not certain, however.

3. In special cases, a colophon indicates: "Sixth tablet of 'He who has seen everything,' Gilgamesh series" (Hunger 1968, 85, no. 255). The later version added twenty-eight lines at the beginning of the prologue. The Old Babylonian version of the Epic of Gilgamesh was thus known by a different incipit: "Surpassing all kings" *(Šūtur eli šarrī)*.

4. Since 2003 there has been a *Journal des Médecines Cunéiformes (Journal of Cuneiform Medicines)* (www.oriental.cam.ac.uk/jmc). See also Attia, Buisson, and Geller 2009.

5. There is even a complete version of the myth of Erra inscribed on a large tablet shaped like a giant amulet (*KAR* 169).

6. I have made two cuts in the long list of texts. Two identical copies of that letter exist; it is therefore not an original, but its authenticity and the fact that the letter comes from Ashurbanipal should not be cast in doubt.

7. See A.3340 (Durand 1988a, 53–54), as well as *ARM* 4 54 (*LAPO* 18 952).

8. Pedersén 1998, 178–179. See the project directed by E. Robson and S. Tinney, *The Geography of Knowledge in Assyria and Babylonia: A Diachronic Analysis of Four Scholarly Libraries* (http://cdl.museum. upenn.edu/gkab/).

9. For example: "On the other hand, at Šaduppûm (Tell Abu Harmal), lexical and literary texts were all recovered from within the temple of Nisaba and her spouse Haja, Sumerian patron-deities of the scribal art" (Lucas 1979, 311).

10. Nabu did not completely replace Nisaba. Rather, the two were sometimes linked together, as in the colophon of *KAR* 31 r. 27: *Nabû u Nisaba bēlê É mumme* (Hunger 1968, no. 192), or in the prohibition: MU ᵈAG *u* ᵈŠE.NAGU MU *šaṭru l*[*a tapaššiṭ*], "By Nabu and Nisaba, do not efface my inscribed name!" (Radner 2005, 170n915).

11. F. Al-Rawi undertook to publish the tablets in collaboration with various colleagues in a series of articles in the review *Iraq* (the oldest is Al-Rawi 1990).

12. References in *CAD* T, 18. The study by Offner (1950) is marred by anachronisms; see more recently the references collected by Hunger 1968, 12–14.

13. *CAD* Ṭ, 114b translates the passage somewhat differently: "Do not mishandle the tablet lest you damage the collection."

14. My apologies to any librarian who reads this—but I have encountered cases of such warped professionalism.

15. A list is provided in his epic (quotation in Fincke 2003–2004, 123–124, no. 108).

16. For statistics concerning the Epic of Gilgamesh, see Sallaberger 2008.

17. By contrast, the situation is largely analogous to that pertaining to literature in Sumerian: the corpora are nearly identical in the different places where manuscripts have been found.

6. MESSAGES FOR THE GODS AND FOR POSTERITY

1. For this chapter, I am greatly indebted to the excellent book by K. Radner (2005), which I reviewed in an article (Charpin forthcoming g).

2. Nazi-Maruttaš *MDP* 2 86; quotation and commentary in Slanski 2003, 41–42, and my remarks on this subject (Charpin 2002b, 176, about Nazi-Maruttaš *MDP* 2 86, and 183n104).

3. For this reading of the title of "musician" (N[AR]), line 4′, see J.-M. Durand in Ziegler 1999, 78n500.

4. A dog cemetery has even been found in the temple of Gula in Isin. An inscription explains there was a kennel there. Dogs were given the task of licking the wounds of the sick (their saliva contains enzymes with a tremendous healing power). Hence the association of dogs with Asklepios in Epidaurus, and even with Catholic churches, where Saint Roch, protector against the plague, is depicted accompanied by a dog. See Charpin forthcoming a.

5. On the back of the dog is a receptacle of sorts; the remedy described by the text was probably inside.

6. For a description of the statuette, currently in the Louvre, see Spycket 1981, 246–247 and fig. 169. This is not a representation of Hammurabi himself, contrary to what is often claimed.

7. The verb used here is *amārum,* "see, read," which could be an indication that Zimri-Lim too can be counted among the literate kings. Otherwise, he might have written: "so that I can have them read to me."

8. Like K. Radner (2005, 134–135), I understand the implicit complement of the verbal phrase "I have dedicated" to be the temple, and not, per A. K. Grayson, the "door socket" on which the inscription appears.

9. See von Dassow 2009.

10. Seminara 2004 is disappointing; see my remarks in Charpin 2006a.

11. The term "year name" is modern and does not altogether correspond to the ancients' way of conceiving things. They did not use the term *šumum,* "name," but rather *nībum,* "appellation" (Radner 2005, 111).

12. The only exception is the famous letter of Sargon to the god Assur; but precisely, this text does not belong to the annals genre.

13. Images, often remaining implicit, compare the historian to a miner who manages to extract from the gangue nuggets of facts, or to an archaeologist who arrives at the important stratum of facts under the mass of ideological and literary spoil earth covering it. Consider for example: "Despite the multi-layered cultural complexity underlying this narrative, the *historical data* therein may be *brought to the light of day* by the modern researcher through a critique of its constituent components and principles" (Fales 1999–2001, 138; my emphasis).

14. For a critique of the supposed greater objectivity of the Babylonian chronicles when compared to the Assyrian annals, see the studies cited in Fales 1999–2001, 120n18.

15. See my commentary in Charpin 2010, chap. 5. For the idea that the expression *ṣalmiya šar mīsarim* refers to the representation of the "king of justice" at the top of the stela, see the references collected in Slanski 2003, 261. The view that there was a statue separate from the stela has been argued most recently by Elsen-Novák and Novák 2006; I do not agree with their analysis, however.

16. And not simply because they were buried: inscribed bricks were usually concealed by the covering on the wall of which they were part (Charpin 2006a, 154 and n7). They are visible at present because they come from

excavated ruins. And such was in fact the ancients' intention, that posterity might learn of them.

17. There is no reason to doubt the veracity of this assertion by Samsi-Addu, *pace* J. G. Westenholz (2004).

CONCLUSION

1. See Linssen 2003. For the second-millennium rituals, see Durand and Guichard 1997. Surprises may yet lie in store, such as that yielded by the *Scherbenloch* of Uruk, where three rituals in Sumerian dating from the time of Rim-Sin were discovered, unfortunately in very poor condition (Cavigneaux 1996b, nos. 122–124).

2. M. A. Powell reconstituted an ingenious scenario according to which the monument was to be attributed to Naram-Sin and not to Manishtushu (1991), but that hypothesis has been invalidated by the manuscript discovered in the library of the temple of Sippar (Al-Rawi and George 1994, 139–148).

3. *TCL* 6 38. Similarly, *SpTU* I 2 is a pseudo-historical document written within the same context, indicating how Shulgi "disrupted the rites of the cult of Anu, the plans of Uruk, and the secret knowledge of the experts." This text dates from 251 B.C., that is, only five years prior to the completion of the Bīt Rēsh.

4. It is in fact by virtue of the syllabic equivalents of Old Babylonian texts that it has been possible to establish the reading of many of the logograms of later divinatory texts.

Bibliography

Abraham, K. 2004. *Business and Politics under the Persian Empire: The Financial Dealings of Marduk-naṣir-apli of the House of Egibi (521–487 B.C.E.).* Bethesda, Md.

Abrahami, P., and L. Coulon. 2008. "De l'usage et de l'archivage des tablettes cunéiformes d'Amarna." In Pantalacci 2008a, 1–26.

Abusch, T. 2002a. *Mesopotamian Witchcraft.* Leiden.

———, ed. 2002b. *Riches Hidden in Secret Places: Ancient Near Eastern Studies in Memory of Thorkild Jacobsen.* Winona Lake, Ind.

Abusch, T., and K. van der Toorn, eds. 1999. *Mesopotamian Magic: Textual, Historical, and Interpretative Perspectives.* Groningen.

Abusch, T. et al., eds. 2001. *Historiography in the Cuneiform World: Proceedings of the XLVe Rencontre Assyriologique Internationale, Part I, Harvard University.* Bethesda, Md.

Al-Jadir, W. 1998. "Découverte d'une bibliothèque dans le temple de la ville de Sippar (Abu Habbah)." *XXXIVe Rencontre assyriologique internationale, 6–10/VII/1987, Istanbul,* 707–715 (and pl. 207–213). Ankara.

Al-Rawi, F. N. H. 1990. "Tablets from the Sippar Library I. The 'Weidner Chronicle': A Supposititious Royal Letter Concerning a Vision." *Iraq* 52: 1–13 and pl. 1.

Al-Rawi, F. N. H., and S. Dalley. 2000. *Old Babylonian Texts from Private Houses at Abu Habbah Ancient Sippir Baghdad University Excavations.* London.

Al-Rawi, F. N. H., and A. R. George. 1994. "Tablets from the Sippar Library III: Two Royal Counterfeits." *Iraq* 56: 135–148.

Alster, B. 1987. "A Note on the Uriah Letter in the Sumerian Sargon Legend." *ZA* 77: 169–173.

———. 1997. *Proverbs of Ancient Sumer: The World's Earliest Proverb Collections.* Bethesda, Md.

———. 2007. *Sumerian Proverbs in the Schoyen Collection.* Bethesda, Md.

Anbar, M. 1975. "Textes de l'époque babylonienne ancienne." *RA* 69: 109–136.

André-Leicknam, B., and C. Ziegler, eds. 1982. *Naissance de l'écriture.* Paris.

Archi, A. 1992. "Transmission of the Mesopotamian Lexical and Literary Texts." *Quaderni di Semitistica* 18: 1–40.

————. 2003. "Archival Record-Keeeping at Ebla 2400–2350 B.C." In Brosius 2003a, 17–36.

Arnaud, D. 1980. "La bibliothèque d'un devin syrien à Meskéné-Emar (Syrie)." *CRAIBL,* 375–388.

————. 1987a. *Textes de la bibliothèque: Transcriptions et traductions, Recherches au pays d'Aštata. Emar 6/4.* Paris.

————. 1987b. "La Syrie du Moyen-Euphrate sous le protectorat hittite: Contrats de droit privé." *AuOr* 5: 211–241.

————. 2007. *Corpus des textes de bibliothèque de Ras Shamra-Ougarit (1936–2000) en sumérien, babylonien et assyrien.* Sabadell, Spain.

Attia, A. et al., eds. 2009. *Advances in Mesopotamian Medicine from Hammurabi to Hippocrates.* Leiden.

Baker, H. 2003. "Record-Keeping Practices as Revealed by the Neo-Babylonian Private Archival Documents." In Brosius 2003a, 241–263.

Battini, L. 1996. "La localisation des archives du palais sud-ouest de Ninive." *RA* 90: 33–40.

Bauer, J., R. K. Englund, and M. Krebernik. 1998. *Mesopotamien: Späturuk-Zeit und Frühdynastische Zeit.* Freibourg and Göttingen.

Bautier, R. H. 1961. "Les archives." In Samaran 1961, 1120–1166.

Beaulieu, P. A. 1989. *The Reign of Nabonidus King of Babylon 556–539 B.C.* New Haven, Conn.

————. 1993. "The Historical Background of the Uruk Prophecy." In Cohen et al. 1993, 41–52.

————. 2000. "The Descendants of Sîn-lēqi-unninni." In Marzahn et al. 2000, 1–16.

————. 2006. "The Astronomers of the Esagil Temple in the Fourth Century B.C." In Guinan et al. 2006, 5–22.

————. 2007. "Late Babylonian Intellectual Life." In Leick 2007, 473–484.

Beckman, G. 1983. "Mesopotamians and Mesopotamian Learning at Ḫattuša." *JCS* 35: 97–114.

————. 1996. *Hittite Diplomatic Text*s. Atlanta.

Beckman, G. et al., eds. 2003. *Hittite Studies in Honor of Harry A. Hoffner Jr. on the Occasion of His Sixty-fifth Birthday.* Winona Lake, Ind.

Behrens, H. et al., eds. 1989. *DUMU-E$_2$-DUB-BA-A: Studies in Honor of Å. W. Sjöberg.* Philadelphia.

Bezold, C. 1889–1899. *Catalogue of the Cuneiform Tablets in the Kouyunjik Collection of the British Museum.* 5 vols. London.

Biga, M. G. 2003. "The Reconstruction of a Relative Chronology for the Ebla Texts." *Orientalia* 72: 345–367.

Biggs, R. D. 1973. "On Regional Cuneiform Handwritings in Third Millennium Mesopotamia." *Orientalia* 42: 39–46.

Birot, M. 1985. "Les chroniques 'assyriennes' de Mari." *MARI* 4: 219–242.

Black, J. A., and G. Spada. 2008. *Texts from Ur Kept in the Iraq Museum and in the British Museum.* Messina.

Bleibtreu, E. 2003. "Bemerkungen zum Griffel des Tontafelschreibers." In Selz 2003, 1–5.

Böck, B. 1996. "'Wenn du zu Nintinuga gesprochen hast. . . .' Untersuchungen zu Aufbau, Inhalt, Sitz-im-Leben und Funktion sumerischer Gottesbriefe." *AoF* 23: 3–23.

———. 2000. *Mesopotamische Morphoskopie.* Vienna.

Bonechi, M. 1992. "Relations amicales syro-palestiniennes: Mari et Haşor au XVIIIe siècle av. J.C." In J.-M. Durand, ed., *Florilegium marianum: Recueil d'études en l'honneur de M. Fleury,* 9–22. Paris.

Bonneterre, D. 1988. "Pour une étude des dermatoglyphes digitaux sur des tablettes cunéiformes." *Akkadica* 59: 26–29.

Bordreuil, P., ed. 1991. *Une bibliothèque au sud de la ville: Les textes de la 34e campagne (1973).* Paris.

Borger, R. 1957–1971. "Geheimwissen." *RlA* 3: 188–191.

———. 1990. "Schlüssel zu M. E. Cohen, *CLAM.*" *BiOr* 47: 5–39.

———. 1996. *Beiträge zum Inschriftenwerk Assurbanipals.* Wiesbaden.

Bottéro, J. 1974. "Symptômes, signes, écritures en Mésopotamie ancienne." In J. P. Vernant et al., *Divination et rationalité,* 70–197. Paris.

———. 1985. *Mythes et rites de Babylone.* Geneva.

———. 1987. *La Mésopotamie: L'écriture, la raison et les dieux.* Paris. Translated into English by Zainab Bahrani and Marc Van De Mieroop as *Mesopotamia: Writing, Reasoning, and the Gods.* Chicago, 1992.

Boyer, G. 1958. *Textes juridiques.* Paris.

Brinkman, J. A. 2006. "Babylonian Royal and Land Grants, Memorials of Financial Interest, and Invocation of the Divine." *JESHO* 49: 1–47.

Brosius, M., ed. 2003a. *Ancient Archives and Archival Traditions.* Oxford.

———. 2003b. "Ancient Archives and Concepts of Record-Keeping: An Introduction." In Brosius 2003a, 1–16.

Brown, D. 2000. *Mesopotamian Planetary Astronomy-Astrology.* Groningen.

Buccellati, G. 1993. "Through a Tablet Darkly: A Reconstruction of Old Ak-kadian Monuments Described in Old Babylonian Copies." In Cohen et al. 1993, 58–71.

Butler, S. A. L. 1998. *Mesopotamian Conceptions of Dreams and Dream Rituals*. Münster.

Cancik-Kirschbaum, E. 1996. *Die Mittelassyrischen Briefe aus Tall Šeh-Ḥamad*. Berlin.

Cancik-Kirschbaum, E., and G. Chambon. 2006. "Les caractères en forme de coins: Le cas du cunéiforme." *RA* 100: 13–40.

Caquot, A., J. M. Tarragon, and J. L. Cunchillos. 1989. *Textes ougaritiques tome II: Textes religieux, rituels, correspondance*. Paris.

Cassin, E. 1987. *Le semblable et le différent: Symbolismes du pouvoir dans le Proche-Orient ancien*. Paris.

Castel, C. 1995. "Contexte archéologique et statut des documents: Les textes retrouvés dans les maisons mésopotamiennes du Ier millénaire av. J. C." *RA* 89: 109–137.

Cavigneaux, A. 1981. *Textes scolaires du temple de Nabû ša harê*. Baghdad.

———. 1982. "Schultexte aus Warka." *BaM* 13: 21–30.

———. 1996a. "Un colophon de Type Nabû ša Harê." *ASJ* 18: 23–30.

———. 1996b. *URUK: Altbabylonische Texte aus dem Planquadrat Pe XVI-4/5 nach Kopien von Adam Falkenstein*. Mainz.

———. 1999a. "Nabû ša harê und die Kinder von Babylon." In J. Renger, ed., *Babylon: Focus mesopotamischer Geschichte, Wiege früher Gelehrsam-keit, Mythos in der Moderne*, 385–391. Saarbrücken.

———. 1999b. "A Scholar's Library in Meturan? With an Edition of the Tab-let H 72 (Texts of Tell Haddad VII)." In Abusch and van der Toorn 1999, 251–273.

Çeçen, S., and K. Hecker. 1995. "*Ina mātīka eblum*: Zu einem neuen Text zum Wegerecht in der Kültepe-Zeit." In Dietrich and Loretz 1995, 31–41.

Chamaza, V. 1992. "Syntaxical and Stylistic Observations on the Text of the Eighth Campaign of Sargon II (TCL 3)." *SAAB* 6: 109–128.

Charpin, D. 1980. *Archives familiales et propriété privée en Babylonie anci-enne: Étude des documents de "Tell Sifr."* Geneva.

———. 1983. "Un inventaire général des trésors du palais de Mari." *MARI* 2: 211–214.

———. 1984. "Nouveaux documents du bureau de l'huile à l'époque assyri-enne." *MARI* 3: 83–126.

—. 1985a. "Les archives d'époque 'assyrienne' dans le palais de Mari." *MARI* 4: 243–268.

—. 1985b. "Les archives du devin Asqudum dans la résidence du 'Chantier A.'" *MARI* 4: 453–462.

—. 1986a. *Le clergé d'Ur au siècle d'Hammurabi (XIXe–XVIIIe siècles av. J.-C.).* Geneva.

—. 1986b. "Transmission des titres de propriété et constitution des archives privées en Babylonie ancienne." In Veenhof 1986a, 121–140.

—. 1987. "Nouveaux documents du bureau de l'huile (suite)." *MARI* 5: 597–599.

—. 1988. "Première partie." In Charpin, Joannès, Lackenbacher, and B. Lafont 1988, 7–232.

—. 1989. "Corrections, ratures, annulations: La pratique des scribes mésopotamiens." In R. Laufer, ed., *Le texte et son inscription,* 57–62. Paris.

—. 1990a. "Les divinités familiales des Babyloniens d'après les légendes de leurs sceaux-cylindres." In Ö. Tunca, ed., *De la Babylonie à la Syrie, en passant par Mari: Mélanges offerts à Monsieur J.-R. Kupper à l'occasion de son 70e anniversaire,* 59–78. Liège.

—. 1990b. "Une alliance contre l'Elam et le rituel du *lipit napištim.*" In F. Vallat, ed., *Contribution à l'histoire de l'Iran: Mélanges offerts à Jean Perrot,* 109–118. Paris.

—. 1991. "Un traité entre Zimri-Lim de Mari et Ibâl-pî-El II d'Ešnunna." In Charpin and Joannès 1991, 139–166.

—. 1992a. "Les malheurs d'un scribe, ou de l'inutilité du sumérien loin de Nippur." In M. Ellis 1992, 7–27.

—. 1992b. "Les légendes de sceaux de Mari: Nouvelles données." In G. Young, ed., *Mari in Retrospect,* 59–76. Winona Lake, Ind.

—. 1992c. Review of Frayne 1990. *RA* 86: 88–91.

—. 1993. "Un souverain éphémère en Ida-Maraṣ: Išme-Addu d'Ašnakkum." *MARI* 7: 165–192.

—. 1994a. "Le sumérien, langue morte parlée." *NABU*: 6.

—. 1994b. "Le sceptre de l'héritier." *NABU*: 8.

—. 1994c. Review of D. Arnaud, *Altbabylonische Rechts- und Verwaltungsurkunde* (Berlin, 1989). *RA* 88: 78–81.

—. 1995a. "'Lies natürlich....' À propos des erreurs de scribes dans les lettres de Mari." In Dietrich and Loretz 1995, 43–56.

—. 1995b. "La fin des archives dans le palais de Mari." *RA* 89: 29–40.

———. 1995c. "Centre et périphérie." *NABU*: 86.

———. 1997a. "Sapîratum, ville du Suhûm." *MARI* 8: 341–366.

———. 1997b. "'Manger un serment.'" In S. Lafont 1997, 85–96.

———. 1997c. "La version mariote de l'"insurrection générale contre Narâm-Sîn.'" In Charpin and Durand 1997a, 9–18.

———. 1999–2002. "Sumer III. Écoles et éducation." *Supplément au Dictionnaire de la Bible* 72: 215–226.

———. 2000a. "Lettres et procès paléo-babyloniens." In Joannès 2000, 69–111.

———. 2000b. "Les prêteurs et le palais: Les édits de *mîšarum* des rois de Babylone et leurs traces dans les archives privées." In A. C. V. M. Bongenaar, ed., *Interdependency of Institutions and Private Entrepreneurs (MOS Studies 2): Proceedings of the Second MOS Symposium (Leiden 1998)*, 185–211. Leiden.

———. 2001. "L'archivage des tablettes dans le palais de Mari: Nouvelles données." In van Soldt 2001a, 13–30.

———. 2002a. "Esquisse d'une diplomatique des documents mésopotamiens." *Bibliothèque de l'École des chartes* 160: 487–511.

———. 2002b. "La commémoration d'actes juridiques: À propos des *kudurrus* babyloniens." *RA* 96: 169–191.

———. 2002c. "Prophètes et rois dans le Proche-Orient amorrite: Nouvelles données, nouvelles perspectives." In D. Charpin and J.-M. Durand, eds., *Florilegium marianum VI: Recueil d'études à la mémoire d'André Parrot*, 7–38. Paris.

———. 2002d. "La politique hydraulique des rois paléo-babyloniens." *Annales, Histoire, Sciences sociales* 57/3: 545–559.

———. 2003. "Le sacrifice de chèvres lors d'alliances sous le règne de Zimri-Lim." *NABU*: 48.

———. 2004a. "Histoire politique du Proche-Orient amorrite (2002–1595)." In Charpin, Edzard, and Stol 2004, 25–480.

———. 2004b. "Données nouvelles sur la région du Petit Zab au XVIIIe siècle av. J.-C." *RA* 98: 151–178.

———. 2005–2006a. Review of M. P. Streck 2000. *AfO* 51: 282–292.

———. 2005–2006b. Review of Heimpel 2003. *AfO* 51: 295–304.

———. 2006a. "Les inscriptions royales suméro-akkadiennes d'époque paléo-babyloniennes." *RA* 100: 131–160.

———. 2006b. "Comment faire connaître la civilisation mésopotamienne." *RA* 100: 107–130.

———. 2007a. "Le 'scribe accroupi' en Mésopotamie." *NABU*: 61.

———. 2007b. Review of Michalowski and Veldhuis 2006. *RA* 101: 186.

———. 2007c. "Les mots et les choses: *Girginakku* 'bibliothèque.'" *NABU*: 60.

———. 2008a. "Tell Hariri / Mari: Textes. II. Les archives de l'époque amorrite." *Supplément au Dictionnaire de la Bible* 14: 233–248.

———. 2008b. "Archivage et classification: Un récapitulatif de créances à Mari sous Zimrî-Lîm." In R. D. Biggs et al., eds., *Proceedings of the 51e Rencontre Assyriologique Internationale held at the Oriental Institute of the University of Chicago July 18–22, 2005*, 1–13. Chicago.

———. 2010. *Writing, Law, and Kingship: Essays on Old Babylonian Mesopotamia*. Chicago.

———. Forthcoming a. "Zur Funktion Mesopotamischer Tempel." In G. J. Selz and K. Wagensonner, eds., *The Empirical Dimension of Ancient Near Eastern Studies*. Münster.

———. Forthcoming b. "Les formulaires juridiques des contrats de Mari à l'époque amorrite: Entre tradition babylonienne et innovation." In S. Démare-Lafont and A. Lemaire, eds., *Trois millénaires de formulaires juridiques ouest-sémitiques*, 13–42. Geneva.

———. Forthcoming c. *La correspondance à l'époque amorrite. Écriture, acheminement et lecture des lettres d'après les archives royales de Mari*.

———. Forthcoming d. "Guerre et paix dans le monde amorrite et postamorrite." In H. Neumann et al., eds., *Krieg und Frieden im Alten Vorderasien*. Wiesbaden.

———. Forthcoming e. "L'historien face aux archives paléo-babyloniennes." English translation in H. D. Baker et al., eds., *Too Much Data? Generalizations and Model-building in Ancient Economic History on the Basis of Large Corpora of Documentary Evidence*. Münster.

———. Forthcoming f. "L'exercice du pouvoir par les rois de la Ière dynastie de Babylone: Problèmes de méthode." In G. Wilhelm, ed., *Organization, Representation and Symbols of Power in the Ancient Near East*. Winona Lake, Ind.

———. Forthcoming g. "Se faire un nom: La louange du roi, la divinisation royale et la quête de l'immortalité en Mésopotamie." *RA* 102.

Charpin, D., and D. Beyer. 1990. "Les sceaux de Yasîm-sûmû." *MARI* 6: 619–624.

Charpin, D., and J.-M. Durand. 1981. *Documents cunéiformes de Strasbourg conservés à la Bibliothèque Nationale et Universitaire*. Vol. 1. Paris.

———. 1985. "La prise du pouvoir par Zimri-Lim." *MARI* 4: 293–343.

———. 1993. "Notes de lecture: Texte aus dem Sînkāšid Palast." *MARI* 7: 367–375.

———, eds. 1994. *Florilegium marianum II: Recueil d'études à la mémoire de Maurice Birot*. Paris.

———, eds. 1997a. *Florilegium marianum III: Recueil d'études à la mémoire de Marie-Thérèse Barrelet*. Paris.

———. 1997b. "Aššur avant l'Assyrie." *MARI* 8: 367–392.

———. 2001. *Mari, Ébla et les Hourrites: Dix ans de travaux. Actes du colloque international (Paris, mai 1993). Deuxième partie*. Paris.

Charpin, D., D. O. Edzard, and M. Stol. 2004. *Mesopotamien: Die altbabylonische Zeit*. Freibourg and Göttingen.

Charpin, D., H. Hunger, and H. Waetzoldt. 2009. "Schreiber (Scribe)." *RlA* 12: 266–269.

Charpin, D., and F. Joannès, eds. 1991. *Marchands, diplomates et empereurs: Études sur la civilisation mésopotamienne offertes à Paul Garelli*. Paris.

———. 1992. *La circulation des biens, des personnes et des idées dans le Proche-Orient ancien: Actes de la XXXVIIIe Rencontre Assyriologique Internationale (Paris, 8–10 juillet 1991)*. Paris.

Charpin D., F. Joannès, S. Lackenbacher, and B. Lafont, 1988. *Archives Epistolaires de Mari I/2*. Paris.

Charpin, D., and N. Ziegler. 2003. *Florilegium marianum V: Mari et le Proche-Orient à l'époque amorrite: Essai d'histoire politique*. Paris.

Civil, M. 1975. "Lexicography." In S. J. Lieberman, ed., *Sumerological Studies in Honor of Thorkild Jacobsen on His Seventieth Birthday*, 123–157. Chicago.

———. 1979. *The Series lú = ša and Related Texts*. Rome.

———. 1983. "An Early Dynastic School Exercise from Lagaš." *BiOr* 40: 559–566.

———. 1985. "Sur les 'livres d'écolier' à l'époque paléo-babylonienne." In Durand and Kupper 1985, 67–78.

———. 1987. "Ur III Bureaucracy: Quantitative Aspects." In M. Gibson and R. D. Biggs, eds., *The Organization of Power*, 43–54. Chicago.

———. 1989. "The Texts from Meskene-Emar." *AuOr* 7: 5–25.

———. 1998. "Bilingual Teaching." In Maul 1998, 1–7.

———. 1999–2000. "Reading Gilgameš." In M. Molina et al., eds., Arbor scientiae: *Estudios del Próximo Oriente Antiguo dedicados a Gregorio* del Olmo Lete con occasión de su 65 aniversario, 179–189. Sabadell, Spain.

———. 2008. *The Early Dynastic Practical Vocabulary A (Archaic HAR-RA A)*. Rome.

Civil, M., O. R. Gurney, and D. Kennedy. 1986. *The Sag-Tablet: Lexical Texts in the Asmolean Museum. Middle Babylonian Grammatical Texts. Miscellaneous Texts*. Rome.

Clancier, P. 2005. *Les bibliothèques en Babylonie dans la deuxième moitié du Ier millénaire av. J.-C.* Münster.

Cohen, M. E. 1988. *The Canonical Lamentations of Ancient Mesopotamia*. Potomac, Md.

Cohen, M. E. et al., eds. 1993. *The Tablet and the Scroll: Near Eastern Studies in Honor of W. W. Hallo*. Bethesda, Md.

Cohen, Y. 2004. "Kidin-Gula—The Foreign Teacher at the Emar Scribal School." *RA* 98: 81–100.

Cole, S. W. 1996. *The Early Neo-Babylonian Governor's Archive from Nippur*. Chicago.

Cooper, J. S. 2006. "Response for the First Session: Origins, Functions, Adaptation, Survival." In Sanders 2006, 83–87.

Cooper, J. S., and W. Heimpel. 1983. "The Sumerian Sargon Legend." *JAOS* 103: 67–82.

Dain, A. 1961. "Introduction à la paléographie." In Samaran 1961, 528–531.

D'Alfonso, L., Y. Cohen, and D. Sürenhagen, eds. 2008. *The City of Emar among the Late Bronze Age Empires: History, Landscape, and Society. Proceedings of the Konstanz Emar Conference, 25.–26.04.2006*. Münster.

Dalley, S. 1973. "Old Babylonian Greeting Formulae and the Iltani's Archive from Rimah." *JCS* 25: 79–88.

Dalley, S., C. B. F. Walker, and D. J. Hawkins. 1976. *The Old Babylonian Tablets from Tell al Rimah*. London.

Daniels, P. T. 1995a. "The Decipherment of Ancient Near Eastern Scripts." In Sasson 1995, 81–93.

———. 1995b. "Cuneiform Calligraphy." In Mattila 1995, 81–90.

Dassow, E. von. 2009. "Narām-Sîn of Uruk: A New King in an Old Shoebox." *JCS* 61: 63–91.

Da Riva, R. 2008. *The Neo-Babylonian Royal Inscriptions: An Introduction*. Münster.

Démare[-Lafont], S. 1987. "L'interprétation de Nb 5,31 à la lumière des droits cunéiformes." In J.-M. Durand, ed., *La femme dans le Proche-Orient* antique: *Compte rendu de la XXXIIIe Rencontre Assyriologique Internationale (Paris, 7–10 juillet 1986), 49–52.* Paris.

Dercksen, J. G., ed. 2004. *Assyria and Beyond: Studies Presented to Mogens Trolle Larsen.* Leiden.

Dick, M. B., ed. 1999. *Born in Heaven, Made on Earth: The Making of the Cult Image in the Ancient Near East.* Winona Lake, Ind.

Dietrich, M. 1990. "Die akkadische Texte der Archive und Bibliotheken von Emar." *UF* 22: 25–48.

———. 2001. "Babylonische Sklaven auf der Schreiberschule. Anspielungen auf *ṭupšarrūtu*-Lehrverträge in *OIP* 114,83 und YOS 19,110." In van Soldt 2001a, 67–81.

Dietrich, M., and O. Loretz, eds. 1995. *Vom Alten Orient zum Alten Testament, Festschrift für Wolfram Freiherrn von Soden zum 85. Geburtstag am 19. Juni 1993.* Neukirchen.

Dombradi, E. 1996. *Die Darstellung des Rechtsaustrags in den altbabylonischen Prozessurkunden.* Stuttgart.

Donbaz, V., and M. W. Stolper. 1997. *Istanbul Murašû Texts.* Leiden.

Dorleijn, G., and H. L. J. Vanstiphout, eds. 2003. *Cultural Repertoires: Structure, Function, and Dynamics.* Leuven.

Driver, G. R. 1976. *Semitic Writing.* 3rd ed. London.

Durand, J.-M. 1982. "Sumérien et Akkadien en pays amorite, I: Un document juridique archaïque de Mari." *MARI* 1: 79–89.

———. 1984. "Trois études sur Mari." *MARI* 3: 127–180.

———. 1985a. "La situation historique des Šakkanakku: Nouvelle approche." *MARI* 4: 147–172.

———. 1985b. "Les dames du palais de Mari à l'époque du royaume de Haute Mésopotamie." *MARI* 4: 385–436.

———. 1987. "Documents pour l'histoire du royaume de Haute-Mésopotamie (I)." *MARI* 5: 155–198.

———. 1988a. *Archives épistolaires de Mari.* Vol. 1. Paris.

———. 1988b. "Lecture d'un texte divinatoire babylonien." In A. M. Christin, ed., *Espaces de la lecture,* 54–59. Paris.

———. 1991. "Précurseurs syriens aux protocoles néo-assyriens: Considérations sur la vie politique aux Bords-de-l'Euphrate." In Charpin and Joannès 1991, 13–72.

———. 1992. "Unité et diversités au Proche-Orient à l'époque amorrite." In Charpin and Joannès 1992, 97–128.

———. 1997. *Les documents épistolaires du palais de Mari.* Vol. 1. Paris.

———. 1998. *Les documents épistolaires du palais de Mari.* Vol. 2. Paris.

———. 2000. *Les documents épistolaires du palais de Mari.* Vol. 3. Paris.

———. 2000–2001. "Assyriologie." *Annuaire du Collège de France:* 693–705.

———. 2003. "La conscience du temps et sa commémoration en Mésopotamie: L'exemple de la documentation mariote." *Akkadica* 124: 1–12.

———. 2006. "La lettre de Labarna au roi de Tigunânum, un réexamen." In G. del Olmo Lete et al., eds., Shapal tibnim mû illakû: *Studies Presented to Joaquín Sanmartín on the Occasion of His Sixty-fifth Birthday,* 219–227. Sabadell, Spain.

———. 2008. "La religion à l'époque amorrite d'après les archives de Mari." In G. del Olmo Lete, ed., *Mythologie et Religion des Sémites Occidentaux.* Vol. 1: *Ebla et Mari,* 161–716. Leuven.

Durand, J.-M., and M. Guichard. 1997. "Les rituels de Mari." In Charpin and Durand 1997a, 19–78.

Durand, J.-M., and J. R. Kupper, eds. 1985. *Miscellanea babylonica: Mélanges offerts à Maurice Birot.* Paris.

Edel, E. 1994. *Die ägyptisch-hethitische Korrespondenz aus Boghazköi in babylonischer und hethitischer Sprache.* Opladen.

———. 1997. *Der Vertrag zwischen Ramses II. von Ägypten und Ḫattušili III. von Ḫatti.* Berlin.

Edzard, D. O. 1976–1980. "Keilschrift." *RlA* 5: 544–568.

———. 1997a. "Le développement de l'écriture cunéiforme: Le fonctionnement de l'écriture sumérienne." In Talon and Van Lerberghe 1997, 33–39.

———. 1997b. *Gudea and His Dynasty.* Toronto.

Eidem, J. 2000. "Northern Jezira in the Eighteenth Century B.C.: Aspects of Geo-Political Patterns." In O. Rouault and M. Wäfler, eds., *La Djéziré et l'Euphrate syriens de la protohistoire à la fin du IIe millénaire av. J. C.: Tendances dans l'interprétation historique des données nouvelles,* 255–264. Turnhout.

———. 2002. "The Clay They Wrote On—Old Babylonian Letters as Artefacts." In L. Al-Gailani Werr et al., eds., *Of Pots and Plans: Papers on the Archaeology and History of Mesopotamia and Syria Presented to David Oates in Honour of His Seventy-fifth Birthday,* 74–81. London.

———. 2008. "Apum: A Kingdom on the Old Assyrian Route." In Veenhof and Eidem 2008, 265–352.

Ellis, M. deJong, ed. 1992. *Nippur at the Centennial: Papers Read at the 35e Rencontre Assyriologique Internationale, Philadelphia 1988.* Philadelphia.

Ellis, R. S. 1968. *Foundation Deposits in Ancient Mesopotamia*. New Haven, Conn.

Elsen-Novák, G., and M. Novák. 2006. "Der 'König der Gerechtigkeit': Zur Ikonologie und Teleologie des 'Codex' Ḫammurapi." *BaM* 37: 131–155.

Englund, R. K. 1998. "Texts from the Late Uruk Period." In Bauer, Englund, and Krebernik 1998, 15–233.

Eph'al, I., and H. Tadmor. 2006. "Observations on Two Inscriptions of Esarhaddon: Prism Nineveh A and the Letter to the God." In Y. Amit et al., eds., *Essays on Ancient Israel in Its Near Eastern Context: A Tribute to Nadav Na'aman*, 155–170. Winona Lake, Ind.

Faivre, X. 1995. "Le recyclage des tablettes cunéiformes." *RA* 89: 57–66.

Fales, F. M. 1986. *Aramaic Epigraphs on Clay Tablets of the Neo-Assyrian Period*. Rome.

———. 1991. "Narrative and Ideological Variations in the Account of Sargon's Eighth Campaign." In M. Cogan and I. Eph'al, eds., *Ah Assyria . . . : Studies in Assyrian History and Ancient Near Eastern Historiography Presented to Hayim Tadmor*, 129–147. Jerusalem.

———. 1999–2001. "Assyrian Royal Inscriptions: Newer Horizons." *SAAB* 13: 115–144.

———. 2007. "Multilingualism on Multiple Media in the Neo-Assyrian Period: A Review of the Evidence." *SAAB* 16: 95–122.

Fales, F. M., and J. N. Postgate. 1992. *Imperial Administrative Records, Part I: Palace and Temple Administration*. Helsinki.

Figulla, H. H. 1953. "Accounts Concerning Allocation of Provisions for Offerings in the Ningal-Temple at Ur." *Iraq* 15: 88–122 and 171–192.

Fincke, J. 2003–2004. "The Babylonian Texts of Nineveh: Report on the British Museum's Ashurbanipal Library Project." *AfO* 50: 111–149.

———. 2006–2007. "Omina, die göttlichen 'Gesetze' der Divination." *JEOL* 40: 131–147.

Finet, A. 1969. "Les symboles du cheveu, du bord du vêtement et de l'ongle en Mésopotamie." In *Eschatologie et Cosmologie*, 101–130. Brussels.

Finkel, I. L. 1988. "Adad-apla-iddina, Esagil-kīn-apli, and the Series SA. GIG." In Leichty et al. 1988, 143–159.

———. 2006. "On an Izbu VII Commentary." In Guinan et al. 2006, 139–148.

Fleming, D. 2000. *Time at Emar: The Cultic Calendar and the Rituals from the Diviner's House*. Winona Lake, Ind.

Foster, B. R. 1986. "Archives and Empire in Sargonic Mesopotamia." In Veenhof 1986a, 46–52.

———. 1991. "On Authorship in Akkadian Literature." *Annali: Rivista del Dipartimento di Studi Asiatici e del Dipartimento di Studi e Ricerche su Africa e Paesia Arabi* 51/1: 17–32.

———. 1993. "Letters and Literature: A Ghost's Entreaty." In Cohen et al. 1993, 98–102.

———. 2003. "Late Babylonian Schooldays: An Archaizing Cylinder." In Selz 2003, 79–87.

———. 2005a. "The Transmission of Knowledge." In D. C. Snell, ed., *A Companion to the Ancient Near East,* 245–252. Oxford.

———. 2005b. "Shuruppak and the Sumerian City State." In L. Kogan et al., eds., *Memoriae Igor M. Diakonoff,* 71–88. Winona Lake, Ind.

———. 2005c. *Before the Muses: An Anthology of Akkadian Literature.* 3rd ed. Bethesda, Md.

———. 2007. *Akkadian Literature of the Late Period.* Münster.

Frahm, E. 1997. *Einleitung in die Sanherib-Inschriften.* Vienna.

———. Forthcoming. *Origins of Interpretation.* Münster.

Frake, C. 1983. "Did Literacy Cause the Great Cognitive Divide?" *American Ethnologist* 10: 369–371.

Frame, G., and A. R. George. 2005. "The Royal Libraries of Nineveh: New Evidence for King Ashurbanipal's Tablet Collecting." *Iraq* 67/1: 265–284.

Frayne, D. R. 1990. *Old Babylonian Period (2003–1595 B.C.).* Toronto.

Freedman, S. M. 1998. *If a City Is Set on a Height: The Akkadian Omen Series Šumma Alu ina Mēlê Šakin.* Vol. 1: *Tablets 1–21.* Philadelphia.

———. 2006a. *If a City Is Set on a Height: The Akkadian Omen Series Šumma Alu ina Mēlê Šakin.* Vol. 2: *Tablets 22–40.* Philadelphia.

———. 2006b. "BM 129092: A Commentary on Snake Omens." In Guinan et al. 2006, 149–166.

Friberg, J. 1987–1990. "Mathematik." *RlA* 7: 531–585.

Fronzaroli, P., and A. Catagnoti. 2003. *Testi di cancelleria: I rapporti con le città.* Rome.

Galter, H. D. 1997. "Assyrische Königsinschriften des 2. Jahrtausends v. Chr. Die Entwicklung einer Textgattung." In Waetzoldt and Hauptmann 1997, 53–59.

Garfinkle, S. J. 2004. "Shepherds, Merchants, and Credit: Some Observations on Lending Practices in Ur III Mesopotamia." *JESHO* 47: 1–30.

Gasche, H., and L. De Meyer. 2006. "Lieu d'enseignement ou atelier de recyclage de terre à tablettes?" In P. Butterlin et al., eds., *Les espaces syromésopotamiens*, 361–373. Turnhout.

Gasche, H. et al., eds. 1994. *Cinquante-deux réflexions sur le Proche-Orient ancien offertes en hommage à Léon De Meyer.* Ghent.

Gavrilov, A. K. 1997. "Techniques of Reading in Classical Antiquity." *Classical Quarterly* 47: 56–73.

Gelb, I. J. 1977. "Typology of Mesopotamian Seal Inscriptions." In Gibson and Biggs 1977, 107–126.

Gelb, I. J., P. Steinkeller, and R. M. Whiting. 1991. *Earliest Land Tenure Systems in the Near East: Ancient Kudurrus.* Chicago.

Geller, M. J. 1997. "The Last Wedge." *ZA* 87: 43–95.

———. 2005. *Renal and Rectal Disease Texts.* Berlin.

George, A. R. 1986. "Sennacherib and the Tablets of Destiny." *Iraq* 48: 133–146.

———. 2003. *The Babylonian Gilgamesh Epic: Introduction, Critical Edition, and Cuneiform Texts.* Oxford.

———. 2003–2004. Review of Gesche 2001. *AfO* 50: 403–406.

———. 2005. "In Search of the *é.dub.ba.a*: The Ancient Mesopotamian School in Literature and Reality." In Y. Sefati et al., eds., *"An Experienced Scribe Who Neglects Nothing": Ancient Near Eastern Studies in Honor of Jacob Klein*, 127–137. Bethesda, Md.

———. 2007a. "The Epic of Gilgameš: Thoughts on Genre and Meaning." In J. Azize and N. Weeks, eds., *Gilgameš and the World of Assyria*, 37–65. Leuven.

———. 2007b. "Gilgamesh and the Literary Traditions of Ancient Mesopotamia." In Leick 2007, 447–457.

———. 2007c. "The Gilgamesh Epic at Ugarit." *Aula Orientalis* 25/2: 237–254.

George, A. R., and I. L. Finkel, eds. 2000. *Wisdom, Gods, and Literature: Studies in Assyriology in Honour of W. G. Lambert.* Winona Lake, Ind.

Gesche, P. D. 2001. *Schulunterricht in Babylonien im ersten Jahrtausend v. Chr.* Münster.

Gibson, M., and R. D. Biggs, eds. 1977. *Seals and Sealing in the Ancient Near East.* Malibu, Calif.

Glassner, J. J. 2004. *Mesopotamian Chronicles.* Atlanta.

Godard, O. 1990. *Le pouvoir de l'écrit: Aux pays des premières écritures.* Paris.

Goddeeris, A. 2002. *Economy and Society in Northern Babylonia in the Early Old Babylonian Period (ca. 2000–1800 B.C.).* Leuven.

Goetze, A. 1947. *Old Babylonian Omen Texts.* New Haven, Conn.

Gorelick, L., and A. J. Gwinnett. 1990. "The Ancient Near Eastern Cylinder Seal as Social Emblem and Status Symbol." *JNES* 49: 45–56.

Gossens, G. 1952. "Introduction à l'archivéconomie de l'Asie Antérieure." *RA* 46: 98–107.

Grayson, A. K. 1980. "Histories and Historians of the Ancient Near East: Assyria and Babylonia." *Orientalia* 49: 140–194.

———. 1987. *Assyrian Rulers of the Third and Second Millennia* B.C. (to 1115 B.C.). Toronto.

———. 1991. *Assyrian Rulers of the Early First Millennium* B.C. Vol. 1: 1114–859. Toronto.

———. 1996. *Assyrian Rulers of the Early First Millennium* B.C. Vol. 2: 858–745 B.C. Toronto.

———. 2000. "Murmuring in Mesopotamia." In George and Finkel 2000, 301–308.

Green, M. W. 1981. "The Construction and Implementation of the Cuneiform Writing System." *Visible Language* 15/4: 345–372.

Greengus, S. 1969. "Old Babylonian Marriage Contracts." *JAOS* 89: 505–532.

Guichard, M. 1994. "Au pays de la Dame de Nagar." In Charpin and Durand 1994, 235–272.

———. 1997. "Violation du serment et casuistique à Mari." In S. Lafont 1997, 71–84.

———. 1999. "Les mentions de la Crète à Mari." In A. Caubet, ed., *L'acrobate au taureau: Les découvertes de Tell el-Dab'a et l'archéologie de la Méditerranée orientale*, 165–177. Paris.

———. 2004. "'La malédiction de cette tablette est très dure!' Sur l'ambassade d'Itûr-Asdû à Babylone en l'an 4 de Zimrî-Lîm." *RA* 98: 13–32.

Guinan, A. K. et al., eds. 2006. *If a Man Builds a Joyful House: Assyriological Studies in Honor of Erle Verdun Leichty*. Leiden.

Günbatti, C. 2001. "The River Ordeal in Ancient Anatolia." In van Soldt 2001a, 151–160.

Gurney, O. 1989. *Literary and Miscellaneous Texts in the Ashmolean Museum*. Oxford.

Hackl, J. 2007. *Der subordinierte Satz in den spätbabylonischen Briefen*. Münster.

Hagenbuchner, A. 1989. *Die Korrespondenz der Hethiter*. Heidelberg.

Hallo, W. W. 1977. "Seals Lost and Found." In Gibson and Biggs 1977, 55–60.

———. 2002. "A Model Court Case Concerning Inheritance." In Abusch 2002b, 141–154.

Hallo, W. W., and I. J. Winter, eds. 2001. *Seals and Seal Impressions: Proceedings of the XLVe Rencontre Assyriologique Internationale, Part II, Yale University*. Bethesda, Md.

Harper, R. F. 1892–1914. *Assyrian and Babylonian Letters Belonging to the Kouyounjik Collection of the British Museum*. London.

Hattori, A. 2001. "Seal Practices in Ur III Nippur." In Hallo and Winter 2001, 71–99.

Heeßel, N. P. 2000. *Babylonisch-assyrische Diagnostik*. Münster.

Heimpel, W. 2003. *Letters to the King of Mari: A New Translation, with Historical Introduction, Notes, and Commentary*. Winona Lake, Ind.

Hilprecht, H. V. 1910. *The Earliest Version of the Babylonian Deluge Story and the Temple Library of Nippur*. Philadelphia.

Horowitz, W., and N. Wasserman. 2004. "From Hazor to Mari and Ekallātum: A Recently Discovered Old-Babylonian Letter from Hazor." In C. Nicolle, ed., *Nomades et sédentaires dans le Proche-Orient ancien: Compte rendu de la XLVIe Rencontre Assyriologique Internationale, Paris, 10–13 juillet 2000*, 335–344. Paris.

Horsnell, M. J. A. 1999. *The Year Names of the First Dynasty of Babylon*. 2 vols. Hamilton, Ontario.

———. 2004. "On the Use of Year Names in Reconstructing the History of the First Dynasty of Babylon." In G. Frame, ed., *From the Upper Sea to the Lower Sea: Studies on History of Assyria and Babylonia in Honor of A. K. Grayson*, 165–186. Leiden.

Howard, M. 1955. "Technical Description of the Ivory Writing-Boards from Nimrud." *Iraq* 17: 14–20.

Huber, F. 2001. "La correspondance royale d'Ur, un corpus apocryphe." *ZA* 91: 169–206.

Hunger, H. 1968. *Babylonische und assyrische Kolophone*. Neukirchen.

———. 1976. *Spätbabylonische Texte aus Uruk*. Vol. 1. Berlin.

Huot, J. L., ed. 1987. *Larsa 10e campagne, 1983 et 'Oueili 4e campagne, 1983: Rapport préliminaire*. Paris.

Ichisar, M. 1981. *Les archives cappadociennes du marchand Imdilum*. Paris.

Ikeda, J. 1999. "Scribes in Emar." In K. Watanabe, ed., *Priests and Officials in the Ancient Near East*, 163–186. Heidelberg.

Janssen, C. 1991. "Samsu-iluna and the Hungry *nadītum*s." *NAPR* 5: 3–40.

———. 1992. "Inanna-mansum et ses fils: Relation d'une succession turbulente dans les archives d'Ur-Utu." *RA* 86: 19–52.

————. 1996. "When the House Is on Fire and the Children Are Gone." In K. R. Veenhof, ed., *Houses and Households in Ancient Mesopotamia: Papers Read at the 40e Rencontre Assyriologique Internationale, Leiden, July 5–8, 1993*, 237–246. Leiden.

Jeyes, U. 1997. "Assurbanipal's *bārûtu*." In Waetzoldt and Hauptmann 1997, 61–65.

Joannès, F. 1984. "Chapitre II: Textes nos. 91 à 245." In G. Bardet et al., *Archives administratives de Mari*, 1:83–226. Paris.

————. 1985. "Nouveaux mémorandums." In Durand and Kupper 1985, 97–113.

————. 1990. *Les tablettes néo-babyloniennes de la Bodleian Library conservées à l'Ashmolean Museum*. Oxford.

————. 1992. "Les archives de Ninurta-aḫḫe-bulliṭ." In M. Ellis 1992, 87–100.

————. 1994. "Un précurseur paléo-babylonien de la série *šumma ālu*." In Gasche et al. 1994, 305–312.

————, ed. 1995. *Les phénomènes de fin d'archives en Mésopotamie. RA* 89.

————. 1997. "Palmyre et les routes du désert au début du deuxième millénaire av. J.-C." *MARI* 8: 393–416.

————, ed. 2000. *Rendre la justice en Mésopotamie*. Paris.

Jonker, G. 1995. *The Topography of Remembrance: The Dead, Tradition, and Collective Memory in Mesopotamia*. Leiden.

Jursa, M. 1997. "'Als König Abi-ešuh gerechte Ordnung hergestellt hat': Eine bemerkenswerte altbabylonische Prozessurkunde." *RA* 91: 135–145.

————. 1999. *Das Archiv des Bēl-rēmanni*. Leiden.

————. 2005. *Neo-Babylonian Legal and Administrative Documents: Typology, Contents, and Archives*. Münster.

Kataja, L. 1987. "A Neo-Assyrian Document on Two Cases of River Ordeal." *SAAB* 1: 65–68.

Kessler, K. 1980. *Untersuchungen zur historischen Topographie Nordmesopotamiens nach keilschriftlichen Quellen des 1. Jahrtausends v. Chr.* Wiesbaden.

Kestemont, G. 1974. *Diplomatique et droit international en Asie occidentale, 1600–1200 av. J. C.* Louvain-la-Neuve.

Kienast, B. 1996. "Mündlichkeit und Schriftlichtkeit im keilschriftlichen Rechtswesen." *Zeitschrift für Altorientalische und Biblische Rechtsgeschichte* 2: 114–130.

Kienast, B., and K. Volk. 1995. *Die sumerischen und akkadischen Briefe des III. Jahrtausends aus der Zeit vor der III. Dynastie von Ur*. Stuttgart.

Kilmer, A. D. 1974. "Symbolic Gestures in Akkadian Contracts from Alalakh." *JAOS* 94: 177–183.

King, L. W. 1914. *Supplement to the Catalogue of the Cuneiform Tablets in the Kouyunjik Collection of the British Museum*. London.

Kitz, A. M. 2004. "An Oath, Its Curse and Anointing Ritual." *JAOS* 124: 315–322.

Klein, J. 1986. "On Writing Monumental Inscriptions in Ur III Scribal Curriculum." *RA* 89: 1–7.

———. 2000. "The Origin and Development of Languages on Earth: The Sumerian versus the Biblical View." In S. Graziani, ed., *Studi sul Vicino Oriente dedicati alla memoria di Luigi Cagni*, 563–584. Naples.

Klein, J., and T. Sharlach. 2007. "A Collection of Model Court Cases from Old Babylonian Nippur (CBS 11324)." *ZA* 97: 1–25.

Klengel, H. 1968. "Eine altbabylonische Verlustanzeige." *Orientalia* 37: 216–219.

———. 1994. "Richter Sippars in der Zeit des Ammiṣaduqa: Ein neuer Text." In H. Gasche, M. Tanret, C. Janssen, and A. Degraeve, eds., *Cinquante-deux réflexions sur le Proche-Orient ancien offertes en hommage à Léon De Meyer*, 169–174. Louvain, 1994.

Klinger, J. 2003. "Zur Paläographie akkadischsprachiger Texte aus Ḫattuša." In Beckman et al. 2003, 237–248.

Koch, U. S. 2005. *Secrets of Extispicy: The Chapter* Multabiltu *of the Babylonian Extispicy Series and* Nisirti barûti *Texts Mainly from Assurbanipal's Library*. Münster.

Koppen, F. van. 2002. "Redeeming a Father's Seal." In C. Wunsch, ed., *Mining the Archives: Festschrift for Christopher Walker on the Occasion of His Sixtieth Birthday*, 147–172. Dresden.

Kraus, F. R. 1973. *Vom mesopotamischen Menschen der altbabylonischen Zeit und seiner Welt*. Amsterdam.

———. 1985a. "Altbabylonische Briefe mit Siegelabrollungen." In Durand and Kupper 1985, 137–145.

———. 1985b. "Eine altbabylonische Buchhaltung aus einem Amtsarchiv in Nippur." *BiOr* 42: 526–542.

Krebernik, M. 2001. *Tall Biʾa/Tuttul*. Vol. 2: *Die altorientalischen Schriftfunde*. Saarbrücken.

Kryszat, G. 2008. "The Use of Writing among the Anatolians." In J. G. Dercksen, ed., *Anatolia and the Jazira during the Old Assyrian Period*, 231–238. Leiden.

Labat, R. 1988 [1948]. *Manuel d'épigraphie akkadienne (signes, syllabaires, idéogrammes)*, edited and corrected by F. Malbran-Labat. 6th rev. ed. Paris.

Lackenbacher, S. 1990. *Le palais sans rival: Le récit de construction en Assyrie*. Paris.

———. 2002. *Textes akkadiens d'Ugarit: Textes provenant des vingt-cinq premières campagnes*. Paris.

Lafont, B. 1990. "Nouvelles lettres du temps des rois d'Ur." *RA* 84: 165–169.

———. 1992. "Messagers et ambassadeurs dans les archives de Mari." In Charpin and Joannès 1992, 167–183.

———. 1997. "Le fonctionnement de la poste et le métier de facteur d'après les textes de Mari." In Young et al. 1997, 315–334.

———. 2000. "Les textes judiciaires sumériens." In Joannès 2000, 35–68.

———. 2001. "Relations internationales, alliances et diplomatie au temps des rois de Mari." In Charpin and Durand 2001, 213–328.

Lafont, S., ed. 1997. *Jurer et maudire: Pratiques politiques et usages juridiques du serment dans le Proche-Orient ancien*. Paris.

———. 1999. *Femmes, droit et justice dans l'Antiquité orientale: Contribution à l'étude du droit pénal au Proche-Orient ancien*. Fribourg and Göttingen.

Lambert, W. G. 1957. "Ancestors, Authors, and Canonicity." *JCS* 11: 1–14.

———. 1960. *Babylonian Wisdom Literature*. Oxford.

———. 1962. "A Catalogue of Texts and Authors." *JCS* 16: 59–77.

———. 1967. "Enmeduranki and Related Matters." *JCS* 21: 126–138.

———. 1989. "The Laws of Hammurabi in the First Millennium." In M. Lebeau and P. Talon, eds., *Reflets des deux fleuves, volume de mélanges offerts à André Finet*, 95–98. Leuven.

———. 1992. *Catalogue of the Cuneiform Tablets in the Kouyunjik Collection of the British Museum: Third Supplement*. London.

———. 1999–2000. "Literary Texts from Nimrud." *AfO* 46–47: 149–155.

———. 2007. *Babylonian Oracle Questions*. Winona Lake, Ind.

Lambert, W. G., and A. L. Millard. 1968. *Second Supplement to Catalogue of the Cuneiform Tablets in the Kouyunjik Collection of the British Museum*. London.

Landsberger, B. 1937. *Die Serie ana ittišu*. Rome.

———. 1960. "Scribal Concepts of Education." In C. H. Kraeling and R. M. Adams, eds., *City Invincible*, 94–123. Chicago.

Larsen, M. T. 1976. *The Old-Assyrian City-State and Its Colonies*. Copenhagen.

———. 1987. "The Babylonian Lukewarm Mind: Reflections on Science, Divination, and Literacy." In Rochberg-Halton 1987, 203–226.

————. 1988. "The Role of Writing and Literacy in the Development of Social and Political Power: Literacy and Social Complexity." In J. Gledhill et al., eds., *State and Society: The Emergence and Development of Social Hierarchy and Political Centralization*, 173–191. London.

————. 1989. "What They Wrote on Clay." In K. Schousboe and M. T. Larsen, eds., *Literacy and Society*, 121–148. Copenhagen.

————. 1996. *The Conquest of Assyria: Excavations in an Antique Land, 1840–1860*. London.

Leemans, W. F. 1960. *Foreign Trade in the Old Babylonian Period*. Leiden.

————. 1982. "La fonction des sceaux apposés à des contrats vieux-babyloniens." In van Driel et al. 1982, 219–244.

————. 1991. "Textes paléo-babyloniens commençant par une liste de personnes." In Charpin and Joannès 1991, 307–332.

Leichty, E. V. 1970. *The Omen Series Šumma Izbu*. New York.

Leichty, E. V. et al., eds. 1988. *A Scientific Humanist: Studies in Memory of Abraham Sachs*. Philadelphia.

Leick, G., ed. 2007. *The Babylonian World*. New York.

Leiderer, R. 1990. *Anatomie der Schafsleber im babylonischen Leberorakel: Eine makroskopisch-analytische Studie*. Munich.

Lemaire, A. 2001. *Nouvelles tablettes araméennes*. Geneva.

Lenzi, A. 2008. *Secrecy and the Gods: Secret Knowledge in Ancient Mesopotamia and Biblical Israel*. Helsinki.

Lieberman, S. J. 1990. "Canonical and Official Cuneiform Texts: Towards an Understanding of Assurbanipal's Personal Tablet Collection." In T. Abusch et al., eds., *Lingering over Words: Studies in Ancient Near Eastern Literature in Honor of William L. Moran*, 305–336. Atlanta.

————. 1992. "Nippur: City of Decisions." In M. Ellis 1992, 127–136.

Linssen, M. J. H. 2003. *The Cults of Uruk and Babylon: The Temple Ritual Texts as Evidence for Hellenistic Cult Practices*. Leiden.

Lion, B. 2001a. "Dame Inanna-ama-mu, scribe à Sippar." *RA* 95: 7–32.

————. 2001b. "Les gouverneurs provinciaux du royaume de Mari à l'époque de Zimrî-Lîm." In Charpin and Durand 2001, 141–210.

Lion, B., and E. Robson. 2005. "Quelques textes scolaires paléo-babyloniens rédigés par des femmes." *JCS* 57: 37–54.

Liverani, M. 1973. "Memorandum on the Approach to Historiographic Texts." *Orientalia* 42: 178–194.

————. 2001. "Mesopotamian Historiography and the Amarna Letters." In Abusch et al. 2001, 303–311.

Livingstone, A. 1999. "The Magic of Time." In Abusch and van der Toorn 1999, 131–138.

———. 2007. "Ashurbanipal: Literate or Not?" *ZA* 97: 98–118.

Loud, G., and C. B. Altman. 1938. *Khorsabad, Part 2: The Citadel and the Town.* Chicago.

Lucas, C. J. 1979. "The Scribal Tablet-House in Ancient Mesopotamia." *History of Education Quarterly* 19/3: 305–332.

Luckenbill, D. D. 1924. *Inscriptions of Sennacherib.* Chicago.

Ludwig, M. C. 1990. *Untersuchungen zu den Hymnen des Išme-Dagan von Isin.* Wiesbaden.

Luukko, M. 2007. "The Administrative Roles of the 'Chief Scribe' and the 'Palace Scribe' in the Neo-Assyrian Period." *SAAB* 16: 227–256.

Luukko, M., and G. Van Buylaere. 2002. *The Political Correspondence of Esarhaddon.* Helsinki.

MacGinnis, J. 2002. "The Use of Writing Boards in the Neo-Babylonian Temple Administration at Sippar." *Iraq* 64: 217–236.

Machinist, P., and H. Tadmor. 1993. "Heavenly Wisdom." In Cohen et al. 1993, 146–151.

Malbran-Labat, F. 1995. *Les inscriptions royales de Suse: Briques de l'époque paléo-élamite à l'Empire néo-élamite.* Paris.

Marazzi, M. 1994. "Ma gli Hittiti scriverano veramente su 'legno?'" In P. Cipriano and P. di Giovine, eds., *Miscellanea di studi linguistici in onore di Walter Berlardi,* 131–160. Rome.

Margueron, J. 1982. *Recherches sur les palais mésopotamiens à l'Âge du Bronze.* Paris.

———. 1986. "Quelques remarques concernant les archives retrouvées dans le palais de Mari." In Veenhof 1986a, 141–152.

———. 1995. "Notes d'archéologie et d'architecture orientales 7.—Feu le four à tablettes de l'ex 'cour V' du palais d'Ugarit." *Syria* 72: 55–69.

Marzahn, J., H. Neumann, and A. Fuchs, eds. 2000. *Assyriologica et Semitica: Festschrift für Joachim Oelsner anläßlich seines 65. Geburtstages am 18. Februar 1997.* Münster.

Matthiae, P. 1986. "The Archives of the Royal Palace G of Ebla: Distribution and Arrangement of the Tablets according to the Archaeological Evidence." In Veenhof 1986a, 53–71.

———. 2008. *Gli Archivi Reali di Ebla: La scoperta, i testi, il significato.* Milan.

Mattila, R., ed. 1995. *Nineveh 612 b.c.: The Glory and Fall of the Assyrian Empire.* Helsinki.

Maul, S. M. 1991. Review of Gurney 1989. *BiOr* 48: 852–860.

———. 1994a. "Die Korrespondenz des Iasīm-Sūmû: Ein Nachtrag zu ARMT XIII 25–57." In Charpin and Durand 1994, 23–54.

———. 1994b. *Zukunftsbewältigung: Eine Untersuchung altorientalischen Denkens anhand der babylonisch-assyrischen Löserituale (Namburbi).* Mainz.

———, ed. 1998. *Festschrift für Rykle Borger zu seinem 65. Geburtstag am 24. Mai 1994* tikip santakki mala bašmu . . . Groningen.

———. 1999. "How the Babylonians Protected Themselves against Calamities Announced by Omens." In Abusch and van der Toorn 1999, 123–130.

———. 2003a. "Omina und Orakel." *RlA* 10: 45–88.

———. 2003b. "Die Reste einer mittelassyrischen Beschwörerbibliothek aus dem Königspalast zu Assur." In Sallaberger et al. 2003, 181–194.

———. 2003c. "Wie die Bibliothek eines Assyrischen Gelehrten wiederersteht." In J. Marzahn and B. Salje, eds., *Wiedererstehendes Assur: 100 Jahre deutsche Ausgrabungen in Assyrien,* 175–182. Mainz.

———. 2005. "Nos 2–18: Bilingual (Sumero-Akkadian) Hymns from the Seleucid-Arsacid Period." In I. Spar and W. G. Lambert, eds., *Literary and Scholastic Texts of the First Millennium b.c.,* 11–116. Turnhout.

Meijer, D. J. W. 2004. "A Scribal Quarter?" In Dercksen 2004, 387–393.

Metman, Y. 1961. "Sigillographie." In Samaran 1961, 393–446.

Michalowski, P. 1981. "Königsbriefe." *RlA* 6: 51–59.

———. 1983. Review of L. Cagni, *Briefe aus dem Iraq Museum (TIM II)* (Leiden, 1980). *JCS* 35: 221–228.

———. 1993. *Letters from Early Mesopotamia.* Atlanta.

———. 1994a. "Writing and Literacy in Early States: A Mesopotamian Perspective." In D. Keller-Cohen, ed., *Literacy: Interdisciplinary Conversations,* 49–70. Cresskill, N.J.

———. 1994b. "The Drinking of Gods: Alcohol in Mesopotamian Ritual and Mythology." In L. Milano, ed., *Drinking in Ancient Society: History and Culture of Drinks in the Ancient Near East. Papers of a Symposium Held in Rome, May 17–19, 1990,* 27–44. Padua.

———. 2003. "The Libraries of Babel: Text, Authority, and Tradition in Ancient Mesopotamia." In Dorleijn and Vanstiphout 2003, 105–129.

———. 2006. "The Lives of the Sumerian Language." In Sanders 2006, 159–184.

———. Forthcoming. *Royal Correspondence of Ur.*

Michalowski, P., and N. Veldhuis, eds. 2006. *Approaches to Sumerian Literature: Studies in Honour of Stip (H. L. J. Vanstiphout).* Leiden.

Michel, C. 2001. *Correspondance des marchands de Kanish.* Paris.

———. 2008. "La correspondance des marchands assyriens du XIXe s. av. J.-C. De l'archivage des lettres commerciales et privées." In Pantalacci 2008a, 117–140.

Miller, J. 2001. "Hattusili I's Expansion into Northern Syria in Light of the Tikunani Letter." In G. Wilhelm, ed., *Akten des IV. Internationalen Kongresses für Hethitologie Würzburg, 4.–8. Oktober 1999,* 410–429. Wiesbaden.

Mittermayer, C. 2006. *Altbabylonische Zeichenliste der sumerisch-literarischen Texte.* Fribourg and Göttingen.

Mora, C., and M. Giorgieri. 2004. *Le lettere tra i re ittiti e i re assiri ritrovate Ḫattuša.* Padua.

Moran, W. L. 1992. *The Amarna Letters.* Baltimore.

———. 2003. *Amarna Studies: Collected Writings.* Winona Lake, Ind.

Morandi, D. 1988. "Stele e statue reali assire: Localizzazione, diffusione, e implicazioni ideologiche." *Mesopotamia* 23: 105–155.

Negri Scafa, P. 1999. "The Scribes of Nuzi." *SCCNH* 10: 63–80.

Nissen, H. J., P. Damerow, and R. K. Englund. 1993. *Archaic Bookkeeping: Writing and Techniques of Economic Administration in the Ancient Near East.* Chicago.

Nougayrol, J. 1955. *Textes accadiens et hourrites des archives est, ouest et centrales.* Paris.

———. 1956. *Textes accadiens des archives sud (Archives internationales).* Paris.

Oettinger, N. 1976. *Die Militärischen Eide der Hethiter.* Wiesbaden.

Offner, G. 1950. "A propos de la sauvegarde des tablettes en Assyro-Babylonie." *RA* 44: 135–143.

Oppenheim, A. L. 1960. "The City of Assur in 714 B.C." *JNES* 19: 133–147.

———. 1964. *Ancient Mesopotamia: Portrait of a Dead Civilization.* Chicago (rev. ed. 1977).

Otten, H. 1988. *Die Bronzetafel aus Bogazköy: Ein Staatsvertrag Tuḫalijas IV.* Wiesbaden.

Ouy, G. 1961. "Les bibliothèques." In Samaran 1961, 1061–1119.

Palaima, T. 2003. "'Archives' and 'Scribes' and Information Hierarchy in Mycenian Greek Linear B Records." In Brosius 2003a, 153–194.

Pantalacci, L., ed. 2008a. *La lettre d'archive.* Cairo.

———. 2008b. "Archivage et scribes dans l'oasis de Dakhla (Égypte) à la fin du IIIe millénaire." In Pantalacci 2008a, 141–153.

Parpola, S. 1983. "Assyrian Library Record." *JNES* 42: 1–29.

———. 1986. "The Royal Archives of Nineveh." In Veenhof 1986a, 223–236.

———. 1987. "The Forlorn Scholar." In Rochberg-Halton 1987, 257–278.

———, ed. 1987–2003. *State Archives of Assyria.* 18 vols. Helsinki.

———. 1993a. *Letters from Assyrian and Babylonian Scholars.* Helsinki.

———. 1993b. "Mesopotamian Astrology and Astronomy as Domains of Mesopotamian 'Wisdom.'" In H. D. Galter, ed., *Die Rolle der Astronomie in den Kulturen Mesopotamiens,* 47–59. Graz.

———. 1995. "The Imperial Archives of Nineveh." In Mattila 1995, 15–25.

———. 1997. "The Man without a Scribe and the Question of Literacy in the Assyrian Empire." In B. Pongratz-Leisten et al., eds., *Ana šadî Labnāni lū allik: Beiträge zu altorientalischen und mittelmeerischen Kulturen. Festschrift für Wolfgang Röllig,* 315–324. Neukirchen.

Parpola, S., and K. Watanabe. 1988. *Neo-Assyrian Treaties and Loyalty Oaths.* Helsinki.

Parrot, A. 1954. "Les fouilles de Mari: Neuvième campagne (automne 1953)." *Syria* 31: 151–171.

Pearce, L. E. 1998. "Babylonian Commentaries and Intellectual Innovation." In J. Prosecky, ed., *Intellectual Life of the Ancient Near East: Papers Presented at the 43e Rencontre assyriologique internationale, Prague, July 1–5, 1996,* 331–338. Prague.

Pedersén, O. 1985–1986. *Archives and Libraries in the City of Assur: A Survey of the Material from the German Excavations.* 2 vols. Uppsala.

———. 1998. *Archives and Libraries in the Ancient Near East 1500–300 b.c.* Bethesda, Md.

———. 2005. *Archive und Bibliothek in Babylon: Die Tontafeln der Grabung Robert Koldeweys 1899–1917.* Saarwellingen.

Poebel, A. 1909. *Babylonian Legal and Business Documents from the Time of the First Dynasty of Babylon Chiefly from Babylonian Nippur.* Philadelphia.

Pomponio, F. 1983. "'Archives' and the Prosopography of Fara." *ASJ* 5: 127–145.

Pongratz-Leisten, B. 1999. *Herrschaftswissen in Mesopotamien: Formen der Kommunikation zwischen Gott und König im 2. und 1. Jahrtausend v. Chr.* Helsinki.

Postgate, J. N. 1976. *Fifty Neo-Assyrian Legal Documents.* Warminster.

———. 1986a. "Middle Assyrian Tablets: The Instruments of Bureaucracy." *AoF* 13: 10–39.

———. 1986b. "Administrative Archives from the City of Assur in the Middle Assyrian Period." In Veenhof 1986a, 168–183.

———. 2003. "Documents in Government under the Middle Assyrian Kingdom." In Brosius 2003a, 124–138.

Potts, D. T. 1990. "Lock and Key in Ancient Mesopotamia." *Mesopotamia* 25: 185–192.

Powell, M. A. 1981. "Three Problems in the History of Cuneiform Writing: Origins, Direction of Script, Literacy." *Visible Language* 15/4: 419–440.

———. 1991. "Narām-Sîn, Son of Sargon: Ancient History, Famous Names, and a Famous Babylonian Forgery." *ZA* 81: 20–30.

Prang, E. 1981. "Sonderbestimmungen in altbabylonischen Erbteilungsurkunden aus Nippur." *ZA* 70: 36–51.

Radner, K. 1995. "The Relation between Format and Content of Neo-Assyrian Texts." In Mattila 1995, 63–77.

———. 2005. *Die Macht des Namens: Altorientalische Strategien zur Selbsterhaltung.* Wiesbaden.

Reade, J. 1986. "Archaeology and the Kuyunjik Archives." In Veenhof 1986a, 213–222.

———. 1998–2001. "Ninive (Nineveh)." *RlA* 9: 388–433.

Reiner, E. 1960. "Plague Amulets and House Blessings." *JNES* 19: 148–155.

———. 1961. "The Etiological Myth of the 'Seven Sages.'" *Orientalia* 30: 1–11.

———. 2004. "Runaway—Seize Him." In Dercksen 2004, 475–482.

———. 2005. *Babylonian Planetary Omens. Part Four.* Leiden.

Renger, J. 1971. "Überlegungen zum akkadischen Syllabar." *ZA* 61: 23–43.

Richardson, S. 2006. "gir₃-gen-na and Šulgi's 'Library': Liver Omen Texts in the Third Millennium B.C. (I)." *CDLJ* 3: 1–9.

Richter, T. 2005. "Qaṭna in the Late Bronze Age: Preliminary Remarks." *SCCNH* 15: 109–126.

Robson, E. 1999. *Mesopotamian Mathematics, 2100–1600 b.c.: Technical Constants in Bureaucracy and Education.* Oxford.

———. 2001. "The Tablet House: A Scribal School in Old Babylonian Nippur." *RA* 95: 39–66.

———. 2008. *Mathematics in Ancient Iraq: A Social History.* Princeton.

Rochberg(-Halton), F. 1984. "Canonicity in Cuneiform Texts." *JCS* 36: 127–144.

———, ed. 1987. *Language, Literature, and History: Philological and Historical Studies Presented to Erica Reiner.* New Haven, Conn.

———. 2000. "Scribes and Scholars: The ṭupšar Enūma Anu Enlil." In Marzahn et al. 2000, 359–375.

———. 2004. *The Heavenly Writing: Divination, Horoscopy, and Astronomy in Mesopotamian Culture.* Cambridge, Mass.

————. 2006. "Old Babylonian Celestial Divination." In Guinan et al. 2006, 337–348. Leiden.

Roth, M. 1995. *Law Collections from Mesopotamia and Asia Minor.* Atlanta.

Rubio, G. 2000 [2005]. "On the Orthography of Sumerian Literary Texts from the Ur-III Period." *ASJ* 22: 203–225.

————. 2006. "Šulgi and the Death of Sumerian." In Michalowski and Veldhuis 2006, 167–179.

Russell, J. M. 1999. *The Writing on the Wall: Studies in the Architectural Context of Late Assyrian Palace Inscriptions.* Winona Lake, Ind.

Rüster, C. 1972. *Hethitische Keilschrift-Paläographie.* Wiesbaden.

Rüster, C., and E. Neu. 1975. *Hethitische Keilschrift-Paläographie II (14./13. Jh. v. Chr.).* Wiesbaden.

Sachs, A. 1976. "The Latest Datable Cuneiform Tablets." In B. L. Eichler, ed., *Kramer Anniversary Volume: Cuneiform Studies in Honor of Samuel Noah Kramer,* 379–398. Neukirchen.

Saggs, H. W. F. 1981. "The Reed Stylus." *Sumer* 37: 127–128.

Sallaberger, W. 1996. "Zu einigen Jahresdaten Enlil-bānis von Isin." *ZA* 86: 177–191.

————. 1999. *"Wenn Du mein Bruder bist . . . :" Interaktion und Textgestaltung in altbabylonischen Alltagsbriefen.* Groningen.

————. 2001. "Die Entwicklung der Keilschrift in Ebla." In J. W. Meyer et al., eds., *Beiträge zur Vorderasiatischen Archäologie Winfried Orthmann gewidmet,* 436–445. Frankfurt.

————. 2004. "Das Ende des Sumerischen: Tod und Nachleben einer altmesopotamischen Sprache." In P. Schrijver and P. A. Mumm, eds., *Sprachtod und Sprachgeburt,* 108–140. Bremen.

————. 2008. *Das Gilgamesh-Epos: Mythos, Werk und Tradition.* Munich.

Sallaberger, W. et al., eds. 2003. *Literatur, Politik und Recht in Mesopotamien: Festschrift für Claus Wilcke.* Wiesbaden.

Salvini, M. 1994. "Una lettera di Ḫattušili I relativa alla spedizione contro Ḫaḫḫum." *SMEA* 34: 61–80.

Samaran, C., ed. 1961. *L'Histoire et ses méthodes.* Paris.

Sanders, S., ed. 2006. *Margins of Writing, Origins of Culture: New Approaches to Writing and Reading in the Ancient Near East.* Chicago.

San Nicolò, M. 1922. *Die Schlussklauseln der altbabylonischen Kauf- und Tauschverträge.* Munich. Second rev. ed. with foreword, notes, and addenda by H. Petschow. Munich. 1974.

Sasson, J. M. 1981. "On Idrimi and Šarruwa, the Scribe." *SCCNH* 1: 309–324.

———. 1982. "Accounting Discrepancies in the Mari NÌ.GUB [NÍG.DU] Texts." In van Driel et al. 1982, 326–341.

———. 1988. "Shunukhra-Khalu." In Leichty et al. 1988, 329–351.

———. 1995. "Water beneath Straw: Adventures of a Prophetic Phrase in the Mari Archives." In Z. Zevit et al., eds., *Solving Riddles and Untying Knots: Biblical, Epigraphic, and Semitic Studies in Honor of Jonas C. Greenfield,* 599–608. Winona Lake, Ind.

———. 1997. "The Vow of Mutiya, King of Shekhna." In Young et al. 1997, 475–490.

———. 1998. "The King and I: A Mari King in Changing Perception." *JAOS* 118: 453–470.

———. 2002. "The Burden of Scribes." In Abusch 2002b, 211–228.

Sasson, J. M. et al., eds. 1995. *Civilizations of the Ancient Near East.* New York.

Schaudig, H. 2002. *Die Inschriften Nabonids von Babylon und Kyros' des Grossen . . .* Münster.

———. 2003. "Nabonid, der 'Archäologe auf dem Königsthron': Zum Geschichtsbild des ausgehenden neubabylonischen Reiches." In Selz 2003, 446–497.

Scheil, J. V. 1937. *Au service de Clio: Notices diverses.* Chalon-sur-Saône.

Seidl, U. 2007. "Assurbanipals Griffel." *ZA* 97: 119–124.

Selz, G., ed. 2003. *Festschrift für Burkhart Kienast zu seinem 70. Geburtstage dargebracht von Freuden, Schülern und Kollegen.* Münster.

Seminara, S. 2004. *Le iscrizioni reali sumero-accadiche d'età paleobabilonese: Un'analisti tipologica e storico-letteraria.* Rome.

Seux, M. J. 1976. *Hymnes et prières aux dieux de Babylonie et d'Assyrie.* Paris.

Shaffer, A. 2000. "A New Look at Some Old Catalogues." In George and Finkel 2000, 429–436.

Sigrist, R. M. 1984. *Les sattukku dans l'Ešumeša durant la période d'Isin et Larsa.* Malibu, Calif.

Singer, I. 2003. "The Great Scribe Taki-Šarruma." In Beckman et al. 2003, 341–348.

Sjöberg, A. 1972. "In Praise of the Scribal Art." *JCS* 24: 126–131.

———. 1973. "Der Vater und sein Missratener Sohn." *JCS* 25: 105–169.

Skaist, A. 1990. "The Sale Contracts from Khafajah." In J. Klein and A. Skaist, eds., *Bar-Ilan Studies in Assyriology Dedicated to Pinḥas Artzi,* 255–276. Bar-Ilan.

———. 1994. *The Old Babylonian Loan Contract: Its History and Geography.* Bar-Ilan.

Slanski, K. E. 2003. *The Babylonian Entitlement* narûs (kudurrus): *A Study in Their Form and Function.* Boston.

———. 2003–2004. "Representation of the Divine on the Babylonian Entitlement Monuments *(kudurrus)*: Part I: Divine Symbols." *AfO* 50: 308–323.

Smith, G. 1876. *The Chaldean Account of Genesis Containing the Description of the Creation, the Fall of Man, the Deluge, the Tower of Babel, the Times of the Patriarchs, and Nimrod.* London.

Sollberger, E. 1966. *Business and Administrative Correspondence under the Kings of Ur.* New York.

———. 1968. "The Cruciform Monument." *JEOL* 20: 50–70.

Sollberger, E., and J. R. Kupper. 1971. *Inscriptions royales sumériennes et akkadiennes.* Paris.

Spada, G. 2007. *Testi economici da Ur di periodo paleo-babilonese.* Messina.

Spycket, A. 1981. *La statuaire du Proche-Orient ancien.* Leiden.

Steinkeller, P. 1989. *Sale Documents of the Ur-III-Period.* Stuttgart.

———. 2003. "Archival Practices at Babylonia in the Third Millennium." In Brosius 2003a, 37–58.

Steve, M. J. 1992. *Syllabaire élamite. Histoire et paléographie.* Neuchâtel.

Stol, M. 1981. *Letters from Yale.* Leiden.

———. 1998. "Einige kurze Wortstudien." In Maul 1998, 343–352.

———. 2001. "A Rescript of an Old Babylonian Letter." In van Soldt 2001a, 457–465.

Stolper, M. 1998. "Inscribed in Egyptian." In M. Brosius and A. Kuhrt, eds., *Studies in Persian History: Essays in Memory of David M. Lewis,* 133–143. Leiden.

Streck, M. 1916. *Assurbanipal und die letzten assyrischen Könige bis zum Untergange Niniveh's.* Leipzig.

Streck, M. P. 2000. *Das Amurritische Onomastikon der altbabylonischen Zeit: Band 1.* Münster.

Suurmeijer, G. 2006–2007. "Loans and Edicts: A Quantitative Analysis of the Temporal Distribution of Loan Documents and Royal Edicts under the Reign of Samsu-iluna." *JEOL* 40: 104–119.

Svenbro, J. 1997. "La Grèce archaïque et classique: L'invention de la lecture silencieuse." In G. Cavallo and R. Chartier, eds., *Histoire de la lecture dans le monde occidental,* 47–77. Paris.

Tadmor, H. 1997. "Propaganda, Literature, Historiography: Cracking the Code of the Assyrian Royal Inscriptions." In S. Parpola and R. M. Whiting, eds., *Assyria 1995,* 325–338. Helsinki.

Talon, P., and K. Van Lerberghe, eds. 1998. *En Syrie aux origines de l'écriture.* Turnhout.

Tanret, M. 2001. "As Years Went by in Sippar-Amnānum . . ." In Abusch et al. 2001, 455–466. Bethesda, Md.

———. 2002. Per aspera ad astra: *L'apprentissage du cunéiforme à Sippar-Amnânum pendant la période paléobabylonienne tardive.* Ghent.

———. 2004. "The Works and the Days . . . : On Scribal Activity in Old Babylonian Sippar-Amnānum." *RA* 98: 33–62.

———. 2005. "Sheqels for the Scribe." *NABU:* 73.

———. 2008. "Find the Tablet-box . . . : New Aspects of Archive-Keeping in Old Babylonian Sippar-Amnānum." In R. van der Spek, ed., *Studies in Ancient Near Eastern World View and Society Presented to Marten Stol on the Occasion of his Sixty-fifth Birthday,* 131–147. Bethesda, Md.

Tanret, M., and K. De Graef. 2003–2004. "Puzzling with Numbers: The Late Old Babylonian SI.BI Clause." *AfO* 50: 56–80.

Teissier, G. 1961. "Diplomatique." In Samaran 1961, 633–676.

Thucydides. 1950. *The History of the Peloponnesian War,* translated by Richard Crawley. New York.

Thureau-Dangin, F. 1912. "Notes assyriologiques XVI: Un jugement sous le règne de Samsu-iluna." *RA* 9: 21–24.

Tinney, S. 1998. "Texts, Tablets and Teaching: Scribal Education in Nippur and Ur." *Expedition* 40/2: 40–50.

———. 1999. "On the Curricular Setting of Sumerian Literature." *Iraq* 61: 159–172.

Ulshöfer, A. M. 1995. *Die altassyrischen Privaturkunden.* Stuttgart.

Van De Mieroop, M. 1997. "On Writing a History of the Ancient Near East." *BiOr* 54: 285–305.

———. 1999. *Cuneiform Texts and the Writing of History.* London.

———. 2000. "Sargon of Agade and His Successors in Anatolia." *SMEA* 42: 133–159.

Van der Toorn, K. 2000. "Cuneiform Documents from Syria-Palestine: Texts, Scribes, and Schools." *Zeitschrift des Deutschen Palästina-Vereins* 116: 97–113.

———. 2007. "Why Wisdom Became a Secret: On Wisdom as a Written Genre." In R. J. Clifford, ed., *Wisdom Literature in Mesopotamia and Israel,* 21–29. Atlanta.

Van Dijk, J. J. 1965. "Une insurrection générale au pays de Larša avant l'avènement de Nūr-Adad." *JCS* 19: 1–25.

Van Dijk, J. J., and W. R. Mayer. 1980. *Texte aus dem Rēš-Heiligtum in Uruk-Warka*. Berlin.

Van Driel, G. 1973. Review of R. Ellis 1968. *JAOS* 93: 67–74.

Van Driel, G. et al., eds. 1982. Zikir šumim: *Assyriological Studies Presented to F. R. Kraus on the Occasion of His Seventieth Birthday*. Leiden.

Van Lerberghe, K. 2003. "Private and Public: The Ur-Utu Archive at Sippar-Amnānum (Tell ed-Dēr)." In Brosius 2003a, 59–77.

Van Lerberghe, K., and G. Voet. 1989. "A Long Lasting Life." In Behrens et al. 1989, 525–538.

———. 1991. "On 'Quasi-Hüllentafeln.'" *NAPR* 6: 3–8.

———. 1994. "An Old Babylonian Clone." In Gasche et al. 1994, 159–168.

Van Soldt, W. H. 1995. "Babylonian Lexical, Religious and Literary Texts, and Scribal Education at Ugarit and Its Implications for the Alphabetic Literary Texts." In M. Dietrich and O. Loretz, eds., *Ugarit: Ein ostmediterranes Kulturzentrum im Alten Orient: Ergebnisse und Perspektiven der Forschung*, 171–212. Münster.

———, ed. 2001a. *Veenhof Anniversary Volume: Studies Presented to Klaas R. Veenhof on the Occasion of His Sixty-fifth Birthday*. Leiden.

———. 2001b. "Nahiš-šalmu, an Assyrian Scribe Working in the 'Southern Palace' at Ugarit." In van Soldt 2001a, 429–444.

Vanstiphout, H. L. J. 1978. "Lipit-Eštar's Praise in Edubba." *JCS* 30: 33–61.

———. 1979. "How Did They Learn Sumerian?" *JCS* 31: 118–126.

———. 1989. "Enmerkar's Invention of Writing Revisited." In Behrens et al. 1989, 515–524.

———. 1995. "On the Old Babylonian Edubba." In J. W. Drijvers and A. A. MacDonald, eds., *Centres of Learning: Learning and Location in Pre-Modern Europe and the Near East*, 3–16. Leiden.

———. 1997. "School Dialogues." In W. W. Hallo and K. L. Younger, eds., *The Context of Scripture*, 1: 589–590. Leiden.

———. 1999. "The Twin Tongues: Theory, Technique, and Practice of Bilingualism in Ancient Mesopotamia." In Vanstiphout et al. 1999, 141–159.

———. 2003a. *Epics of Sumerian Kings: The Matter of Aratta*. Atlanta.

———. 2003b. "The Old Babylonian Literary Canon: Structure, Function, and Intention." In Dorleijn and Vanstiphout 2003, 1–28.

Vanstiphout, H. L. J. et al., eds. 1999. *All Those Nations . . . : Cultural Encounters within and with the Near East*. Groningen.

Veenhof, K. R. 1966. Review of E. Kutsch, *Salbung als Rechtakt im Alten Testament und im Alten Orient* (Berlin, 1963). *BiOr* 23: 308–313.

———, ed. 1986a. *Cuneiform Archives and Libraries: Papers Read at the 30e Rencontre Assyriologique Internationale, Leiden, 4–8 July 1983*. Leiden.

———. 1986b. "Cuneiform Archives: An Introduction." In Veenhof 1986a, 1–36.

———. 1987. "'Dying Tablets' and 'Hungry Silver': Elements of Figurative Language in Akkadian Commercial Terminology." In M. Mindlin et al., eds., *Figurative Language in the Ancient Near East*, 41–75. London.

———. 2003a. "Archives of Old Assyrian Traders." In Brosius 2003a, 78–123.

———. 2003b. "Fatherhood Is a Matter of Opinion: An Old Babylonian Trial on Filiation and Service Duties." In Sallaberger et al. 2003, 313–332.

———. 2008. "The Old Assyrian Period." In Veenhof and Eidem 2008, 13–264.

Veenhof, K. R., and J. Eidem. 2008. *Mesopotamia: The Old Assyrian Period*. Fribourg and Göttingen.

Veldhuis, N. 1997. *Elementary Education at Nippur*. Groningen.

———. 1997–1998. Review of Cavigneaux 1996. *AfO* 44–45: 360–363.

———. 1999a. "Reading the Signs." In Vanstiphout et al. 1999, 161–174.

———. 1999b. "The Poetry of Magic." In Abusch and van der Toorn 1999, 35–48.

———. 2000a. "Sumerian Proverbs in Their Curricular Context." *JAOS* 120: 383–399.

———. 2000b. "Kassite Exercices: Literary and Lexical Extracts." *JCS* 52: 67–94.

———. 2003. "On the Curriculum of the Neo-Babylonian School." *JAOS* 123: 627–633.

———. 2006. "How Did They Learn Cuneiform? Tribute/Word List C as an Elementary Exercise." In Michalowski and Veldhuis 2006, 181–200.

Verbrugghe, G. P., and J. M. Wickersham. 1996. *Berossos and Manetho, Introduced and Translated: Native Traditions in Ancient Mesopotamia and Egypt*. Ann Arbor, Mich.

Villard, P. 1992. "Parade militaire dans les jardins de Babylone." In J.-M. Durand, ed., *Florilegium marianum: Recueil d'études en l'honneur de M. Fleury*, 137–152. Paris.

———. 1995. "Les derniers rapports des devins néo-assyriens." *RA* 89: 97–107.

———. 1997. "L'éducation d'Assurbanipal." *Ktèma* 22: 135–149.

———. 2006. "Acheminement et réception de la correspondance royale dans l'empire néo-assyrien." In L. Capdetray and J. Nelis-Clément, eds., *La circulation de l'information dans les États antiques*, 17–32. Bordeaux.

———. 2008. "Les lettres du temple d'Aššur." In Pantalacci 2008a, 179–191.

Vincente, C. A. 1995. "The Tall Leilān Recension of the Sumerian King List." *ZA* 85: 234–270.

Visicato, G. 2000. *The Power and the Writing: The Early Scribes of Mesopotamia*. Bethesda, Md.

Voet, G., and K. Van Lerberghe. 1993. "Sealing in Philadelphia and Elsewhere." *Acta Archaeologica Lovaniensia* 32: 43–58.

———. 1994. "Comments." *BiOr* 51: 441.

Volk, K. 1996. "Methoden altmesopotamischer Erziehung nach Quellen der altbabylonischen Zeit." *Saeculum* 47: 178–216.

———. 2000. "Edubba'a und Edubba'a-Literatur: Rätsel und Lösungen." *ZA* 90: 1–30.

Von Weiher, E. 1983–1998. *Spätbabylonische Texte aus Uruk*. Vols. 2–5. Berlin.

Waetzoldt, H. 1986. "Keilschrift und Schulen in Mesopotamien und Ebla." In *Erziehungs- und Unterrichtsmethoden im historischen Wandel*, 36–50. Bad Heilbrunn.

———. 1991. Review of M. Gibson and R. D. Biggs, eds., *The Organization of Power: Aspects of Bureaucracy in the Ancient Near East* (Chicago, 1987). *JAOS* 111: 637–641.

Waetzoldt, H., and H. Hauptmann, eds. 1997. *Assyrien im Wandel der Zeiten*. Heidelberg.

Walker, C. B. F. 1987a. *Cuneiform: Reading the Past*. London.

———. 1987b. "The Kouyunjik Collection of Cuneiform Texts: Formation, Problems, and Prospects." In M. F. Fales and B. J. Hickey, eds., *Austen Henry Layard tra l'Oriente e Venezia*, 183–193. Rome.

Walker, C. B. F., and M. Dick. 2001. *The Induction of the Cult Image in Ancient Mesopotamia: The Mesopotamian mis pi Ritual*. Winona Lake, Ind.

Watanabe, K. 1985. "Die Briefe der neuassyrischen Könige." *ASJ* 7: 139–156.

Watson, W. G. E., and N. Wyatt, eds. 1999. *Handbook of Ugaritic Studies*. Leiden.

Weisberg, D. B. 1969. "An Old Babylonian Forerunner to *šumma ālu*." *Hebrew Union College Annual* 40: 87–104.

Westbrook, R. 1988. *Old Babylonian Marriage Law*. Horn, Austria.

Westenholz, A. 2007. "The Graeco-Babyloniaca Once Again." *ZA* 97: 262–313.

Westenholz, J. G. 1993. "Writing for Posterity: Naram-Sin and Enmerkar." In A. F. Rainey, ed., *kinattūtu ša dārâti: Raphael Kutscher Memorial Volume*, 205–218. Tel Aviv.

———. 1997. *Legends of the Kings of Akkade: The Texts*. Winona Lake, Ind.

———. 2004. "The Old Akkadian Presence at Nineveh: Fact or Fiction." *Iraq* 66: 7–18.

Whiting, R. M. 1977. "Sealing Practices on House and Land Sale Documents at Eshnunna in the Isin-Larsa Period." In Gibson and Biggs 1977, 67–74.

———. 1987. *Old Babylonian Letters from Tell Asmar*. Chicago.

Wilcke, C. 2000. *Wer las und schrieb in Babylonien und Assyrien: Überlegungen zur Literalität im Alten Zweistromland*. Munich.

———. 2006. "Die Hymne auf das Heiligtum Keš: Zu Struktur und 'Gattung' einer altsumerischen Dichtung und zu ihrer Literaturtheorie." In Michalowski and Veldhuis 2006, 181–237.

Wilhelm, G. 1970. *Untersuchungen zum Ḫurro-Akkadischen von Nuzi*. Neukirchen.

———. 1991. "A Hurrian Letter from Tell Brak." *Iraq* 53: 153–168.

Wiseman, D. J. 1955. "Assyrian Writing-Boards." *Iraq* 17: 3–13.

Wiseman, D. J., and J. A. Black. 1996. *Literary Texts from the Temple of Nabû*. London.

Woodard R. D., ed. 2004. *The Cambridge Encyclopedia of the World's Ancient Languages*. Cambridge, Mass.

Woods, C. 2006. "Bilingualism, Scribal Learning, and the Death of Sumerian." In Sanders 2006, 91–120.

Wunsch, C. 2000. *Das Egibi-Archiv I: Die Felder und Gärten*. Groningen.

Xenophon. 1914. *Cyropaedia*, with an English translation by Walter Miller. 2 vols. London.

Yon, M., and D. Arnaud, eds. 2001. *Études ougaritiques I: Travaux 1985–1995*. Paris.

Young, G. D. et al., eds. 1997. *Crossing Boundaries and Linking Horizons: Studies in Honor of M. C. Astour on His Eightieth Birthday*. Bethesda, Md.

Ziegler, N. 1999. *Florilegium marianum IV: Le harem de Zimrî-Lîm*. Paris.

———. 2000. "Aspects économiques des guerres de Samsî-Addu." In J. Andreau et al., eds., *Economie antique: La guerre dans les économies antiques*, 14–33. Saint-Bertrand-de-Comminges.

———, ed. 2006. *La musique au Proche-Orient ancien*. Dijon.

———. 2007. *Florilegium Marianum IX: Les musiciens et la musique d'après les archives de Mari*. Paris.

Ziegler, N., and D. Charpin. 2004. "Une lettre de Samsî-Addu découverte à Hazor?" *NABU*: 84.

———. 2007. "Amurritisch lernen." In *Festschrift für Hermann Hunger zum 65. Geburtstag gewidmet von seinen Freunden, Kollegen und Schülern* (*WZKM* 97), 55–77. Vienna.

Index

Note: Page numbers followed by *f* indicate figures.